Richard Wagner

ALSO BY OR EDITED BY JOHN LOUIS DIGAETANI
AND FROM MCFARLAND

Wagner Outside the Ring: *Essays on the Operas, Their Performance and Their Connections with Other Arts* (2009)

Stages of Struggle: Modern Playwrights and Their Psychological Inspirations (2008)

Inside the Ring: Essays on Wagner's Opera Cycle (2006)

Wagner and Suicide (2003)

Carlo Gozzi: A Life in the 18th Century Venetian Theater, an Afterlife in Opera (2000)

Richard Wagner
New Light on a Musical Life

John Louis DiGaetani

McFarland & Company, Inc., Publishers
Jefferson, North Carolina

LIBRARY OF CONGRESS CATALOGUING-IN-PUBLICATION DATA

DiGaetani, John Louis, 1943–, author.
  Richard Wagner : new light on a
musical life / John Louis DiGaetani.
           p.   cm.
  Includes bibliographical references and index.

ISBN 978-0-7864-4544-8
softcover : acid free paper ∞

  1. Wagner, Richard, 1813–1883.
  2. Composers—Germany—Biography. I. Title.
ML410.W1D56 2014   782.1092—dc23   [B]   2013039869

BRITISH LIBRARY CATALOGUING DATA ARE AVAILABLE

© 2014 John Louis DiGaetani. All rights reserved

*No part of this book may be reproduced or transmitted in any form
or by any means, electronic or mechanical, including photocopying
or recording, or by any information storage and retrieval system,
without permission in writing from the publisher.*

On the cover: *Richard Wagner and King Ludwig II*, color lithograph
by Michael Mathias Prechtl (courtesy of the Stadtmuseum Amberg)

Manufactured in the United States of America

*McFarland & Company, Inc., Publishers
Box 611, Jefferson, North Carolina 28640
www.mcfarlandpub.com*

To my sister
Annette

Table of Contents

Acknowledgements ix
Preface 1
Introduction 3

1. A Child of War: 1813–1821 9
2. The Child as Victim: 1821–1830 23
3. Student in Leipzig: 1823–1833 33
4. Minna and Magdeburg: 1833–1840 44
5. Russia, England and Paris (First Sojourn): 1837–1842 54
6. Kapellmeister in Dresden — Premieres of *Rienzi*, *The Flying Dutchman* and *Tannhäuser:* 1840–1849 64
7. Revolution in Dresden: 1848–1850 75
8. Wagner and Liszt — The Premiere of *Lohengrin:* 1849–1850 82
9. Refuge in Zurich — The Development of Big Plans: 1850–1857 90
10. The Idea of the Ring: Italy: 1857–1858 98
11. The Wesendoncks: 1858–1859 107
12. Venice, Switzerland and Paris: 1859–1861 113
13. Paris and *Tannhäuser:* 1860–1861 122
14. Vienna, Russia and Matrimonial Crisis: 1861–1864 131
15. The Rescue by King Ludwig II of Bavaria: 1864–1865 139
16. *Tristan* in Munich: 1864–1865 147
17. The Triangle in Triebschen: 1865–1870 153
18. *Meistersinger* Premiere in Munich: 1868–1871 162

Table of Contents

19. Hans, Cosima and King Ludwig: 1870–1874 169
20. The Idea of Bayreuth — The Premiere of the Ring: 1873–1876 175
21. Wagner and Nietzsche: 1876–1880 182
22. *Parsifal*: 1881–1882 191
23. Death in Venice: 1883 201

Conclusion: A Life of Extremes 207
Bibliography 211
Index 215

Acknowledgments

I would like to thank Hofstra University for granting me a sabbatical and travel funds to work on this book.

I would also like to thank the Richard Wagner Museum at Bayreuth and the Geheimnis (Secret) Archive of the Bavarian State Library for help in researching this book. The New York Public Library kindly provided illustrations for this book.

Finally, I would like to thank Elayne Horn and Maribeth Bobeck for their encouragement.

Preface

There have been more books written about Richard Wagner than any other composer. There is a Wagner industry out there and Wagner societies all over the world. The year 2013 marks the two hundredth anniversary of his birth, and we are living during a Wagner Renaissance when virtually every opera company in the world wants to stage a Ring cycle. Still a controversial figure, Wagner has survived Adolf Hitler's criminal abuses of him. Theodore Herzl, the founder of Zionism and also a racist, was a fan of Wagnerian opera. Wagner has survived Zionist attempts to turn him into a Nazi, even though he died in 1883, fifty years before the Nazis came to power in 1933. Despite efforts to demonize Wagner and his art, the ultimate sign of maturity for any opera company in the world has become its ability to stage Wagner's Ring cycle, the top achievement in the genre of opera. Increasingly, only provincial opera companies are unable to stage a Ring cycle. As part of London's Olympics in the summer of 2012, the Royal Opera staged four complete Ring cycles. Clearly Wagner has become an international celebrity, even extending to the world of sport.

In writing a new biography of Wagner, I am indebted to all previous biographies, particularly Ernest Newman's still definitive four-volume work. Gregor-Dellin's biography and Chancellor's biography of the composer were also very useful. I am also indebted to Stewart Spencer and Barry Millington's collection of translations of the letters of Wagner. But a new century and new information has necessitated a new one-volume biography of this most controversial but most wonderful and esteemed of opera composers. While the earliest biographers of Wagner idolized him, biographies published after World War II demonized him. It is time to look at him in a more realistic way for what he was and what he accomplished. The 21st century can finally see Wagner more clearly and more objectively.

Wagner's life became one of wandering and of finding what seemed like perfect locations for himself and his creativity—a safe nest, which he then destroyed. The self-destructive part of the composer existed alongside the constructive and creative sides of him. Wagner's needs and the self-destructive and creative aspects of his personality were as complicated as the rest of us, and complicated even further by the demands of his genius. Wagner simultaneously held the noblest views of human rights and human equality and anti–Semitic racism, and Wagner's self-contradictory personality created both friends and enemies for him. But his operas have endured his own personality to become icons in the history of musical theater. A new look at his life and personality will reveal new aspects of that personality and new aspects of those ten wonderful operas. I am also trying to present both the positive and negative aspects of Wagner's complex personality — as complex as the rest of us.

Whether it is his *Flying Dutchman* or his *Tristan und Isolde* or his comedy *Die Meistersinger von Nürnberg*, all his operas reveal various aspects of his complexity — and ours. Wagner's ten great operas reflect the mind of their creator, and the many positive aspects of his personality have for too long been ignored in an effort to demonize him. Wagner's complex personality remains the source for his great operas.

Introduction

Why another biography of this German composer when there are three in English — plus four others in German? There is currently no biography of the composer in print in English, and I feel there is a real need for a new one-volume biography since the biographies which have appeared since World War II have discussed Wagner in the shadow of that war. Even the film biography of the composer by Tony Palmer demonized him, and the man who played him in that film, Richard Burton, complained that the negative view of the composer in the film's script made it almost impossible to create a genuinely human character for him to play. Burton realized that the positive aspects of the life and personality of Wagner were not enough known and not present in the script of the film, and attempts to demonize him — like attempts to idolize him — were ultimately over-simplifications of a vastly complex personality. That personality had both positive and negative qualities.

The worst thing that ever happened to Wagner's reputation was the sad fact that Adolf Hitler became a great fan of Wagner's operas and said that to understand National Socialism one had to understand Wagner's operas — not that Hitler himself ever did or he would never have done what he did. Wagner's pacifist themes in both his Ring cycle and his final opera *Parsifal* never seem to have been understood by Hitler. Given the realities of World War II and the Holocaust, most biographers of Wagner — especially Robert Gutman and Joachim Koehler — have tried to turn Wagner into a Nazi. Gutman even argues in his book that the central theme of Wagnerian opera remains anti–Semitism and all the villains in Wagner's operas are really Jews. Wagner also had a prejudice against Catholics and one can just as easily see hidden Catholics in all Wagner's operatic villains. He also had a prejudice against Italians and one can equally argue that all the villains in Wagner's operas are hidden Italians. It is often difficult to figure out who is the villain in a Wagnerian opera and many modern productions of these works raise questions about who the real villain is. Who creates more evil in the Ring — Alberich or Wotan? Who creates greater unhappiness in *Lohengrin*— Telramund or Lohengrin? Who is the real villain in *Tannhäuser*— Venus or Elizabeth? Wagner's characters resist easy categorization, which adds to their fascination for us.

An accusatory and a limited approach to the composer fails to understand that Wagner died in 1883, fifty years before Hitler came to power in Germany in 1933, and Wagner's brand of anti–Semitism (tragic though it was) reflects his period and not Hitler's. As one earlier biographer said, Wagner was anti–Semitic in theory but never in practice. Modern

Introduction

productions of these operas have done much to indicate their subtlety and Wagner's concept of *Mitleid*— sympathy for all the peoples of the world. This concept also appears in Wagner's works and his correspondence. His writings about his aims for his new theater in Bayreuth, Germany, especially indicate that this was to be a place welcome to all the peoples of the world who were interested in his art of the future, and that great art transcends racial and religious differences. Wagner frequently employed Jewish artists like Herman Levi and Josef Rubinstein and both men were quick to defend Wagner and to say how much he added to their lives and artistic careers.

Certainly one of the tragedies of the 21st century is the appearance of a new kind of anti–Semitism. Zionists often argued that all Arabs are "terrorists" and so Israel is correct to deny them civil rights, steal their land, and murder them or push them into refugee camps. Zionists often argue that pushing Palestinians into concentration camps like Gaza and then killing them is part of their "war on terror." When the United Nations voted that Zionism was a form of racism, it pointed out a new form of anti–Semitism which wants to see all Arabs, the largest group of Semitic people in the world, or all Muslims, as genetically inferior and criminal people. So clearly newer forms of anti–Semitism have become as criminal as the older versions. Some extreme Zionists want to massacre all Arabs or all Muslims since they are all "terrorists," rather like members of the Ku Klux Klan who consider all African Americans "niggers" who need to be denied civil rights and turned into slaves or murdered. Many of the very writers who present Wagner's own tragic anti–Semitism fully support Israeli apartheid and the Israeli government's determination to push most Palestinians into refugee camps and deny them civil rights in Israel because of their race and religion. Is another form of genocide — Palestinian genocide — occurring? As the first president of Israel, Chaim Wiezmann, said, "There is no such thing as Palestinians. They are just Negroes."

Another reason for a new biography of Wagner is all the new documents which have come to light since his death and within the last twenty years. More and more of Wagner's correspondence has been released at the Wagner archives at Bayreuth and Munich — much of it still has not been published since more and more of it is appearing. The composer was such an inexhaustible writer that he wrote not just thirteen operas and ten volumes of essays, but he also thousands of letters to hundreds of people, both friends and enemies. Hundreds of these letters have recently been published and many have yet to be published. Just his letters to Franz Liszt fill two volumes, and this is not the complete correspondence between these two giants of 19th century music. Wagner's correspondence with Ludwig II has not yet been fully published since there is a secret cabinet of documents in Munich's Wittelsbach archives.

Newly discovered correspondence indicates the complexities of Wagner's relationships with members of his own immediate family. His father (Wagner) and stepfather (Ludwig Geyer) both died before he was eight years old, and he spent much of his life looking for a father figure. His mother Johanna Rosine kept abandoning him to pursue her own interests so that he was often placed with relatives or with teachers who housed their students, so he often felt abandoned by his mother as well. He was born in Leipzig in 1813 during

Introduction

the Battle of Leipzig and the Napoleonic occupation of that city, and his father's death because of typhoid fever was a direct result of that French occupation. In the midst of warfare and familial abandonment, Wagner often became an angry and insecure child who doubted that his family members were interested in him. He never got the unconditional love and protection which every child deserves, and that generated an anger in him which recurred throughout his life. He always felt cheated as a result of his loveless childhood. For most of his childhood, Wagner was a fatherless little boy whose mother was moving him from relative to relative to avoid her own responsibility to the boy. Did Johanna Rosine ever love her youngest son? Probably, but only at a distance and certainly not unconditionally.

In many ways, Wagner's own important early relationships were with his siblings and especially his older sisters who in many ways became the parental figures he lacked. Another important substitute for a secure family became his relationships with some of his teachers and uncles, especially his uncle Adolf Wagner, who provided the encouragement and nurturing that his parents could not provide. Many of these early teachers found in Wagner a passionate interest in drama and music which they encouraged. His stepfather Ludwig Geyer also performed with the local theater companies, and he encouraged Richard to perform on stage and see the theater as a source of entertainment and even a possible profession.

Newly discovered correspondence indicates the complexity of his relationship with his first wife Minna Planer, who became a mother-substitute for the composer but also encouraged Wagner to believe that he could have a career not just as a chorus master or conductor, which he had done in the beginning of his career, but also as an opera composer. She saw his dual interests in both drama and music as leading to a career as an opera composer, and a uniquely gifted opera composer who could also write his own librettos. Minna encouraged him to believe in his abilities both to write librettos and to compose music and so compose a new kind of opera which was uniquely dramatic. She told him he had special gifts and he felt he could reform opera and return it to its ancient roots in Greek tragedy — a unique combination of drama and music in which the music did not just please the ear of the audience but could actually further the drama. She also felt that he was qualified to write this new kind of opera and please the audiences of his time. Wagner's mother never provided him with such encouragement; instead, she wanted him to become a lawyer or a teacher since these were much more stable careers. She thought his interest in theater and opera was a waste of time, and the fact that several of his siblings pursued such careers added to Rosine's annoyance with her son Richard.

Thanks to Minna, Wagner tried to compose his own kinds of operas and get them staged. After two flops, he finally achieved success with *Rienzi*, which at its 1842 premiere in Dresden became a resounding success. It was soon staged in other opera houses in Germany. Excerpts of this opera, especially its famous overture, were soon being played in Italy, England, France, and the United States. Wagner was so encouraged with stories of his music being performed in America that he repeatedly considered immigrating there, which eight million Germans were doing in the 19th century. Because of revolutions,

Introduction

political instability, and economic problems, millions of Germans fled their homeland for America — even before Germany finally became a unified country in 1871. Germans were a large part of the migration of millions of Europeans to America in the 19th century.

I am certainly indebted to all the previous biographies of the composer, especially Ernest Newman's massive four volumes. This huge biography tries to balance the pleasant with the unpleasant aspects of the composer's often narcissistic personality and to avoid demonizing him. More has been written on Wagner than any other composer — and not just biographies but also analyses of his theories and operas. Despite this deluge of material in both German and English (and French and Italian and Spanish), there remains a need for a one-volume biography of Wagner in English which presents him in a sympathetic light.

Now that we are in the 21st century, we can see Wagner more objectively. The earlier biographies by people like Glasenapp and Chamberlain wanted to use biography in the Victorian period to create a flattering monument to the composer and avoided mentioning any of his obvious blemishes, and most of the biographies after World War II presented him as totally evil if not a proto–Nazi. So the time has come for a new and more objective life of the composer. Chancellor's biography tries to avoid demonizing Wagner, but mistakenly states that he had a normal and happy childhood. More recent evidence proves that this was not the case. We need to see Wagner in a sympathetic light while still understanding his faults, but in terms of the 19th century and not the 20th. Racism was a tragic aspect of 19th and 20th century culture, and other racists of the period like Charles Dickens, F. Scott Fitzgerald, George Bernard Shaw, and George Eliot have received much more sympathetic treatment from history. Shakespeare's racism remains glaring in his *Merchant of Venice,* indicating how much racism remained a part of European history and culture. Even earlier, Chaucer's *Canterbury Tales*

Richard Wagner, an 1895 photogravure portrait by Hubert Herkomer (Music Division, New York Public Library for the Performing Arts, Astor, Lenox and Tilden Foundations).

includes the anti–Semitism of "The Prioress' Tale." In Dickens' *Oliver Twist,* the villain Fagin was, in the novel's original edition, called "Fagin the Jew." Racism, especially anti–Semitism, has had a long and tragic history in European and American literatures. Racism of course remains a problem all over the world. Israel keeps pushing Palestinians into refugee camps and stealing their property because of their race and religion.

This becomes especially important now, when we are living in a period of a Wagner renaissance. Thirty years ago only two opera companies in the United States, the Metropolitan Opera and the San Francisco Opera, ever staged Wagner's Ring cycle, and not very frequently. Now every opera company in the United States and the world wants to stage a Ring cycle and many of them are succeeding. In the first decade of the 21st century alone, the Met, the Seattle Opera, the San Francisco Opera, the Los Angeles Opera, and the Washington Opera staged complete Ring cycles. Wagner's time has clearly come.

One cannot help noticing that Wagner's life was one of extremes: He spent time in debtor's prison in Paris yet he became by the end of his life the most famous opera composer of the 19th century (rivaled only by Verdi). He was born in a time of war; he yearned for a peace that would include all of Europe and the world. He was hounded by creditors; he yearned for someone who would save him from his own anger and his own debts, all self-imposed. He wandered all over Europe, but he wanted a home with a wife and family, which he came to hate once he got them. He was a man doomed to be unhappy, yet he created some of the greatest art the world has ever seen. The middle road was never to be Wagner's road in life. He wanted to revolutionize the arts, especially opera, and he did that. He was always attracted to extreme rather than centrist positions — often in a bipolar way. So we need a new approach to this highly complex and yet tantalizing artist.

Such a book would encourage new readers and new audiences to see Wagner's ten major operas, especially his Ring cycle, in terms of their greatness — and their composer as a complex and often sympathetic man. Like the rest of us, Wagner was a combination of good qualities and bad qualities, but to see only the bad qualities is to ignore the realities of his very human personality, not to mention his tragic childhood and his kindness to his many loyal friends.

Freud wrote that analyzing a person was like peeling an onion, layer by layer. So I will use this approach to try to understand Wagner, and each chapter will have a different theory or a different aspect of Wagner's personality. Each will try to present another side of the complicated, multi-leveled reality that was Richard Wagner.

Wagner became the greatest artistic genius of the 19th century and had a greater effect on the arts of the 20th century than anyone else. He caused suffering, but he suffered as well, and he also created great art and great happiness for others, rarely for himself. It is not coincidental that Thomas Mann's essay on Wagner is called "The Sufferings and Greatness of Richard Wagner" because the composer suffered much in his life and in his career—a career that swept all over Europe and influenced all the other arts.

1

A Child of War: 1813–1821

"My father, Friedrich Wagner, died in October during the wartime unrest of the battle of Leipzig, after catching typhoid fever in what had become an epidemic."
— Richard Wagner, *My Life*

Richard Wagner was born on May 22, 1813, in the Red and White Lion Inn in Leipzig in der Bruhl, then a Jewish section of town. This was a very tense period since the Napoleonic wars were being waged often in Germany. Richard was baptized in the Thomaskirche in Leipzig two days later. The Battle of Borodino had occurred the previous year, a draw between Napoleon and the Russian czar, but Napoleon was soon driven out of Russia after the loss of millions of Russian and French and some German lives. Within six months of Wagner's birth, bombs were dropping on his native city of Leipzig, and it was occupied by the French. The Battle of Leipzig, called the Battle of Nations, one of the bloodiest of the Napoleonic wars, was at Wagner's doorstep when he was an infant. He really became in many ways a victim of that war, and his early childhood traumas were connected with the Battle of Leipzig.

All the major armies of Europe (Russian, Prussian, British, and Swedish) were there trying to defeat Napoleon and the French. The Napoleonic wars are often considered by historians as the First World War since it included most of Europe, North Africa, and parts of the Americas. A massive war, it resulted in the death of millions of people all over Europe and the world. Europe would not see another war like this until World War I in 1914, and then of course the even more terrible World War II in 1939. The Napoleonic wars clearly brought unprecedented carnage to Europe, due to Napoleon Bonaparte and his determination to dominate all of Europe. Bonaparte called for the liberation of all of Europe and spreading the wonders of the French revolution and its liberty, fraternity, and equality throughout the world, but in fact he wanted power over all of Europe and the world and was responsible for the deaths of millions of people, particularly in Germany, Russia, and Spain — not to mention France.

Wagner's family members were victims of this mass invasion and slaughter since much of the Napoleonic wars occurred in the then disunified country of Germany. One of the reasons for the movement to unify Germany during the 19th century was its victimization by France during the early part of the century and even earlier, during the 17th and 18th centuries. Germans increasingly felt that if they were not a unified country, France would invade again and again.

Richard Wagner

Two years after the Battle of Leipzig, another defeat for Napoleon, the 1815 battle of Waterloo took place in Belgium with the ultimate defeat of Napoleon and the victory of the Allied forces, led by Wellington and Blücher. Napoleon spent his final years on the Island of Saint Helena as a prisoner of the English, who were determined that he would never again threaten the peace of the world. Napoleon had claimed to be a great liberator of Europe but was really a great murderer. Carlo Gozzi, in his *Memorie Inutili*, describes the reaction in his native Venice, where many liberals saw Napoleon as the great liberator and freedom fighter when he conquered Venice, only to weep as Napoleon's army sacked Venice and stole most of its art treasures. Gozzi also wept as he saw his city being sacked and stripped of its treasures while fools were dancing around the tree of liberty in Piazza San Marco. In his writings he had predicted what "French Liberty" would lead to: the destruction of the rest of Europe. But since the fall of Venice in 1797, Napoleon had begun losing more and more battles.

He remains a very controversial figure, some (especially the French) seeing him as a liberator, others as an early version of Adolf Hitler, responsible for starting the first real world war. The Napoleonic wars spread beyond Europe to Africa and North America, where the Americans fought the British in Canada and elsewhere in the newly formed United States, until Napoleon was finally defeated.

While the French tend to glorify Napoleon as the great liberator of Europe, and Paris is dotted with monuments to the little general, other, more scientific histories see him as an equivalent to Hitler. The German federation also saw millions of people dead thanks to Napoleon's invasion of the German-speaking independent states. He always talked about all the liberation he was bringing to Europe — spreading the benefits of the French revolution — but these were wars of conquest, not liberation, as the conquered nations soon saw after they were dominated by Napoleon. Napoleon did create the Code Napoleon, a legal document which granted liberal rights to most citizens, but he also started one war after another and caused land and sea battles all over the Mediterranean and also with America. This Napoleonic bloodbath did not end until the little general was finally defeated.

Gozzi wrote about the irony behind Napoleon's claims of spreading democracy and liberating the population. Gozzi was in Venice when Napoleon "liberated" the city — but what Gozzi saw was the sacking of his beloved city, with most of its artistic treasures ripped out of churches and palaces and sent to Paris. In his *Memorie Inutili*, Gozzi describes what happened to Venice to Napoleon's invasion. The city was not bombed, as was Leipzig, but it was sacked and its treasures shipped to Paris for public display. The Venetians eventually got some of the art back but certainly not all the art that the French stole from Venice. At least they got the four bronze horses back onto the front of San Marco Cathedral, which the Venetians themselves stole from Constantinople.

Leipzig saw the spread of diseases like typhoid fever as a result of the Napoleonic occupation. Wagner's father Friedrich died of the disease. He had been an employee of the city but died within six months of Richard's birth. Soon afterwards, Richard's mother married Ludwig Geyer, a family friend in Dresden. Geyer himself died seven years later

1. A Child of War: 1813–1821

when Richard was only eight years old. It is no wonder that orphans, and being an orphan, became major themes in the operas of Wagner—the most famous orphans being Siegmund, Sieglinde, Siegfried, Tristan, and Parsifal. "Who are my parents?" these orphans often wonder, just as Wagner himself must have wondered.

On a most basic level, the war made Wagner a lifelong Francophobe, always suspicious of the French because of what they did to his hometown. Repeatedly in his writings and correspondence he voices this prejudice against France and the French—their language, their culture, and their condescending attitude toward the Germans. He came to see Napoleon as a pseudo-liberator who presented himself as representing the rights of men but killing millions of them as a result of his wars of conquest. These realities were complicated by the fact that in Wagner's life the capital of opera was Paris, though the two greatest opera composers of the 19th century (Wagner and Verdi) both had primarily failure in Paris, and neither liked the main Paris opera house very much. Verdi referred to it as "la Boutique"—in other words, a place for selling rather than producing art. Minor composers, especially of Jewish descent, tended to succeed in Paris thanks to the critics in the city and the taste of the period. Most of the operas that were wildly popular in Paris in the 19th century (operas by Meyerbeer, Adam, and Halevy) are now rarely performed and not in the standard repertory of even the French opera houses. French operatic taste was different from our own, though some of the composers living in Paris at the time, especially Rossini, made wonderful and lasting contributions to the medium of opera or musical theater. And Paris remained a state threatening war with its neighbors even after Napoleon. Napoleon III would invade Prussia yet again in 1870.

The war affected Wagner's childhood in many ways, all adverse. His father, or the person he thought of as his father, died within six months after his birth in the fall of 1813. That death left his mother a frantic widow, with eight children to support and just trying to survive the Battle of Leipzig and the post-war situation in devastated Leipzig. She wrote letters to family and friends begging for financial help. She and Carl Friedrich had had nine children in all, eight surviving into adulthood. These were Albert, Carl Gustav, Rosalie, Carl Julius, Luise, Klara, Maria Theresia (who died as a child in 1814), Ottilie, and Wilhelm Richard (the composer).

But who was the composer's real father? On the first page of his autobiography, Wagner leaves a hint that he thought maybe Geyer was when he reports:

> [My father's] fondness for the theater was also evidenced by his selection of the actor Ludwig Geyer as an intimate friend of the family. While his choice of such a friend was surely attributable mainly to this love of the theater, he thereby bestowed upon his family a most noble benefactor, inasmuch as this modest artist, through heartfelt concern with the destiny of the numerous offspring of his unexpectedly deceased friend Wagner, was moved to devote the rest of his life most strenuously to the support and upbringing of this family. Even while the police official was spending his evenings in the theater, this admirable actor generally filled his place in the bosom of his family, and it appears that he was often obliged to soothe my mother when she complained, rightly or wrongly, about the flightiness of her husband. How deep was the need of this homeless, hard-pressed, and buffeted artist to be at home within a

sympathetic family environment was proved a year after his friend's death, when he married the widow and henceforth became a most solicitous father to the seven surviving children.

Wagner is hinting right from the first page of his autobiography that perhaps his stepfather was his real father.

In her panic, the widow Wagner left her children and went through all those armies to a man who was a close family friend, Ludwig Geyer, and married him the following year, he having promised to support her and her children. Richard's mother's flight was the first of many abandonments which he suffered in his childhood. By the time Wagner was eight years old, both his fathers had died and his mother was not able to mother him very well because of her own traumas connected with the war and her two widowhoods. As a child, Wagner must have connected family life with death and abandonment. His sister Theresia died the year following his birth, which must have been very traumatic for his mother. He was a sickly, difficult, unhappy child whom his mother avoided when possible. There are no villains in this sad situation, just various victims. Wagner would have agreed with the American playwright Eugene O'Neill, who said on several occasions, "There is no hell quite like the family."

Wagner opens his autobiography *Mein Leben* with a description of his family and how the Battle of Leipzig influenced him and his family:

> Born May 22, 1813, in Leipzig, two flights up in a house on the Bruhl known as "The Red and White Lion," I was christened two days later in St. Thomas Church with the name Wilhelm Richard. My father Friedrich Wagner, at the time of my birth the registrar of police in Leipzig with the expectation of becoming director of police, died in October of the same year, following the great exertions imposed by overwhelming load of official duties during the wartime unrest and the battle of Leipzig, after catching typhoid fever in what had become an epidemic. As to his own father's situation in life, I learned much later that he had distinguished himself among composers in his humble municipal post of toll collector at the Ranstaedter Gate by giving his sons a higher education having one of them, my father Friedrich, study law and the younger one, Adolf, study theology. My uncle subsequently came to exert a not insignificant influence on my development; we will meet him again in a decisive phase of the story of my youth. About my father whom I lost so early I learned later that he was in general very much interested in poetry and literature, and particularly accorded an almost passionate devotion to the theater, at that time much patronized by the educated classes. My mother told me among other things that he took her to Lauchstaedt to the first performance of *Die Braut von Messina* and pointed out Schiller and Goethe to her on the promenade, enthusiastically setting her straight as to her ignorance of those great men. He seems to have been not entirely free of a certain amorous interest in actresses. My mother used to complain jokingly that she frequently had to hold lunch for him... His fondness for the theater was also evidenced by his selection of the actor Ludwig Geyer as an intimate friend of the family [Wagner, *My Life*, 3].

This passage emphasizes the upheaval of war during his birth, his connections with the men in his family, especially his uncle Adolf, and his anger at his mother, whom he connects with ignorance. War and abandonment would be the central problems of his childhood, along with anger as a result of these traumas. He often wondered if his mother Johanna Rosina Wagner ever really loved him, or whether she wished he were dead. He

1. A Child of War: 1813–1821

often felt as a child that his mother found him impossible and wanted him far away from her.

It appears that Wagner was not sure who his real father was. How was Ludwig Geyer "joining the family" when Carl Friedrich was away with actresses? Does this passage suggest that Geyer was having an affair with his mother Johanna Rosina while Carl Friedrich was having an affair with some actress? Does this passage suggest that Wagner's real father was Geyer? The passage does suggest this in an enigmatic way. Part of this reaction may have been caused by his mother's neglect of him and his difficult relationship with her.

One of a child's greatest fears is the fear of abandonment by his parents, especially his mother, and this became a repeated fear in the childhood of Richard Wagner—a fear of being abandoned by his parents, and this happened. His mother kept dumping him with family and tutors so that young Wagner must have felt constantly abandoned in the most basic ways. He was abandoned especially by his mother, who found him very difficult and overwhelming. Little Richard must have often felt like an orphan as a child — a father dead and a mother who did not like him much. During the 19th century, Charles Dickens often wrote about orphans, especially in his *Oliver Twist*. Dickens himself was not an orphan, but he often felt like an orphan because of parental neglect. Dickens as a writer intuited that people with two parents were very interested in his orphan boys because they also felt like orphans, even though they had their own parents. Bad and neglectful parents often leave their children feeling unwanted, unloved, unprotected and feeling like orphans even though they are not orphans.

Wagner's mother had many children, and she must have had her hands full with them. She also was undoubtedly traumatized by the death of her four-year-old daughter Theresia. The death may have complicated her relationship with little Richard. Plus she had a habit of suddenly abandoning them, which must have been very traumatic for the children, especially the smaller ones. Johanna Rosina Wagner, born Patz, must have had a difficult time of it with two husbands dying on her, left a widow twice, and the Napoleonic wars to deal with. It is amazing that all but one of her children lived to adulthood, especially given the grim nature of the war of the time, but they did. On one level she must have been a very good mother, but on another she must have been overwhelmed by what she had to deal with.

At age 15, before she married Carl Friedrich, she had an affair with an aristocrat. Was she a rape victim or a victim of a sexual assault or the victim of a pedophile aristocrat? Girls of 15 are considered children now but in the 19th century they would have been considered adults, and some aristocrats thought of poor women, especially very young women, as their preferred sexual partners. Poor women were sometimes preyed upon by rich aristocrats who would never marry such a girl but might have preferred them as sexual partners. Such girls were often victims of wealthy aristocrats, forced to have illegitimate children by such men. Given the unjust laws of the time, these girls would have had virtually no legal protection since poor people were stripped of most legal rights.

But who then was Wagner's father? Legally, he was the son of Wagner, but the only father he really knew was Ludwig Geyer, and in fact he used the last name of Geyer on his school certificate when he entered primary school. Was Geyer his real father? To his dying day he was never completely sure. And the section of Leipzig where he was raised was the Jewish quarter, the Buhl as it was called then, and his last name of Geyer was not typically German but perhaps Jewish so there were always rumors about who his father was and whether he was Jewish or not. Most biographers of Wagner, especially Newman, argued that Wagner was most probably Christian but his paternity was in doubt. But Nietzsche repeatedly suggested that Wagner was Jewish and in fact looked Jewish — short, large head, large nose, and he was often trying to get money from people to stage his operas or to buy luxuries (the negative stereotype of the Jew presented by anti–Semites). In the cartoons of the period, Wagner was sometimes depicted with stereotypically Jewish features so this must have been a constant rumor about him from his childhood.

Clearly young Richard really loved Geyer and at age eight was certainly traumatized by his death. His fears of abandonment were exacerbated by yet another death of a father figure. Wagner must have felt like an orphan — again. Death and abandonment were the two traumas of Wagner's childhood, and these traumas were repeated over and over again on the little orphan boy Richard Wagner. These themes would also appear in Wagner's operas.

When Ludwig Geyer was sick in bed and slowly dying, Wagner tried to cheer him up by playing some tunes on the piano; Geyer turned to his wife and said, "Perhaps he has some musical talent?" That story became very important to the composer because it showed that his stepfather detected something special in him and loved him. The boy was devastated by Geyer's death. A portrait of Geyer was in Wagner's possession and eventually was hung in Wagner's house in Bayreuth, Wahnfried.

Wagner's mother became so traumatized by the battle of Leipzig and its effects on her family that her ability to be a mother was compromised. Wagner in his autobiography mentioned having no memories of ever being touched by her. When he was very sick as a child, he reports that his mother did not think he would survive the illness and perhaps she did not want him to survive. Touching is the only way a child feels love, and to be raised by a mother who never touched him must have been very traumatic for Wagner.

Wagner's mother seems to have been a neglectful mother when it comes to her last son Richard. Partially of course her mothering skills would have been diminished by the battle going on around her and the death of her daughter. Also, the death of her husband and her marriage to Geyer, who may have been her lover, would have also diminished her ability to mother her youngest son. That she found Richard such a difficult child may have complicated the situation even more, though that difficulty may have been the result of her inability to mother this child. Difficult children are often the result of maternal neglect: Children discover that making problems regains a mother's attention, though often in a negative way.

Wagner was really raised in chaos, as Luigi Pirandello once said of his own childhood, and he must have felt fatherless and motherless for much of his childhood. His

1. A Child of War: 1813–1821

father was dead and his mother was trying to get rid of him by shipping him to one relative or another or putting him into some boarding school. She must have spent much of the time trying to foist her children on relatives and friends. Given all the children she had and the wartime realities she had to live with, this is all understandable, but the situation must have left her feeling completely overwhelmed and her children, particularly her younger children, feeling abandoned and without a home. If Wagner as an adult often complained of being without a home, that was the condition of his childhood as well. How traumatic that must have been for him as a child, with a burning sense of abandonment and with a great need for attention. It is amazing that most of the Wagner children survived, and this was primarily due to his mother's efforts and also the efforts of the family's greatest friend Geyer, who managed to save most of the children, then marry the mother, and then die soon afterwards in 1821. Johanna did not get any sort of pension from the state from either of her marriages and so must have been financially overwhelmed by her dire economic situation.

It is surely significant that Wagner's operas, especially his later ones, present us with orphaned sons. This must indicate something about his feelings about his own past. Siegfried remains the prime example of an orphan always wondering who his parents are, and Siegmund and Sieglinde in the Ring are also without parents. Parsifal in Wagner's final opera is yet another orphaned child not knowing his own parents. Tristan too lost both his parents as a child and was raised by his uncle, King Mark. All these orphans must have arisen from Wagner's deep feelings of abandonment.

A child who feels like an orphan will spend much of his adult life looking for a father and a mother, and this is precisely what little Richard did. And he found them, for a while. His natural need for love was exaggerated by his feelings of being without parents and without a home. His childhood trauma would haunt him for all of his life, as childhood traumas generally do. In many ways Wagner was like an orphan from a war, and that is precisely how he felt for the duration of his life. He also suffered from lack of object constancy—so he panicked when he was alone and felt that no one in the world liked him or cared about him. He was not able to endure isolation very well because he did not remember all the friends in his life but felt totally isolated and abandoned—something he often felt as a child.

But two years after he was born, his sister Cecilia was born, and they had a particularly close bond. They clung to each other because they were all they felt they had. Cecilia was Wagner's favorite sibling. When children are raised in a family with absent or incompetent parents, they often develop particularly close bonds with their siblings and turn them into parent substitutes. Wagner's relationship with Cecilia became one of those relationships. They spent hours together, trying to find some love and support in each other.

Wagner was raised in the Bruhl, the Jewish area of Leipzig. Did he think he himself was Jewish? Most of his neighbors were, and as an adult he looked like the negative stereotype of the Jew: short, hump-backed, with a big head and a big nose, a person who was always trying to get money out of people. That was how Wagner must have looked like as an adult, and he *was* often trying to get money out of people — money to borrow from them or money so that he could stage one of his new operas. Hans von Bülow once said that Wagner was really a genius of finance, and in a way he *was*, since he rarely paid back what he owed and he got other people to stage his operas all his life. That he also happened to be a genius, the greatest operatic genius of his time, added to the complexity, not to mention the comedy, of the situation. Was Wagner's anti–Semitism a way of throwing off the assumption that many people must have made, that he himself was a Jew? Many newspaper cartoons of Wagner during his lifetime presented him as a caricatured Jew. Was his stepfather Ludwig Geyer a Jew? Not really, but the name is Jewish. Anti-Semitism became one of the major neuroses in European culture in the 19th century.

Most of the evidence suggests that both Wagner's parents come from Christian backgrounds — many of Carl Friedrich's relatives were teachers or servants of the church in some way. The Geyer relatives were often connected with the theater and were also often teachers, though poor. But racism occurred on many levels in European and American society at the time, especially against the Jews. The 19th century became the age of imperialism in Europe, especially in Britain and France, and imperialism is based on racism.

Wagner as a child also suffered from nightmares, certainly a sign of an unhappy, neglected child. His mother avoided him and locked him in his room so everybody else got some sleep, which would add to a child's sense of abandonment. But Wagner did have some very warm memories of his stepfather Geyer, as he recounts in his autobiography:

> The earliest recollections of my childhood are fixed on this stepfather and pass from him to the theater. I remember well that my father would have been very happy to see a talent for painting in me; his studies, with the easels and paintings upon them, did not ... fail to make an impression on me; I remember, in fact, that I tried to copy a portrait of King Friedrich August of Saxony, with a child's eagerness to imitate; but as soon as I expected to go beyond this simple playing with paint to a serious study of drawing, I did not persevere, possibly scared off by the pedantic ways of my teacher (a boring cousin of mine). After one of the common ailments of infancy, which made me so sick that my mother, as she later told me, almost wished me dead owing to my seemingly helpless condition, I seem to have surprised my parents by thriving. On this occasion, as well, I was told, my admirable stepfather played a splendid part, never despairing despite the cares and complaints of such a large family, remaining patient, and never giving up the hope that I could be pulled through" [Wagner, *My Life*, 4–5].

This passage seems to suggest that Wagner's mother rather wished he had died, but his stepfather never lost hope. His stepfather teasingly called him "the Cossack," suggesting his rough, masculine character as a little boy.

Despite maternal neglect, Wagner grew and in some cases thrived so he must have had an iron constitution and a subconscious determination to live and grow. His mother kept sending him out to be raised by distant relations or teachers and tutors so his childhood reflected constant moving. A child would have certainly seen all these moves as abandonments by his parents, especially his mother. His mother seemed to think of him as a very difficult child who had nightmares and must be isolated from the rest of the

1. A Child of War: 1813–1821

family. You would think the mother would have tried harder to comfort her last son when he had nightmares, but she was probably overwhelmed by the demands of her other children, a new husband, and the situation in Leipzig, a city trying to recover from the Napoleonic occupation. Much of the Napoleonic wars were fought in Germany with many of the German city states humiliated and invaded by the French, who thought of Germany as a weak, disunified country and thought of that country with contempt, which would explain Wagner's suspicions of Paris and the French in Germany and the German sense of inferiority and anger at the French and their condescending view of a supposedly weak and backward neighbor. The French had a very condescending view of the Germans, and we can see this very clearly in Voltaire's view of his time in Potsdam and the royal patronage of Friedrich the Great. In Voltaire's great work *Candide*, we can see his condescending and comic presentation of all things German. Germans are presented as fat, stupid people speaking a ridiculous language with ridiculous customs and costumes — aping French costumes in a comic way. Germans were beginning to resent the French insistence that Germany was a backward country full of backward people — fat and ugly and with an ugly language. The Germans were also resenting that the French had invaded their country so often since it was not a unified country and "easy pickings" for the unified French. Most of the castles along the Rhine are ruins because of French invasions, culminating in Wagner's time in the Napoleon wars and the repeated sacking of the German towns Leipzig and Dresden — both in Wagner's home province of Saxony, the center of Europe, and so an easy and strategic target of invaders of a country which was not unified and so often defenseless.

Certainly Wagner's mother was under extreme pressure as a result of this war and its effect in Leipzig. There is one particularly interesting passage in Wagner's autobiography in which he talks about his mother:

> The anxious and trying relations with a large family (of which I was the seventh surviving member), the difficulties in providing the necessities of life, and the fulfillment of a certain desire to keep up appearances even with very limited means, were not conducive to a comforting tone of motherly solicitude in her; I hardly remember ever being caressed by her, just as outpourings of affection did not take place in our family at all; on the contrary, quite naturally a certain impetuous, even loud and boisterous manner characterized our behavior. In those circumstances I remember it as epoch-making one night being taken to bed and looking up at her with tearful eyes when she gazed back at me fondly and spoke of me to a visitor with a certain amount of tenderness. What particularly struck me about her was the strange zeal with which she spoke, in almost histrionic tones, of the great and beautiful in art. She would never let me suppose that she included dramatic art in this category, but rather solely poetry, music and painting, and often in fact came close to threatening me with her curse if ever I too would think of going into the theater [*My Life*, 11–12].

This passage states that Wagner had virtually no memories of his mother caressing him as a child, but the one time she did, it was in connection with art and the creation of art, though not with theater, the one art he eventually contributed to, and so significantly. Perhaps in his mind, creating some sort of art was the only way he could get his mother's approval, though the only art he had talent for was musical theater, which his mother did not regard as art. Was Wagner's whole career an expression of both love and defiance toward his mother? But in the midst of all this, war and its aftermath in Leipzig were the realities.

Because of the Napoleonic wars, many Germans felt that they should be in a unified country. The move for German reunification grew right after Waterloo as more and more Germans felt that their fatherland had to be unified and had to be strong to defend itself against its neighbors, especially France, which had invaded Germany several times. Most of the castles along the Rhine river were destroyed by repeated French invasions. Germany, in the middle of Europe, had been invaded by the Swedes in the 17th and 18th centuries and by the French in the 19th century. Many Germans, including Wagner, were angry about the wars which were fought on German lands and the millions of Germans who had died in those wars — the Hundred Years War, the Thirty Years War, the Napoleonic wars — and in all these wars Germany was a victim of destruction and humiliation from foreign invasions, especially and most recently from France.

Despite this, the little Cossack grew and also learned, but he was haunted by illnesses and nightmares. In his own memoirs, Wagner talks about his howling at night:

> From earliest childhood certain mysterious and uncanny phenomena produced undue effects on me; I remember, whenever I was alone in a room for any length of time and looked fixedly at such inanimate objects as pieces of furniture, suddenly bursting into a loud shriek, because they seemed to me to come alive. Until late in my boyhood no night passed without my awakening with a frightful scream from some dream about ghosts, which would end only when a human voice bade me be quiet. Severe scoldings or even corporal punishment would then seem to me redeeming kindness. None of my brothers and sisters wanted to sleep near me; they tried to bed me down as far from the others as possible, not stopping to think that by doing so my nocturnal calls to be saved from ghosts would become even louder and more enduring, until they finally accustomed themselves to this nightly calamity.

These nightly screams clearly indicate the fears of abandonment by a child, and his mother did not comfort him and assure him of her presence and love; instead, she beat him. The most dreaded fear of childhood is the fear of abandonment, and this was little Richard's fear. Throughout his life, Wagner went into a panic when he was by himself and felt that not one person in the world loved him or even liked him. This is what psychologists called lack of object constancy. As a child, he clearly did not feel that he was getting much love and attention from his mother, yet being away from her caused panic.

His other family members did not want to sleep in the same room with him, certainly not his mother, who seems to have thought of him as her biggest problem. He seems to have been isolated from the family since at night at least no one wanted to be near him. Why would he have such terrible dreams unless he was haunted by visions of monsters who were trying to consume him? Probably these monsters were symbols of his parental figures that seemed to be so powerful yet were abandoning him. That must have generated tremendous anger in this boy, which would also explain his mother's difficulties with him. He was clearly most angry at her for not meeting his basic needs and comforting and loving him.

1. A Child of War: 1813–1821

Wagner clearly did not get the unconditional love which all children need from their parents, and this affected him for the rest of his life. He was often looking for unconditional love from people, which is a kind of love which no adult can give another adult and which if one does not get as a child, one never will get from anyone else. If one does not get unconditional love from one's parents, one will feel that deficit for the rest of one's life because one can never get such love from anyone but a parent, and not from other adults when one is a grown-up and deficient in that area.

Wagner was a determined survivor with a will of steel when it came to his artistic aims. He suffered from nervous discords all his life and various psychosomatic illnesses like skin diseases and allergies but he must have had a determination to survive and overcome despite his frequently mentioned desire to kill himself, so his parents must have provided him with some good support despite their own battles with war and mortality. Wagner was a sickly child, and often a sickly adult with many illnesses connected with skin diseases and allergies, diseases which would now be considered psychogenic in origin. As with so many sickly people, he lived to be 69 and so must have had healthy genes, or at least the ability to work through an illness, whether it is physical or psychological. But skin diseases, especially erysipelas, a very painful inflammation of the facial muscles and skin, made him suffer for much of his life. Many of his symptoms now sound like allergic reactions, and these attacks could have been psychogenic. The tensions and conflicts in his life, and his recurrent fears of abandonment, undoubtedly triggered these allergic reactions and skin eruptions, plus his stomach problems. He frequently went to baths and spas throughout his life to find relief from these problems.

Wagner's mother, we have recently found out, was once the mistress to one of the younger sons of the Saxon royal family. They were both teenagers at the time and she was in a private school for a while, thanks to this royal patron. No pregnancy developed, from what we know so far, and she eventually married Friedrich Wagner, who was a town employee. Ernest Newman's biography indicates that he was a musical and theatrical amateur despite his day job. He worked for the police department in Leipzig as a writer of official documents, probably like a secretary. It was not a particularly wonderful job, but he had a steady income, which was needed since he and Johanna had eight children. He liked to keep his family entertained with stories from the theaters and the opera houses. In English-speaking countries we tend to think of opera as a branch of music, but in Germany and Italy opera is more often thought of as a branch of theater, or musical drama, as Wagner would eventually call it.

This was even truer of Wagner's second father, Ludwig Geyer, who was a major fan of opera and theater and even staged them for family birthdays and Christmas celebrations, with the children in costume and given parts. Wagner would continue this tradition in his own family at Triebschen and eventually at Bayreuth with the children often dressed up as Wagnerian characters. Family celebrations always included pantomimes and plays with the children getting to play roles for the amusement and entertainment of the whole family. Despite the traumas of Wagner's childhood, there were also happy memories, especially those around the theater and theater people.

Richard Wagner

The composer developed a very close bond with Ludwig Geyer and always thought of him as his real father since he had no recollections of Friedrich Wagner. But a horrible tragedy occurred when Geyer suddenly died when Richard was eight. It was a major trauma for Richard because he felt fatherless — yet again — and eventually for the rest of his life. Luckily he had some father substitutes like his uncles and older brothers, but Geyer's death left him bereft of his major parent since his mother seemed not very interested in him. Wagner felt like an orphan for much of his life; these were not the realities, but this is how he felt. And Wagner felt a kind of love *and* rage toward his parents, his mother for her neglect of him and his fathers for dying and leaving him.

What was family life like for little Richard? From what we can tell from his autobiography *My Life*, upheaval and parental neglect and sadism were the major characteristics. Aside from the battle of Leipzig, there were moves from Leipzig to Dresden and back, plus his being placed in various foster care environments, so clearly the little boy had nightmares about monsters and abandonment since he felt abandoned so often himself.

Neglect naturally left its traumas on the composer and he spent the rest of his life looking for parental figures, especially mother figures. The women he fell in love with tended to be surrounded by children and tended to be very maternal, which certainly suited Wagner's needs. He was also often looking for father figures, older men who would help him and take care of him.

Clearly Wagner did not enjoy a particularly happy, secure childhood and that left scars on his personality. He was the victim of a war going on over his head and various traumas within the family. He was often described as a sickly child, and one gets the feeling that his mother did not much want him to survive. She was undoubtedly overwhelmed by being a widow and trying to provide for the children she already had by Friedrich Wagner. Then once she married Ludwig Geyer — in August of 1814 — she had one more child. Most women would have been overwhelmed with so many children, and I am sure Rosalie Wagner did her best, but Wagner especially was adversely affected by the Napoleonic invasion of Leipzig and the upheavals within his family.

Despite his physical delicacy, Richard did develop an iron will and a determination to live his life and accomplish what he wanted to accomplish. He had an amazing ability to work on his compositions despite the trauma around him, in spite of them in fact. Wagner may have been delicate and traumatized, but he was also determined to do what he wanted to do despite the problems.

His siblings helped him in ways that his parents did not. He was raised in a house full of older (and one younger) sisters and he formed particularly close attachments to his sisters, especially Rosalie and Cecilia. These girls were the parental figures for him which his parents did not seem able to be. His relationships with his sisters helped little Richard to feel less isolated, less unloved, and more a part of a family unit, though hardly a typical family unit. There were happy moments too in his traumatic childhood, and one of the family jokes was when he as a child appeared on stage in a local production. He was only four and did not do well, but the situation and the place were remembered by him. Clearly even as a child he was fascinated with the theater and would eventually

1. A Child of War: 1813–1821

become a great reformer of the theater, especially in his own theater at Bayreuth for the Bayreuth festival, which was started in 1876 for the premiere of the Ring cycle.

Wagner survived and overcame the difficulties of his home life since within his delicate little frame existed someone who would overcome difficulties, even the difficulties which he himself created. He developed an ability to work despite his depressions and mood swings and his allergies. While most people would have been prostrate and unable to get out of bed with all their grief, Wagner was able to work no matter what catastrophes were occurring around him. Even when he was in debtors' prison in Paris, he was working on his new opera.

One way of understanding Wagner is as a victim of war, his family and his childhood marred by death and the other trauma of war like diseases, social upheaval, and even the death of a parent. Perhaps it left him insecure and a bit paranoid, fearful that nothing was safe and nobody was to be trusted, not even his parents, and that people were plotting against him. Nothing was safe, least of all family life. He both yearned for family life and companionship and dreaded it because of the traumas of his earliest life.

One can very easily see Wagner traumatized by a lack of a father figure so that he spent the rest of his life looking for a father. He kept trying to turn men into father-figures, especially Franz Liszt, who was actually only two years older than Wagner. When one examines the correspondence between the two men, Wagner is constantly playing the role of the wayward son, constantly appealing to Liszt as a father figure who will save him from his problems. And Liszt responded very generously to most of Wagner's appeals for money and advice.

Wagner often behaved in a child-like manner around older men, or sometimes even younger men like Otto Wesendonck — he acted often like a precocious child who was brilliant but wayward and needed a father to take care of him — and that was how he was feeling around men. He was always on the subconscious lookout for a father-figure, and he hated himself at the same time for behaving that way. He both wanted a father-figure and hated that need within himself because he knew he was behaving like a child, but subconscious forces were driving him. On another level he yearned to *be* a father and was overjoyed when he had children near the end of his life, when he was old enough to be their grandfather.

Wagner would spend much of his life looking for parental figures and often playing the truant child, the irresponsible child, desperate for a parental figure that would take care of him. For a while that would be his first wife Minna, but only for a while. He was strongly attracted to women, especially mother figures, for much of his life. He needed maternal attention since he really did not get much from his neglectful and distracted mother.

But something else Wagner inherited from his dysfunctional family was a love of the arts. Both his fathers were very interested in the arts, especially theater, and when he said he wanted a career in the arts, his mother (though she did not approve) did send him to teachers of music. As his stepfather was dying Richard played some piano music for him, and Geyer commented to Johanna that perhaps the boy had some musical talent. Clearly both his parents encouraged his interest in the arts and tried to provide him with some education so that he could have a career in the arts.

Amazingly enough, they mostly did survive, except for his legal father and his sister Theresia; both died as the indirect result of this invasion because the bombardment of Leipzig resulted in typhoid fever being introduced to the local populace due to lack of sanitary facilities.

First Wagner wanted to be a playwright and wrote a play, *Leubald*, which he read dramatically to his sisters, who found it comic. Since his play was a tragedy, he thought this was most discouraging. But this early play indicates that Wagner had a taste for Shakespeare and an interest in writing for the theater. It was the Romantic writers who first saw the greatness in Shakespeare's plays, including the German romantics like Goethe and E.T.A. Hoffmann, and here Wagner was a typical Romantic in terms of his love of Shakespeare. Verdi too was typically Romantic in that regard since he turned Shakespeare's *Macbeth, Othello,* and *Merry Wives of Windsor* into operas. Since Wagner's whole family, especially his stepfather, were very fond of theater and had friends who were working in the theater, this indicated some encouragement. Geyer himself sometimes appeared onstage as an actor — rather like participating in community theater. Geyer encouraged the boy's interest in theater, and on his deathbed encouraged his musical abilities. So there were some positive aspects of his war-torn childhood. There was even a family story that Wagner as a child appeared in a play and ruined his lines and caused comedy and some problems while on stage.

Wagner was as self-contradictory as the rest of mankind, and his operas would be marked by complex, self-contradictory characters who can be interpreted many different ways and who continue to fascinate us and drive us to see Wagner's operas over and over again to see different interpretations of his operas and his complex characters. Suicide also reappeared in his operas, especially the Ring and *Tristan und Isolde.*

What did Wagner look like as a child? There seemed to be a grotesque quality to his appearance and this continued into his adult years. He was short, with a very large head and a slight hump on his back, and a big nose. He had a rather dwarf-like appearance — actually something like the anti–Semitic view of the appearance of Jews as short people with big noses. Did Wagner see his appearance as Jewish? He was raised in a Jewish neighborhood in Leipzig. And did this appearance in part explain his notorious anti–Semitism? When caricatures of him appeared in newspaper articles of his period, he was often presented with a Jewish appearance. Did other people often suspect that he was Jewish? His friend Friedrich Nietzsche suspected this, and he wrote about it when he became an enemy of Wagner. Clearly the whole Jewish theme was one of the weird obsessions of 19th century Germany — in fact, of 19th century Europe and America in general. And from his childhood Wagner was suspected of being a Jew, which added to the neurosis he developed with anti–Semitism, which may have been a form of self-hatred — though it was, alas, a typical prejudice of the period all over Europe and America. Wagner did not have a happy childhood, but then artists rarely do.

2

The Child as Victim: 1821–1830

"Where is home?"— Wagner

Children are always victims but some are more victimized than others. By the time Richard was eight years old, Geyer was dead and Richard's mother did not seem to like him very much. Perhaps she had too many children — nine in all, considered a large family even at the time. Perhaps if she had a husband who had survived and could help her with the raising of her children, perhaps if Napoleon had not invaded Saxony and bombed Leipzig, perhaps if ... Richard's mother often complained to relatives that little Richard was driving her crazy. And he probably was! Even Geyer called him "the Cossack," suggesting his mischief-making capacity. But Wagner's mother seemed annoyed when her little boy did what all little boys do: They are curious and sometimes mischievous but not malicious. Wagner's mother seemed to panic when her son Richard did the things that all little boys do — and she tended to demonize him as an evil child when he was just a typical little boy who craved love and attention from his mother.

Ludwig Geyer had some success in the theater. His play *The Murder of the Innocents* premiered in Dresden on February 20, 1821, and was a real success. In fact, it was staged in several other towns in Germany, including Breslau, and was a success. From his stepfather, Wagner first got the idea of the life of a freelance artist, moving around, performing, and living by his wits. Wagner himself would lead such a life. Another artist in the family was his father's brother, Adolf Wagner, who was a translator and scholar who scraped by with his freelance career — and without an academic position. Richard was absorbing lessons on survival from the men in his life. While his father Carl Friedrich was a salaried employee of the city of Leipzig, Geyer and his uncle were freelancers. These were his father-figures in his childhood and they had an influence on the boy. His life would be modeled on theirs.

Wagner's nightmares would have suggested to a modern psychologist that he feared the adults around him and he feared abandonment. "Where was home?" he must have wondered as a child, and who if anyone loved him? He had no memory of his legal father and Ludwig Geyer, the only father he had any memory of, died on Richard when he was eight. This would have left most children enraged and convinced that everyone was abandoning him, and also convinced that he himself was the problem and the reason why all of his significant adult figures were abandoning him. Children are naïve enough to believe what the adults around them tell them, and Wagner's mother was telling him that he was a bad boy. This would have generated deep feelings of doubt and self-hatred, and resulted in an insecure narcissism, an attempt to handle all these insecurities with an overpowering sense of self-confidence. As an adult he always appeared self-confident and sure of his own value as a composer, but this was all probably based on insecurities.

Wagner's mother was constantly sending him off to other family members, especially his uncles, and to various teachers, who housed him and taught him. His mother clearly wanted to get rid of him any chance she could. When he was eight years old and in school at Possendorf, his teacher walked with him to Dresden in time to visit Geyer on his deathbed; he died the very next day. Then Wagner was sent with his teacher back to his school at Possendorf. What a traumatic event this must have been for little Richard, and his mother did not comfort him because he was back to school immediately after the death, which left his mother a widow for the second time. This incident must have left the eight-year-old Richard Wagner (then called Richard Geyer) fatherless and attached to a mother who did not comfort or love him.

By the time Wagner was nine years old, some stability entered his life when he was enrolled in the old Dresden Kreuzsschule under the name of his stepfather—Wilhelm Richard Geyer—which would have added to his paternal confusion. At least Wagner now had a regular school to go to, though he was not a Wunderkind but an average student who seemed to do well only in classes he was interested in, especially in literature and drama. Greek literature, especially drama, particularly interested him and he enjoyed reading it. Very soon Wagner became known as a boy who liked to read and discuss literature, especially drama.

By his teen years, Wagner's intelligence and his musical abilities were already becoming apparent. Several of his teachers were telling his mother about his ability with the arts. This was not an ability his mother encouraged since she knew the uncertainties and difficulties of the life of a freelance artist, especially a theater writer or composer. But it was becoming clear that little Richard had a great interest in theater, like his father, his uncle, and his stepfather, and abilities to write and to compose music. His earliest music teachers noticed this in him, in addition to his uncles, especially Adolf Wagner, his father's brother. He had corresponded with people like Goethe and Schiller so he clearly had a significant reputation by the early years of the 19th century, though he certainly was not a major literary figure. But he was a productive writer who had translated all of Carlo Gozzi's great plays into German. Wagner in later life said he learned from only two people, Adolf Wagner and his second wife Cosima.

Richard rarely had anything positive to say about his mother. She must have often thought that her life would have been much easier if he was dead, and maybe he got the message that she wanted him dead. Certainly in many of his operas there is a character who yearns for death—especially Wotan, Tristan, Isolde, Kundy, and Amfortas. Perhaps Wagner got the idea that his own death would greatly please his mother. Death was somehow always connected in his mind with the search for a mother and this appears often in his operas, particularly *Tristan und Isolde*, the Ring cycle, and *Parsifal*. The orphaned boy yearning to connect with a lost mother reappears in these Wagnerian operas. Loving

2. The Child as Victim: 1821–1830

female characters are often motherly figures as well—we see this in Venus, Elisabeth, Isolde, Brunnhilde, and Kundry. A man who had a bad relationship with his own mother is doomed to look for mothers for the rest of his life. People who have had happy relationships with their mothers go on with their lives and can form more mature relationships with women and men.

The Congress of Vienna in 1818 tried to reestablish the conservative monarchies of Europe and create a lasting peace, which by and large it did, at least for a while. Germany and Italy were left as a series of city-states though many people in both countries yearned for independence and unity, which happened at the end of the 19th century. Certainly, the warfare and political situation would affect the two greatest opera composers of the 19th century, Wagner and Verdi, both born in 1813 and both ardent admirers of their respective countries' desire for unity and independence at last. Verdi's nationalism is seen as okay while Wagner's is seen with suspicion, though why is not clear. Some biographers want to connect Wagner with Hitler because of anti–Semitism, but this is clearly unfair. Both Verdi and Wagner wrote music which reflects their countries' yearning for unity and independence. When Verdi's *Attila* presents a hero yearning for Italy, this is okay; when Wagner presents an opera talking about Germany, this becomes suspect. Wagner shared the same fate as Nietzsche, who was also turned into a Nazi by Hitler, with the cooperation of Nietzsche's sister Elisabeth. Wagner's daughter-in-law Winifred, Siegfried Wagner's wife, also became a Nazi. After Wagner's death, Cosima Wagner turned Bayreuth into a center of anti–Semitism, though Wagner would not have approved. Both Nietzsche and Richard Wagner were long dead by the time the Nazi period arrived so they could not defend themselves from such criminal abuse. Wagner died fifty years before the Nazi period, but that did not render his reputation safe from those criminals.

But Wagner was raised in both Leipzig and then mostly in Dresden, both Saxon cities with musical pasts. Leipzig was the city of Bach, and Wagner went to the famous Thomasschule, which was connected with the Thomaskirche, where Bach himself was a composer, organist, and music director for the church, and where Wagner was baptized. Dresden's orchestra and opera were already famous in the 19th century, and this was the city of Carl Maria von Weber (though he moved to London and in fact died there). Wagner very soon became fond of the operas of Dresden's native son, especially *Die Freischütz*, and he alerted his little sister Cecilia whenever he saw Weber pass by their house—or enter into it, since he was a family friend. As a child he soon learned the popular tunes from that opera and began to idolize Weber as the father figure he rarely had in his own childhood. In fact, Weber became a family friend, and Wagner soon saw him as a truly great man. When Wagner became a conductor of the Saxon State Opera twenty years later, he was responsible for moving Weber's remains from a cemetery in London to one in his native Dresden and to have a monument erected to him near the Opera House. Weber became Wagner's favorite composer and a model to the teenage Wagner, a model of a new kind of German composer who was writing operas in German based on German folklore and mythology. Even as a teenager, Wagner was attracted to mythology as a subject for opera rather than realism, but also as a teenager Wagner discovered the intensity and attraction of theater. He also discovered the music of Beethoven. Even as a teenager, Wagner had a dream of connecting his favorite composer, Beethoven, with his favorite dramatist, Shakespeare.

In both Leipzig and Dresden, both Saxon cities, Wagner had a series of tutors who tried to give him the rudiments of musical composition, but most of his teachers reported that little Richard had tremendous enthusiasm and talent but not much discipline. That's hardly unusual in a child; most children are not known for their abilities to be disciplined. Several specific teachers, like Christian Mueller and Theodor Weinlig, saw Wagner as a bright boy with real musical talent and even ability in composition despite the fact that he was not a very disciplined student. He did not do well in a classroom but needed the individual attention which a private tutor or a musical conservatory could provide, even though there were not any musical conservatories in Saxony when he was a child. All this was before the state felt any obligation to educate its citizens — this being seen as the responsibility of the family, not the general public.

Wagner first studied music with Christian Mueller and he was already being taken to concerts. In Leipzig, Wagner got to hear Beethoven's 7th symphony and immediately became a Beethoven fan. He was a precocious child, especially interested in music and drama.

Wagner was lucky to be living in Dresden or Leipzig since he was able to get a much better education there than in most of Germany. Both cities had orchestras and opera companies by the early years of the 19th century. Germany did not become a unified country until 1871; before that it was a series of independent kingdoms, the two biggest being Protestant Prussia and Catholic Bavaria. Saxony was between the two giants and had its own traditions and even its own dialect of German, which Wagner never lost throughout his life. As a son of Saxony, how was Wagner to get an education? Back then, the state felt that this was his parents' responsibility, not theirs. There were some state school but these were for exceptional children, and Wagner was one of those exceptional children. Very early in his teen years Wagner was seen as an intelligent and gifted little boy, which would have been due not only to his native intelligence but also to his mother's efforts on his behalf to get him accepted into state schools. She realized that her son was bright and needed and deserved an education, even if she could not afford to provide him with one. Adolf Wagner helped with money to get little Richard an education.

One of the things that marked Wagner's childhood was the moving his mother did — Leipzig, Dresden, Prague, and Leipzig again, Dresden. Much of the Czech Republic and Poland were under the control of Saxony so Wagner would have seen these cities as part of his own country though they spoke a different language. Saxony remained an independent country when Wagner was born, though the largest German states were Prussia, followed by Bavaria — with the conflict still of the Protestant Prussian state versus Catholic Bavaria, a conflict which still exists in a unified Germany. Sometimes Wagner's mother moved the family but left her son Richard in the charge of some relative so that he could continue his education. As an adult, Wagner complained about living like a wandering Jew but that was the life he chose for himself in many ways, though he always saw himself

2. The Child as Victim: 1821–1830

as the victim of forces beyond his control and always looking for a home. In fact, he developed a pattern of getting a home and then doing something to blow it up and force himself to leave and find a new home, which he would subsequently blow up — literally or figuratively. Stability became something he both yearned for and dreaded throughout his life. The greatest stability in his life, first in Triebschen and then Bayreuth, was due to his second wife Cosima. He came to love her for giving him this stability, and also resented her for it. Wagner's love always came mixed with hate, a common human situation according to Freud. Wagner realized before Freud how complicated we all are, and every emotion includes its opposite, and that love and hate come together for humanity. Wagner both loved and hated the women he fell in love with — reflecting Freud's theories before he wrote them. Freud always said that the artists understood psychoanalysis before he tried to put it on a scientific basis, but Freud was not an opera fan and so did not know much about Wagner and his operas, even though he was living in two of the operatic capitals of Europe, Vienna and London. But Wagner had an uncanny ability to provide his operatic characters with both good and bad qualities so that some of his villains are his most sympathetic characters — for example, Kundry, Alberich, Hagen, and Venus. One of the questions his operas often present is the difficulty of telling who are the heroes and who are the villains — which of course adds to the audience's fascination with his operas. Wagnerian opera presents human complexity in all its positive and self-destructive qualities. Wagner's characters reflect Freud's theories about human complexities which make "heroes" and "villains" seem simple-minded.

Wagner's family also lived for a while in an area called the Buhl, a Jewish quarter, so Wagner as a child must have had some Jewish friends. Here too a love-hate relationship developed since he must have been both cherished and rejected by them. They were welcome into his Protestant church, but he was not welcome in their synagogue since he was the wrong race. He must have felt this as another one of the many rejections he felt as a child. Such incidents also doomed him to being anti–Semitic and seeing Jews as racists whose religion was based on exclusion — this was before Reformed Judaism developed. We certainly see this exclusion as well in the expulsion by force of millions of Palestinians, and the massacres of them as well, as a result of the creation of the state of Israel in 1948. Israeli democracy was intended only for the Chosen People — not everyone living there — and this state was called an apartheid state by the United Nations.

But despite these problems, and despite his many childhood illnesses, some of them grave, he survived and grew up. You don't have to love and cherish children, but you do have to feed them, and Wagner was fed — the bare minimum that a parent can do. As Wagner grew and survived, he developed an iron will and an iron determination to get what he wanted, no matter what the obstacles, and he developed this tendency probably from his need and determination to get some attention from his often distracted mother.

Though he was born in Leipzig, the family moved to Dresden, and then back again to Leipzig so he was raised between those two Saxon cities. Dresden was certainly the more beautiful city with a famous opera house, but Leipzig also had the Thomaskirche and the tradition of Bach and his Baroque music. The musical tradition of Leipzig and the operatic tradition of Dresden both influenced Wagner. He would live to connect the symphonic and operatic traditions of Leipzig and Dresden with the theatrical traditions of ancient Greece. But as a child he was especially fond of theater since so many members of his family were involved in the theater. His father was a theater fan, his stepfather was often in plays as an actor and even wrote plays; several of his brothers and sisters were already making careers in the theater so it was no wonder that Wagner developed an interest in the theater—and music as well. The connection of theater and music Wagner as a child found irresistible, and this became his vision of the theater of the future. It is interesting even now that people who don't much like theater do want to see a Broadway musical—that combination of music and theater is irresistible even for theaterphobes. At a time when film and television are the most popular of art forms, people still like musicals as the only form of live theater they want to see. And film and television are forms of theater most basically.

Very soon Wagner saw himself as a child of the theater, pushed onstage at an early stage to help with the family's precarious financial situation, and also to please Ludwig Geyer. The family would joke about little Richard's acting debut at the age of seven and his fascination with theater props and costumes. He was furnished with a little toy-theater as a child and encouraged to play with dolls dressed in theatrical costumes as Hamlet or Faust. The boy soon came to read the plays of Goethe and Shakespeare, the two most popular playwrights of the period.

His mother did not encourage this since she knew the uncertainties of a life in the theater. Like most mothers, she wanted him to be an educated, professional man, like a lawyer, a profession which certainly offered much more security than acting or composing. She wanted him to go to the university and not have the insecurity of the life of a musician or actor, especially since several of her older children were doing that, especially her son Albert. The mother wanted greater wealth and security for her youngest son, hardly an unusual feeling for a mother.

For a time, Richard lived with his uncle Adolf Wagner, a confirmed old bachelor for most of his life, perhaps homosexual, very scholarly and a writer fascinated with theater. He took to the boy and tried to educate him. He found in Richard a ready student who was very interested in reading, especially plays. The uncle was also a scholar and writer who was particularly interested in translation and theater. In the early years of the 19th century, long after Carlo Gozzi's plays no longer attracted interest in his native Italy, a "Gozzi vogue" became established in German-speaking lands. In the German states and Austria, Gozzi's plays were being staged, often in the translations of Wagner's uncle.

Certainly Gozzi's plays had a profound effect on Mozart's *The Magic Flute*. A troupe of actors performed Gozzi's plays in Vienna in German, and they often used Adolf Wagner's translations. Richard learned from his uncle about these Italian plays; Wagner's first completed opera, *Die Feen*, is based on Gozzi's *La Donna Serpente*. While Wagner came to think of his first three operas—*Die Feen, Das Liebesverbot,* and *Rienzi*—as juvenilia which he did not want performed at Bayreuth, it is certainly significant that his first opera was based on an Italian fairy tale play by Gozzi. And this first opera was the only one of

2. The Child as Victim: 1821–1830

the three true to Wagner's vision of opera. This clearly indicates the influence Wagner's uncle had on the young composer.

Wagner seemed immediately drawn to mythology rather than realism in the theater and opera house, and indeed his mature operas all involve myth. Later, he wrote a famous essay on the attractions of myth versus history and reality and chose in favor of mythology, something most other opera composers would have avoided, certainly his great Italian rival, Giuseppe Verdi. But Wagner was in many ways a typical Romantic in his fascination with mythology as the source of all art — as with the ancient Greeks and Greek tragedies, which also used myths for drama. Verdi was both Romantic and anti–Romantic in his fondness for the theater of his own time, a realistic, melodramatic theater with playwrights like Byron, Schiller, Shakespeare, and Gutierez. Wagner's interest in dreams became the essence of his art. In *Die Meistersinger von Nüremberg*, the elderly Hans Sachs has a highly significant talk with the young artist Walter von Stolzing in the last act, and Hans states that art comes from the artist's dreams the night before. This sounds like Andre Breton's theories of surrealism, which appeared in France almost fifty years after Wagner presented them in his operas.

While Verdi was usually attracted to realism and history, Wagner remained the mythic artist and composer. While both were great composers of operas, very early in their careers both showed signs of very different temperaments and interests. Both composers were born in 1813 and both became the most famous opera composers of their centuries, indeed of all time, but the differences remained. Right from the beginning, Verdi was a very realistic composer, aware of his audience and what he could expect from his performers. Wagner was more idealistic, writing operas for the ideal musical forces and ideal audiences which he rarely got except toward the end of his career. Verdi came from the Italian tradition of bel canto operas and composers like Rossini, Donizetti, and Bellini, while Wagner was much more interested in the German tradition of Beethoven's symphonies, Weber's operas, and Goethe's mythic plays like *Faust*.

Neither Verdi not Wagner had an easy time of it, but life was more difficult for Wagner. The copyright laws in Italy made it easier for Verdi to become wealthy rather early in his career. Wagner was a victim of the German copyright laws, which varied from region to region since it did not become a unified country until 1871. Most regions of Germany — like Prussia or Bavaria — paid a one-time fee to the composer for a new opera, which meant that it was difficult for German composers to make much money from their works through royalties from repeated performances, though opera remained the most lucrative of musical compositions and most composers dreamed of success in the theater, opera being considered a branch of theater which used music, so a form of music theater. Artists and composers often had to depend on a wealthy patron or the Church to get commissions; the theater was the only source of great wealth for a composer since a popular hit could generate much income for a playwright or composer.

Verdi was always more generous to his great rival to the north than Wagner ever was to Verdi. Wagner's insecurities as an adult made him very ungenerous to other composers of opera, with very few exceptions. He liked Bellini but that's because Bellini was already dead and so did not become a competitor. Wagner ultimately felt that there were only three great composers in the 19th century — himself, Liszt, and Berlioz. The fact that he did not include his great Italian rival Verdi, or Bellini, Donizetti, and Rossini, indicated something of Wagner's arrogance and also his insecurity. For Wagner the essence of opera was theater, with music helping the drama, though Wagner often contradicted himself here.

Wagner remained interested in theater as a child, primarily because this was the family business, or at least the family obsession of his father, his stepfather, and his brothers and sisters. His father figures died early but they were all theater fans, and perhaps Wagner's early interest in theater was a subconscious desire to find a father there. Some of Wagner's siblings were already theater people, making a living as directors, actors, and singers. Wagner's brother Albert and niece Elizabeth would all become significant players in theater and opera. Despite his mother's desires for him for be an educated, professional man, as a child Wagner must have been drawn to the excitement of show business since it was much more exciting for a child to visit a theater than a lawyer's office. Wagner's brother Albert was making a life in the theater, and his sister Rosalie would eventually become an opera singer, as did his niece Joanna — who would sing in some of her uncle's operas like *Tannhäuser* and *Lohengrin*.

And clearly this boy had artistic talent, and artistic talent in several directions, writing, acting, music, etc. His teachers commented on his many talents, though they often noticed that he often got bored if he was not the center of attention. In many ways Wagner very early displayed the narcissism often connected with the artistic child, a desire to be the center of attention and noticed and talked about — and loved.

His uncle Adolf encouraged Richard's interest in literature and theater and Adolf's library soon became a source of fascination for Richard. This library really became his university education because it was here that he developed his love of reading — something he did all his life — and his love of literature, especially theater. World literature, especially Shakespeare and Goethe, became lifelong fascinations for Wagner. In his uncle's library he also found Dante, Cervantes, and even Carlo Gozzi and his rival in Venice, Carlo Goldoni.

This uncle had a rather bad reputation in the family as the black sheep. Could it be that he was gay? He married late in life and rather quietly and secretly, but Wagner all his life had a fondness for the society of gay men, and he might have developed this as a result of the kind attention and encouragement he got from Adolf.

Parental absence and parental neglect were the main elements of Wagner's childhood, but perhaps that is good for an artist since the artist — unlike the rest of us — can turn such suffering into great works of art. The traumas of childhood cause much suffering for most people, but the artist can turn such pain into art, and this was certainly true of Wagner, where abandonment and neglect and yearning would become major themes in his operas. The abandoned boy Siegfried, raised by a sadistic, manipulative dwarf, the abandoned boy Parsifal, who does not even know his own name, the abandoned Kundry, manipulated by the sadistic Klingsor — these would become fascinating characters in Wagner's Ring cycle and *Parsifal*. Love and mother would become major themes in these operas as well, in addition to *Tannhäuser* and *The Flying Dutchman*. Redemption through the love of a woman, a major theme in Wagnerian opera, was a product of Wagner's yearning for a mother figure throughout his life.

In many ways, Wagner felt like an orphan for most of his adult life, constantly looking for mother figures to help him. Most of the women he subsequently met and fell in love with — Minna, Mathilde Wesendonck, and Cosima — were mothers surrounded by their own children. This could not have been a coincidence but clearly indicated Wagner's need for maternal figures in the women he fell in love with. Wagner connected sexual love with maternal love, not uniquely, and he sought maternal figures in most of the women he fell in love with — not exactly a unique male reaction. But if one has had a loving relationship with one's mother, this all becomes much easier than if the relationship is full of anger and resentments and a feeling of being cheated and victimized. Wagner had lifelong mother issues which had negative effects on his personality and his view of himself, and his search for loving women.

Wagner was an undisciplined student, but not the kind of student who refused to do his work; once he was interested in something, he did the assigned reading and writing in spades. Reading and writing would become the main pleasures of his adult life, and early in his childhood his teachers reported that he was a bright and curious child. If his music teachers assigned him to compose something, he did. He made friends, and at home he had sisters who doted on him. Sister-brother relationships would often appear in his operas, and he always presented them as loving relationships — especially in *Rienzi*, *Lohengrin*, and *Die Walküre*. Sibling relationships were often more powerful and loving than parental relationship in his operas.

Orphans often appeared in his operas — characters like Tristan, Siegmund, Sieglinde, Siegfried, and Parsifal. This was because Wagner himself often felt like an orphan, alone and abandoned, even when he had a wife and his own children. That sense of childhood abandonment haunted him his entire life, rather like his English contemporary Charles Dickens, who was always writing about orphans because he felt like an orphan even though he had parents. Both men were accused of anti–Semitism — Dickens presenting Fagin the Jew (in the original edition of *Oliver Twist*) as a Jew who lived by exploiting Christian boys and turning them into pickpockets. Did the sense of parental abandonment connect with a desire to find a national villain — the Jew? From the Middle Ages, Jews were accused of exploiting or killing Christian children — as in Chaucer's "The Prioress's Tale," when the Christian child Hugh of Lincoln was killed by the Jews. Such horrible anti–Semitism is part, alas, of European and American culture. This tragic pattern continues when people consider all Arabs to be "terrorists," another Semitic group often targeted by Zionist Jews. The tragic pattern of anti–Semitism seems to continue despite the horrors of the Holocaust.

The teen years are difficult for all children, but they were especially difficult for the very talented but very troubled Richard Wagner. Of course 19th century Europe did not have a conception of teenagers; their idea was that once you were 14 years old and had

had your confirmation, you were now an adult and could legally get married. Girls especially were often married by the time they were 15 or 16 years old, and boys could legally marry then as well. While we would now consider Wagner a teenager then, his contemporaries would have considered him an adult and a student.

Despite all these traumas, Wagner survived his childhood and entered the more difficult period of adolescence with more than his fair share of the usual problems of his age.

3

Student in Leipzig: 1823–1833

"To live only for love!" — *Tristan und Isolde*

Wagner entered the difficult period of adolescence with more pain than most children, and these problems and his new sexuality undoubtedly complicated all this.

He was sent to school at this time in Germany when there were no state-sponsored schools, and parents had to hire tutors to educate their children, the state not feeling that it was the duty of the state to educate any but the royal children. Laissez faire economics meant that the state did not feel any responsibility to educate poor people's children. If there were any state-sponsored schools, they were for the children of the aristocracy. Some religious orders like the Jesuits ran their own schools, but such private school depended on tuition, which poor families could not afford.

It must have been very difficult for Rosina Wagner, a poor widow with many children. Luckily her older children were now old enough to work, if they could find work, and as a result give some money to her. But most of her older children wanted careers in the arts — singing or acting or theater management — and such careers are notoriously difficult to maintain and they rarely earned much money. As the playwright Robert Anderson once said, in the theater you can make a killing but not a living. Some performers got very rich in the theater or opera — people like Wilhelmina Schroeder-Devrient and Enrico Caruso — but most people in the theater and opera at the time considered themselves lucky if they got regular work through a court theater in Germany, which was supported by a particular king or aristocrat. The performing arts were always a precarious existence for their followers and performers. This was undoubtedly true all over Europe and not just Germany.

The Wagner-Geyer household was in desperate financial straits after the death of Ludwig Geyer. Johanna and the rest of the family survived thanks to her older children and her extended family. Some of her relations, especially Adolf Wagner, provided some money for her and the children and housed some of the children, especially little Richard, with the uncle and his new wife. Adolf felt that Richard was very talented in the arts and so was willing to help any way he could in supporting the boy.

Richard's oldest sister Rosalie took over when Johanna was having an emotional collapse. She got an acting job and helped to support the family, brother Julius got a job as an apprentice goldsmith, and sister Klara got a job as a singer, despite her lack of training. Wagner's older brother Albert got a job as a manager of an opera company — a useful contact for a young composer.

Richard Wagner

Geyer's nickname for little Richard was always "the Cossack" because he was mischievous and full of energy, dashing around the apartment and pleading for attention. Unsurprisingly, he became one of those movers and shakers who could initiate projects which would come to fruition, whether it was arrange a picnic for the family or stage an opera in Bayreuth. Especially when it came to marketing himself and his career and his operas, Wagner was a go-getter with organizational skills. His fathers kept dying and his mother kept avoiding him, but somehow he absorbed from them artistic ability and organizational skills and genius.

The nineteenth century in many European countries was a time of great emigration as millions of Germans and Englishmen and French and Italian people tried to avoid the dire poverty in much of Europe by emigrating to America — or South America or Australia or New Zealand. Millions fled Europe because of the grinding poverty or political opposition, and Wagner himself often thought of joining those millions of Germans fleeing their fatherland and immigrating to America. He had offers of contracts from America later in life, especially to compose music for its centennial in 1876. Would Wagner have been better off emigrating to America? There was already a large German population all over America, especially in New York, Minnesota, New Orleans, Chicago, Milwaukee, St. Louis, and Texas. Wagner often wondered about this given all his difficulties establishing a career in Europe — Paris, the operatic capital, was certainly not very welcoming to him. He once developed a plan of emigrating to Minnesota and staging his Ring cycle there. Could Minneapolis have supported him in the middle of the 19th century? I doubt it, but maybe New York City could have supported him given the arts organization already in existence there, like its opera and symphony and the large community of German musicians there and in Chicago.

But in the meantime he had to convince his mother to let him be a university student, something he really wanted to do. His uncle Adolf Wagner was willing to give some money to support the boy as a student at the university, and this was very hard for the uncle since he was a freelance writer who often could not pay his bills. Wagner's life remained feast or famine, typical of a life in the theater. Being a freelance composer is always difficult, even if you are a genius.

Wagner told Cosima, as reported in her diary, that the only people he really learned from were her and his uncle, Adolf Wagner. Adolf was a man who lived by his writing — he wrote books, he wrote translations, and he corresponded with people like Goethe. He was a freelance literary man who had a reputation and had a hard life but survived and took a kindly interest in his nephew. Wagner subconsciously used him as a model for the life which he himself would eventually have as a freelance writer and composer who lived by his wits and survived and had to do all sorts of financial wheeling and dealing to survive.

In 1820, when Wagner was eight years old, he was sent to Possendorf to study the piano with Christian Wetzel. In 1822, Richard Geyer (as he was called then) entered the Dresden Keurzschule to study. This was then one of the best schools in Dresden so Wagner would have gotten some real education there. In 1826 the family moved to Prague

3. Student in Leipzig: 1823–1833

(then part of Saxony) but Richard was boarded out in Dresden so he could continue his education, and this must have been very traumatic for him since he was without a family though only eleven years old. But the next year the family moved back to Leipzig.

In 1828 Wagner entered the Nicholaischule in Leipzig, so this was another move for the child. He was now called Richard Wagner instead of Richard Geyer. In this year Wagner also studied as a private student with Christian Mueller, and he was studying music and harmony. In the next year, 1829, he wrote two piano sonatas and a concert aria and a string quartet. All of these compositions were lost, but they were probably really juvenilia since Wagner was only about fifteen years old when he wrote them. But there are not many teenagers who are writing piano sonatas so clearly Wagner had a real musical interest and musical talent as well. Johanna recognized the boy's talents and tried to get an education for him, though he did not always cooperate. But it was difficult for him to develop the discipline, especially the internal discipline, needed for a life as a composer. (Of course, which child has much discipline?)

By 1830 Wagner remained at the St. Nicholas school in Leipzig, and he was also studying violin and music in general. He talked about theater and actors with his family members, especially Cecilia, but his education included a lot of music as well. Given all the upheavals inherent in a life in the arts, especially theater, Rosine probably did not encourage such a life for her son, but she soon learned that she did not have much control of him.

By now Wagner was a teenager and undoubtedly experienced all the new trauma of that period of development. He discovered his newly budding sexuality, the joys and embarrassments of masturbation, and the new discovery of women and their place in the development of reproduction. The search for love began in him too. Did his mother ever explain the realities of human sexuality to him? Probably one of his teachers or siblings did this, but it must have been very confusing for him, as it is for any other adolescent. He may have been attracted to the girls in the neighborhood, though the family moved around so much one wonders what neighborhood that would be.

Wagner always yearned to be a university student and his dream came through in 1831 when he was accepted as a student at Leipzig University, one of the oldest universities in Germany (it was founded in the medieval period). He was finally that thing he had wanted to be for so long, a real university student, with all the rights and privileges to such a position, including the right to drink and gamble and be considered a grown-up and even a rake. He also started taking lessons in music and musical composition with Theodor Weinlig, the Kantor (musical director) of the Thomaskirsche in Leipzig and one of the famous local composers. Weinlig's recollections of Wagner indicated that he was not such a very good student: very enthusiastic and talented but not very disciplined. Weinlig never thought that Wagner would become the most famous opera composer in the history of German opera, but then what do teachers know? Wagner was not the kind of Wunderkind that Mozart and his sister had been in the 18th century.

Wagner's two years attending Leipzig University did not result in a degree, though he had entered as a student of the law — at his mother's insistence. His own reminiscences of his student years in *My Life* indicate that he did not learn much because he found most of the lecturers very dull, and he was not disciplined enough to get his degree. His heart at this point was already in theater and music rather than the law so he ultimately followed his heart and started composing. University education in the early years of the 19th century involved going to lectures (sometimes in Latin), reading and taking long exams to qualify for a degree. Wagner discovered that he liked to read but in German and not Latin — but this he knew about himself already. But he soon found that he did not like attending scholarly lectures and he found that if he already liked something, he could go to the library and read about it for hours, but he needed individual attention and did not do well in large lecture classes. His yearning for attention, and being the center of attention, indicated that a career as an actor would be perfect for him.

Wagner did have some fond memories of his stay at the University of Leipzig, but those mostly involved gambling, sexual experiences, drinking, and other major concerns of bad students. Bad university students have not changed so much through the years, and Wagner was clearly one of those bad but brilliant students. He was too obsessed with music and theater and his plans for future works to do the work required of a university student so it came as no surprise that he did not get his degree but essentially flunked out. One is reminded of how F. Scott Fitzgerald performed as a student at Princeton: He too flunked because of terrible behavior as a drunken gambler there. In any case, flunking out of a university led both Fitzgerald and Wagner to brilliant careers as artists. Artistic geniuses are rarely famous for being good students or for having particularly stable and disciplined personalities. Their genius tends to make them self-obsessed, and anything which is not connected to their current projects tends to bore them.

If a teacher captured Wagner's enthusiasm, he could be a wonderful student, but he learned much more in his uncle's library than at the university, which specialized in courses in which he was not much interested, least of all the major point of his studies, the law.

In the following passage from his autobiography, Wagner describes his life as a university student:

> My passion for gambling grew to almost manic intensity out of despair at my bad luck; insensible to everything that had attracted me in student life, senselessly indifferent to the judgment of my former companions, I disappeared entirely from their horizon and lost myself in the smaller gambling dens of Leipzig with the scum of the student body. I even bore with obtuse disregard the contempt of my sister Rosalie, who like my mother hardly deigned to accord the baffling young wastrel, whom she saw only at rare intervals, looking pale and wan, as much as a glance. In my growing despair, I finally seized the means to improve my lot by confronting my hostile fortune boldly. I was of the opinion that profits could only be achieved by upping the size of my stakes and to this end determined to make use of a not inconsiderable sum in cash that was in my safe-keeping, to wit my mother's pension, which I had collected for her. That night I lost it all, right down to one last taler: the new excitement with which I staked that last coin on a card was something new for me, even after everything else I had experienced in my young life: without having eaten a bite, I was forced to leave the gambling table repeatedly to throw up. With this last taler I staked my life: for there was no question of returning home; I could see myself in the grey dawn fleeing through fields and woods into a

3. Student in Leipzig: 1823–1833

wide blue yonder like a lost prodigal. This despairing mood held me so forcibly that when my card won, I left my winnings on the board and continued to do so time after time, until I had won a really substantial amount. I now began to win continuously. My luck became so conspicuous that the bank thought it best to close. I had actually regained not only all the money I had previously lost in this one night but also enough to pay all my past debts. The growing elation I felt during this whole process was utterly sacred. With the turn in my luck I clearly sensed God or His angels as if standing beside me and whispering words of warning and consolation. One again I had to climb over the courtyard gate at daybreak to get into my home: there I fell into a deep and energizing sleep, from which I awakened late, strengthened and as if born again. No sense of shame deterred me from voluntarily telling my mother, to whom I remitted her money, about the events of this decisive night and of my dereliction with her property. She folded her hands and gave thanks to God for this sign of His grace, and expressed her confidence that I had been saved and would never again relapse into similar sins. And temptation really lost its power over me for all time. The world through which I had reeled and staggered now stuck me as the most incomprehensible and unattractive one imaginable: the gambling mania had already made me indifferent to other student vanities; once I was liberated from this compulsion as well I found myself suddenly in another world, and to this world I belong henceforth by devoting myself with previously unknown dedication to the new phase, that of truly serious study, upon which my musical education now entered. Even in this wildest period of my life my musical development had not remained entirely at a standstill; on the contrary, music had become most decidedly the only direction for which I had a marked bent" [*My Life*, 50–51].

In 1833 while still a Leipzig student, he started work on his first opera, *Die Feen*, which was based on Carlo Gozzi's play *La Donna Serpente*. He completed it in January of 1834, and he wrote both the libretto and the music, though he never succeeded in getting it staged in his lifetime, and he ultimately did not think much of it. He did not want this opera performed at the Bayreuth Festival since he felt that he found himself as a composer only with his fourth opera, *The Flying Dutchman*, and he wanted that opera and his subsequent operas staged at Bayreuth and decidedly not his first three operas.

But Wagner's first opera has been staged in modern times with some success, though it is clearly juvenilia. *Die Feen* was based on a Gozzi play which had been translated into German by Adolf Wagner. This first opera does prefigure many later developments in Wagnerian opera. The plot involves magic and fairies rather than realism and features a magic sword, a magic cup, a conflict between the gods and humanity, and a mother who keeps turning into a snake — themes Wagner would spend his later career developing and putting to music.

Gozzi was one of the most popular of playwrights in 18th century Venice, having driven his rival Carlo Goldoni out of town. From 1860 when Gozzi's first play *The Love of Three Oranges* was first staged in Venice and was a hit, his fame spread all over Italy. When the Italian audiences got tired of Gozzi's plays, the Germans discovered him, and his plays became very popular all over Germany and Austria, especially Vienna. Mozart undoubtedly got the idea for *The Magic Flute* from the plays of Gozzi. And indeed Gozzi is now much more famous in opera than in theater since so many of his plays became famous operas.

Gozzi called these plays "fiabe," or fairy tale plays, and they were clearly anti-realistic and intended as a vehicle to revive his beloved *commedia dell'arte*, which Goldoni had tried to replace with his own realistic theater. The three greatest Gozzi plays, *The Love of Three Oranges, The Snake Lady*, and *Turandot*, had all been great successes at their premieres in Venice and toured around the Italian peninsula. But it was his anti-realistic, fairy tale plays which inspired Wagner to write his first opera, *Die Feen*, a play about a group of fairies and their influence on the life of humans. It is surely significant that the central character in this piece is the snake lady, and one is never sure if she is a good wife and mother to her children or if she is a witch who keeps turning into a snake lady.

About fifty years earlier, Wolfgang Amadeus Mozart had become fascinated with the Gozzi plays that were being staged in Vienna and his final opera, *The Magic Flute,* was undoubtedly a product of Gozzi's fairy tale plays. Even in the 20th century, Gozzi's plays had a greater influence on opera than theater. Prokofiev's *The Love of Three Oranges* is based on Gozzi's first play, and Puccini's final opera *Turandot* is based on Gozzi's play. Hans Werner Henze's *The Stag King* is based on *Re Corvo* of Gozzi so Gozzi had a greater influence on subsequent opera composers than on theater critics or playwrights. Wagner's uncle, Adolf Wagner, was one of the major translators of Gozzi's plays so it was only natural that Wagner would begin his career as a composer with an operatic version of a play by Gozzi, one of his uncle's favorite playwrights.

As an adult, Wagner considered this first opera junk, but *Die Feen* does foreshadow some of his major themes — non-realistic and mythic opera, the world of the humans vs. the world of the gods (the Ring), and the search for the resolution of polar opposites through fulfillment and redemption. It is certainly significant that Wagner's first opera was based on mythology from Gozzi, indicating Wagner's subsequent obsessions with various Scandinavian and German myths rather than on realism. Wagner would ultimately become a mythic, idealistic composer rather than an essentially realistic one, like Giuseppe Verdi. While Verdi wrote some kind things about Wagner, Wagner wrote nothing kind about Verdi. The only Italian opera composers he ever seems to have really liked were Bellini and Rossini, though his compliments to even them were often mixed with some negativity as well. Wagner rarely said kind things about his contemporary composers, one of the few exceptions being both Liszt and Berlioz. Wagner much preferred dead composers like Beethoven since they would not be competing with him for attention with the public. Wagner's insecurities as a composer meant that he could rarely say kind things about other living composers, which is sad as this tended to isolate him from people who could have been his friends and helped his career. Both Wagner's narcissism and insecurities kept him isolated from most of the composers of his generation, alas. He also presented himself as sure of his genius, but he had private moments of insecurity as well.

It can be argued that of all Wagner's juvenilia (*Die Feen, Das Liebesverbot,* and *Rienzi*), only his first opera, *Die Feen*, was essentially Wagnerian for it involved fairy tale and mythology, subjects which would obsessed Wagner and appear in his operas for the rest of his creative life. *Die Feen* also involved a mother-figure, Caressani, who keeps turning herself into a snake. Does this reflect Wagner's own suspicions about the true nature of his own mother?

3. Student in Leipzig: 1823–1833

Around this time Wagner developed a close relationship with his uncle Adolf Wagner. After the popularity of Gozzi's operas had faded in Venice, a Gozzi craze developed in Germany and Austria, though Gozzi got no royalties from this; he died in Venice in 1806. Given the German copyright laws, Gozzi's work was not protected, and neither would Wagner's work be protected in Germany. Some historians have commented that if Wagner had in Germany the same copyright laws which protected Verdi in Italy, Wagner would have been a very wealthy man, though he probably would have spent the money as quickly as he earned it given Wagner's track record with money. But Wagner's uncle encouraged the boy in his literary interests, something his mother did not do. This uncle was also the closest things to a stable father-figure which Wagner ever got. This uncle was also famous for financial shenanigans, something Wagner would also become infamous for as he matured. Hans von Bülow once said that Wagner was a genius of finance because of his ability to get money out of people, including his final patron, King Ludwig II of Bavaria.

Once Wagner was 20 years old and did not want to be a student any longer, he had to get a job, and a job in the theater seemed to attract him as the most exciting prospect. He had to start earning a living and could no longer expect his family to keep supporting him. He began by asking his family members if they could help him find a job somewhere. His brother Albert had a job as a tenor, but when his voice failed him he began managing a theater in Wurzburg, and that opera company needed a choral director. Richard said he could do such a job. The theater did not pay much, but it was a real job, a start in the profession, and he felt himself a lucky young man. Wagner would develop many family contacts connected with theater and opera, due primarily to his brother and his niece Johanna, who eventually became a very famous soprano. Wagner used his family contacts throughout his career to help him, and he always seemed to need help, though most of his financial problems were of his own making of course. But Wagner soon developed very expensive tastes and he went on manic spending binges which threatened to ruin him.

These binges got him hounded by creditors and even got him into debtors' prison while he was living in Paris. But even while he was in debtor's prison, he was working on a new opera. Wagner soon got to know money-lenders, many of them Jewish, and these people naturally wanted their money back, which Wagner promised to do but soon became unable to do. Why was Wagner always going to Jewish moneylenders? Rumors soon spread in the operatic community that Wagner was always borrowing money from friends to buy trinkets he did not need. Wagner also became obsessed with exquisite clothing; he developed a love of satins and silks. He soon developed a reputation as a clothes horse among the other members of that little opera company where he first developed into an opera professional. He also developed a reputation as a work horse who could write filler music, conduct a rehearsal, and get things done.

Wagner had the uncanny ability to keep writing, either prose or poetry or music, despite the chaos all around him — often chaos he himself created. Situations which would place most people in mental hospitals did not interfere with his composition. Hans von Bülow, a great friend who ultimately became a great enemy, once said that Wagner was really a genius of finance, and indeed he induced all sorts of people to give him money, even when they had none of their own. King Ludwig II of Bavaria became famous for giving him money, and the king's financial largess to Wagner was one of the reasons he was ultimately forced to abdicate in 1886; he committed suicide soon afterwards in Lake Starnberg near Munich.

Already Wagner had about him the atmosphere of the narcissistic young artist who did not know how to handle money but expected other people to provide it for him. Wagner always had a great sense of entitlement: Because he was a great artist in both literature and music, people had to provide for him. He was a bit like a naughty little boy who was looking for indulgent, wealthy, and protective parents to provide for him.

Some would call Wagner a user and parasite who was incapable of gratitude, but others would see the musical and theatrical genius who could create unique and universal works of art which would survive them all. The composer Liszt remained particularly generous to Wagner, who would eventually make Liszt's daughter Cosima his second wife after his first wife Minna died.

Wagner was developing into the personality of the narcissistic artist, who was willing to use anyone if he felt that person would help his art. His art always came first in his life, and he felt that his art was the greatest around. All other people had to serve his art. In many ways, Wagner would become the typical narcissistic artist whose life revolved around himself and his current operatic project. His obsession was his needs and his current project, and everything else came in second. In many ways, Wagner became a Byronic hero, so popular in his period. There are of course many people like this with absolutely no artistic skills, but Wagner was able to deliver the goods, the kind of enthralling, fascinating major art works which would leave operatic audiences in wonder — or dying of boredom. Wagner's music generated extreme reactions in audiences — love or hate. But right from the beginning, Wagner developed bands of followers who believed in him and his art, and some of those people were even willing to subsidize Wagner in his pursuit of his art. Very early in his career, Wagner was able to find women who were willing to support him in exchange for sharing the limelight of his art — and one of the first was his first wife Minna Planer.

Even as a teenager, the composer Wagner was curious about love and sex — in other words, a normal and typical teenager. On a trip to Prague (then part of the kingdom of Saxony), he fell in love with the lovely Pachta sisters, especially one of them. When they both dumped him for an older and richer man, Richard learned something about how some women could be faithless and materialistic, just as Wagner himself could be. But his need for women became apparent early in his teen years, and he soon felt that he could not live without them. He was not destined to be a bachelor with a healthy sense of his own power and independence, like Schubert or Brahms. His need for love and sexuality became quite apparent in his teen years. It is certainly significant that his second opera, *Das Liebesverbot*, involved the Ban on Love, and the power of the human need for love and sexuality — in many ways a typical Romantic theme, and Wagner was in many ways a typical Romantic writer and composer. One of the major concerns of the Young

3. Student in Leipzig: 1823–1833

Germany movement at the time was the power of love. And basic humanity is reflected here since we all feel the need for love and sexuality, and the power of our human needs.

These are of course typical adolescent themes but they also connected with the young Germany movement developing around him with young poets who were dreaming of a unified and liberated Germany that could develop its own literature and art and not merely reflect the latest theories and movements coming from Paris. Could Wagner be one of those new breed of artists who could create a new kind of German Romantic art? He wondered about and of course ultimately became the greatest artist of his period of German Romanticism. And the search for love and sexuality has remained a recurrent and popular theme throughout the history of art, especially drama. The Greek and Roman comedies and the comedies of Shakespeare use the power of sexuality and love as the foundations of the drama; after all, the classic ending of comedy is marriage, often multiple marriages, as in *A Midsummer Night's Dream*, which would become the basis of Wagner's great comedy *Die Meistersinger von Nürnberg*.

The desire for love and sexual experience was hardly an original theme in art— Shakespeare himself repeatedly used it. But the young Germany movement was particularly interested in love and sexuality as topics for art and how people find this kind of fulfillment, and what the barriers to sexual fulfillment were. These were all themes that would interest Wagner, especially for his next opera, *Das Liebesverbot*— or the Ban on Love— which was based on Shakespeare's *Measure for Measure*. The erotic impulse would become a major issue for Wagnerian opera, as it was a major issue for Wagner himself. He was a needy man, and in many ways a man desperate for love since he got so little of it in his childhood. We learn about love in our relationships with our parents, and Wagner's relationship with his parents was very troubled.

Love and sexuality became major themes in Wagnerian opera, and Wagner was soon credited with writing the most erotic music in opera. Such blatant sexuality, especially in *Tannhäuser, Tristan und Isolde*, and the Ring, had a polarizing effect on audiences. Some audience members loved this in Wagner's music and others were repelled by it. Wagner very soon got a group of fans who considered his operas mesmerizing and also a group of enemies who considered them immoral. The rejection of sexuality became a major theme in Wagner's final opera *Parsifal*, where the code of celibacy of the Grail Knights becomes central to the opera's mythology.

Wagner certainly enjoyed reading, and in many ways he was a student for the rest of his life. He was a reader who liked ideas and theories which he could discuss with his family and friends. He did not want to sit around and drink all day but always accumulated a considerable library, though he sometimes had to pawn his books to pay his debts. He liked books throughout his life and he liked in particular reading the classic authors Goethe, Schiller, and Shakespeare, and these writers would affect his operas. Here he was very similar to his great Italian contemporary, Giuseppe Verdi. Wagner also kept abreast of new trends in philosophy, especially David Strauss and Schopenhauer.

Another transforming event during his early years occurred when he saw Wilhemine Schroeder-Devrient perform opera roles in Leipzig or Dresden. Wagner's autobiography is especially interesting when he describes the force of her performances. He first saw her in *Fidelio* while a student in Leipzig and he found her performance of Leonora unique and electrifyingly real. She showed him how opera can be centrally about the drama.

Here Wagner got an idea of how powerful singing and acting can be when they are done in combination by a real acting singer like Schroeder-Devrient. These performances occurred in Leipzig, and from them Wagner got the idea of becoming a composer and wrote to her. She kept the letter and showed it to him when she sang Senta in the original performance of *The Flying Dutchman* in Dresden, and she was the original Venus in *Tannhäuser* several years later — opposite the Elisabeth of Johanna Wagner, his niece. Ultimately they quarreled over money, but Schroeder-Devrient remained one of the major influences on his life as a composer of operas. Wagner borrowed money from her — as he did with many other people he knew. But Wilhelmine Schroeder-Devrient showed him the power of an acting singer, a singer who knew how to use her voice but also had the acting ability to move her audience with the drama on stage, an ability to become not just a singer but a character onstage. She had the ability to convince an audience she was a character in front of them — despite some vocal problems, especially towards the end of her career.

Another inspiration for the young Wagner was the composer Carl Maria von Weber, whose operas greatly impressed the young composer, particularly *Die Freischütz*. This was a romantic work in German, a singspiel, with spoken text, which used German mythology to tell a mythic tale about a magic bullet and a devil incarnate. Wagner as a young man was fascinated with this opera and this composer, and when he was a Kappelmeister in Dresden he moved the dead Weber's body from London, where he had died, to Dresden, where his operas had been staged and had become famous at the local opera house. Wagner felt greatly indebted to Weber, a man who had visited his family when he was a boy and who had encouraged him.

Wagner had finally found his true vocation, to write operas for the German stage, while he was working in Wutzburg, and he would eventually become the greatest German opera composer ever. That is what he felt would be his destiny. He was attracted to theater and musical theater, but he wanted to combine Shakespeare with Beethoven, to use Shakespearean drama, along with Greek tragedy, which he also admired, and combine it with Beethoven's use of the orchestra — to combine the German symphonic tradition with the English and Greek dramatic traditions. That would be quite an accomplishment but he did it. But not right away since first he had to compose a work which someone would actually sing and stage. That would be his first challenge as a composer — to write a musical drama which some people thought was stage worthy, if not quite yet Beethoven-like.

He did not have to find a librettist to write the text of his new work since he would write both text and music. Not even Mozart or Weber could do that! Neither great composer, and Wagner was especially fond of Weber, wrote his own librettos. But Wagner felt himself uniquely gifted with both words and music, and he felt that a great work of operatic art had to come out of one mind rather than be a collaboration of two minds, which was the tradition for all the other operas he had experienced. Never before had one

3. Student in Leipzig: 1823–1833

person been able to write both words and music, but this is what Wagner decided he would do — create a truly unified work of musical drama. This unity of vision was his aim.

When Wagner was 13 years old and living in Leipzig, there occurred a public execution of a man who murdered his common-law wife, named Marie. The man was a soldier named Wozzeck, and about a hundred years later Alban Berg would create an opera based on Buchner's play of the incident. Berg used Wagner's leitmotifs and large and subtle orchestration techniques in this opera. Did Wagner actually witness this public execution? We can't be sure but he was a teenager in Leipzig when the soldier was publicly hanged.

4

Minna and Magdeburg: 1833–1840

"All my riches I will give to you if you give me a home with you!" — *The Flying Dutchman*

The best way to get a job is through family contacts, and that is how Wagner got his first job and launched his career in musical theater. Wagner's older brother Albert had a job singing and helping to manage an opera company in Wurzburg, then a very small town with an interest in opera and theater. Albert was singing baritone parts with the company, though he did not have much training, and he got a job for his younger brother Richard to direct the chorus and stage manage. There was not much of a salary with this job, but Albert and his wife offered to house Richard and keep an eye on him so the mother sent him to Wurzburg. By now Richard was 20 years old and felt he was a man and had to get a job and not be supported by his family any more, something his mother heartily agreed with. He did not get a degree at the University of Leipzig, but after two years he had had enough of the life of the student.

Wagner lasted only about a year in Wurzburg, but he found that he liked life in an opera company and had become a useful member of the troupe. He was not only conducting the chorus but also moving scenery and coaching singers and being useful behind the scenes in a working opera house. He had found his vocation, and he liked a life in the musical theater. He discovered he was becoming a man of the theater — specifically the world of music theater, or opera. While he was living in Wurzburg, he continued work on his first opera *Die Feen*, which is now considered juvenilia. This opera was based on a play by Gozzi in a German translation by his uncle Adolf but the text of the opera was by the composer. In his maturity Wagner considered this work junk and did not want it performed at Bayreuth, and it certainly is juvenilia. He was in his early twenties when he wrote it and could never get it staged at the time in either Wurzburg or Magdeburg. By the end of his life, he was working on it again but was never really pleased with it. He was very disappointed at not being able to get his first opera staged, but as always when that happened, he started work on another opera and hoped it would receive a better reception. At the time of its composition in 1834, Wagner was full of enthusiasm for his first opera and desperate to get it staged. He developed manic visions of the opera having a very successful premiere, being staged in Paris, then the operatic capital of Europe, and then being staged all over the world. He wanted to revolutionize opera. Most operas, he felt, were written for tired businessmen and included some nice tunes to make

4. Minna and Magdeburg: 1833–1840

for a pleasant stay in the opera house. Wagner had a vision of opera as a real music drama — combining symphonic music rather than merely orchestral accompaniment of the singers with fascinating and significant drama which included captivating characters and relevant ideas.

Wagner had a lot of energy and enthusiasm, and he found that opera composition was something he could do and the only form of musical composition that really excited him. He had found his métier, but could he make a living at it? He knew he was a genius but he was not sure that the world would agree with him. In the meantime, he was discovering how lonely he was as a bachelor. His uncle Adolf had spent most of his life as a bachelor and seemed to enjoy living alone, but for Richard it was a very lonely life since he felt that no one in the world loved or even liked him. He suffered so much when alone that he soon realized that he was a man who needed to live with a woman — perhaps more than one.

Wagner soon became known as a workaholic since he was a one-man opera company. He seemed to have perfect pitch and could tell when a singer or an orchestral player was performing out of pitch — a useful talent in an opera house!! He even wrote arias for popular operas when a particular singer wanted an extra aria not in the opera — this was typical operatic practice at the time. He soon developed a reputation of being able to do anything and everything in the opera house, but he also developed a reputation of being unable to handle money without going into debt and getting involved with Jewish and non–Jewish money lenders and becoming an embarrassment to the opera house and its staff.

He soon developed real sympathy for the common man, especially after reading the French socialist Proudhon, but he wanted to live like an aristocrat and soon became notorious for manic spending binges for luxuries he felt he could not live without. (According to Proudhon, property was theft and money was a way of controlling the poor.)

Then Richard got an offer from an opera company in Magdeburg. His reputation as a useful man to have in an opera company was spreading, though still not a reputation as an opera composer. The rumors soon spread that he had a good musical ear and could direct a rehearsal, conduct and direct a chorus, and even conduct an orchestra and hold a performances together, despite the fact that he was in his early 20s still. He could even write music to supplement roles — as he did for one of his favorite operas, Bellini's *Norma*. The basso wanted another short aria in the opera, which Wagner produced for the singer in the correct Bellini style.

While Wagner was in Magdeburg, he started work on his second opera, *Das Liebesverbot*, which was based on Shakespeare's *Measure for Measure*. A play he was particularly fond of, *Measure for Measure* was about the power of love and sexuality — something that would become one of his major themes. His opera also involved sexual hypocrisy, and an attempt to deny the power of sexuality and love. He was begging people to listen to parts of it as he was working on it, and he was trying to get the Magdeburg opera company to stage its premiere. In 1836 the Magdeburg Opera Company staged the premiere of *Liebesverbot*, and it was a resounding flop. Partially this occurred because the opera had not been properly rehearsed and staged, and the singers barely knew the roles in the opera, but the singers undoubtedly knew a stinker when they saw one, so after two booed performances the opera was withdrawn, much to Wagner's disappointment. As was so typical of him, he was devastated for a day or two, and then he started work on his next opera. Wagner had an amazing ability to have confidence in himself, to recover quickly from failure, and to find a new project when he was finished with one. As Hume once said, despair not, but if you do, work on in despair. This could have been Wagner's motto as well. Wagner had this amazing ability to work on his essays or his operas no matter what problems were occurring in his personal life. An amazingly productive man, he could compose prose, poetry (in his librettos), or music no matter the crises going on around him. He was also a voracious reader, and the only composer who actually enjoyed reading philosophy as well as history, drama, and poetry. His library at Bayreuth, in addition to his earlier libraries, indicates an extremely intellectual reader who had many interests and who remembered just about everything he read.

Magdeburg was inevitably connected in Wagner's mind with Minna Planer, his first wife. He had had several affairs with women, but as he was approaching thirty, and like most men he wanted to marry and have a sexual partner and a life partner, and also raise a family. He already knew that he could not live alone since he tended to go into a panic when he was alone for long periods. He was an intensely social animal, that he already knew about himself, especially in an opera company. He liked having groups of friends around him. By this time he felt he was a genius but he was a genius full of insecurities and one of them was that he was not properly educated so he continued to read. He was more interested in the theory of the art he practiced, opera composition, than most artists of the period.

Minna Wagner, Richard's first wife, photograph by August Weger, ca. 1892. Their marriage began happily, but eventually became very bitter (Music Division, The New York Public Library for the Performing Arts, Astor, Lenox and Tilden Foundations).

He did not seem much interested in the light, singspiel musical theater of the time, forms like operetta with spoken texts between songs, which was understandable given his love of Beethoven and symphonic music. He had clearly read and seen some of Schiller's plays, and Schiller had said that theater was the center of a country's civilization — something a narcissist like Wagner would have wanted to believe. Wagner shared Schiller's concepts of theater. But for Wagner, theater was also the family busi-

4. Minna and Magdeburg: 1833–1840

ness. Schiller also glorified the Greek tragic playwrights—Aeschylus, Sophocles, and Euripides—and felt that they had originated drama and brought it to its greatest heights. Wagner wanted to create art on that level, with music, and Wagner knew that Greek tragedy had a musical component, though the music has been lost.

Richard was particularly fond of Weber and Beethoven. (When Richard was a child, he actually got to meet Weber, before the composer moved to London, where he died.) Wagner was also attracted to Beethoven's opera *Fidelio* and his symphonies, especially his Ninth symphony. Early on, he was obsessed with Beethoven's symphonies and dreamed to connect the German symphonic tradition with Shakespeare's plays—something he eventually accomplished, especially in his opera *Die Meistersinger*, which is clearly based on Shakespeare's *A Midsummer Night's Dream*, but with Wagner's symphonic use of the orchestra.

So the logical thing for Wagner to do would be to get a job in the theater and write an opera based on a play by Carlo Gozzi. His play *La Donne Serpente* became the basis of Wagner's first completed opera, *Die Feen*. Wagner's first opera tells us much about him and his theatrical interests even though this opera was never staged in Wagner's lifetime (Wagner undoubtedly tried to get it staged). He was certainly following some of the musical and operatic successes of the time, especially Rossini and Donizetti. But Wagner was also imitating the music of Carl Maria von Weber and his interest in German folk legends, though here Wagner was using Italian mythology via Gozzi.

It is significant that Wagner's first opera was based on an Italian fairy tale play since mythology and mythological subject would become the basis for all of his subsequent mature operas. It involved the interaction between human beings and gods, a subject that would recur in most of his subsequent operas. While the music in this opera is trying to be Italian or French, we already notice in the score some Wagnerian elements, especially the subtle use of the orchestra. By this point Wagner knew that he wanted to combine Beethoven with Shakespeare but in this first opera clearly he has not found his operatic voice yet, though there are some interesting moments, especially some of the quasi–Italian arias which are not really Italian but still sometimes interesting. The opera also contains the problematic figure of Cerestani, a mother who keeps turning into a snake. And Wagner started a lifelong pattern here too since he wrote the libretto himself rather than trying to hire a librettist, the typical pattern for operatic composers.

Wagner remains the only major opera composer who was able to write his own librettos. He felt that a unified work of art had to come from one mind, his own, but no other major opera composers have been able to do this: Mozart depended on librettists, especially Da Ponte, Verdi depended on librettists, Puccini drove his librettists crazy with his constantly changing directions, and Strauss depended on Hugo von Hofmannsthal and once he died was especially desperate to find good librettists. Strauss wrote one of his own librettos, for *Intermezzo*, based on his marriage to his difficult wife Pauline, but this work has never been a favorite with opera audiences though it does contain some wonderful music. Wagner remains unique as an opera composer who was able to write his own librettos and this gives his operas a wonderful unity of vision and effect. And we see this immediately with his first opera *Die Feen*, though it is a very minor work.

While Wagner was working as a chorus master in Wurzburg, still a lovely town famous for its Tiepolo ceiling fresco in the main royal building and town hall, he was also working on his own first operas. He was leading the chorus and sometimes conducting some of the popular operas of the 1830s, which meant Rossini, Auber, etc. Wagner got to know these operas of the standard repertory of the time through conducting them, and his musical memory was impressive to his colleagues. Clearly, Wagner was a man who knew the score: He could read a score intelligently and even edit it if necessary, and it soon became apparent in Madgeburg that he could also conduct an opera's orchestra in addition to its chorus. As a chorus master with an excellent musical memory for scores, he was called upon to conduct performances when the main conductor got sick or wanted a day off. So Wagner began his music career with four duties: composer, conductor, stage director, and vocal coach. He would continue to juggle all four of these balls for the rest of his career, until the last five years when he was too old to do all this simultaneously.

While in Wurzburg, he first became remarkable for his Wagnerian energy. He could combine the energies of four people into one, especially when it came to promoting his own work and his own ideas. He could not only conduct the chorus but very soon the whole orchestra. He could also reorchestrate works. He could even compose occasional pieces for gala performances. He could compose music in various musical styles to help the opera company when it needed some filler music when a scene was being staged but the stage hands needed more time to change the sets or properties. He could compose operas, even if they were not staged, as *Die Feen* was not staged until after his death in Munich in 1888. In his maturity Wagner continued to work on his first works, juvenilia though they were. Wagner was a master organizer and could promote concerts. He became a real dynamo, though he soon developed enemies as well. In addition, rumors were soon spreading about his going to pawnbrokers and creating tremendous debts; debt collectors were soon appearing backstage and demanding repayment from Wagner, which generated embarrassment for both Wagner and the opera company. He was always begging people for more money, though he was beginning to get decent salaries.

Wagner was next engaged by Heinrich Bethmann in a touring opera company that was currently in Königsburg (now called Kaliningrad in Russia). There he met his first wife, Minna Planer, who was a very popular comic actress in the town. While Minna never really developed national importance as an actress, she was making a career for herself and Wagner soon fell in love with her. She was popular with the troupe and with audiences. Also, she was a motherly woman since she was always concerned about her younger sister Nathalie, and Wagner was always attracted to mother figures because of his own difficult relationship with his own mother. A man who has had a bad relationship with his own mother is doomed to spend the rest of his life looking for a mother substitute. Some of these men become gay but certainly not all of them. Looking for a mother-figure is almost as popular as looking for a father-figure among women.

Wagner first met Minna in a theater. She had become a very liberated woman of her

4. Minna and Magdeburg: 1833–1840

time—she was never the Victorian ideal of the virginal and naïve young beauty. Also, she seemed to love him, just as he was falling in love with her.

There must have been rumors in the company about the nature of the relationship between Minna and Nathalie. Even though Minna kept referring to Nathalie as her younger sister, most of the people in the theater company must have done the math and concluded that in fact Nathalie was Minna's illegitimate daughter, and Wagner must have been told or figured out for himself the reality of the situation. But while many men of the period would have been repelled by a woman with an illegitimate child, Wagner kept Minna's secret. This indicated his sympathy with women's liberation before it was fashionable and his own need for maternal care and his attraction to maternal women. Wagner inevitably fell in love with women who had children—someone else's children. Wagner never revealed this family secret even when he no longer lived with Minna and became involved with other women. At a time when many wealthy men looked to servants for sexual release, Wagner did not do this. There was clearly an honorable element in Wagner, a sympathy with working class people, and a willingness to keep family secrets like Nathalie's illegitimacy. He also did not exploit poor women and use them for his sexual needs, something often done by men in the 19th century. Hardy's Victorian novel *Tess of the D'Urbervilles* involved a wealthy, aristocratic man raping a poor woman, and the horrendous effect on the woman's life.

Richard proposed to Minna, despite her past, was accepted, and they married on November 2, 1836, in Koenigsburg. Soon afterwards she ran off with a Jewish merchant; Wagner's desperately lonely letters convinced her to come back to him, but this initial infidelity became a bad omen for a marriage which would become very ugly as the years progressed.

The marriage lasted for over twenty-five years, though it certainly ended bitterly with her living in Dresden and he living with Cosima in Triebschen. But Wagner rarely said nasty things about Minna since he knew that he loved her for many years and that they were happily married for many years. He also knew that she had suffered much thanks to him, and that she had followed him to London, to Paris, and even to Switzerland after fleeing from Dresden thanks to his revolutionary activities there. He felt a great deal of gratitude to her, though he also felt that the marriage had become hell towards the end of their time together. When they were young, it worked out pretty well, but as they got older she got more bitter and tired of all the wandering, and angry with him for destroying their happy situation in Dresden as Kappelmsister. But Wagner and Minna were never able to produce children, and Wagner did yearn for a family. Why was the marriage infertile? There were various rumors, and Minna already had a daughter, Nathalie. Wagner had three children with Cosima von Bülow. One rumor was that Minna had suffered some damage to her reproductive organs due to an injury while fleeing out of Russia thanks to Richard's debts and his creditors' pursuit of him.

But Wagner always retained many good memories of Minna when their marriage worked. She was a fiercely maternal woman who loved him and encouraged his art; she also nursed him through his episodes of erysipelas, a skin condition which was an allergic reaction to stress, and Wagner lived a very stressful life. Wagner suffered from physical problems due in part to psychological problems, and he tended to fall in love with the women who provided him with the maternal care which he needed. All his skin eruptions were very painful, but Minna helped with his salves and other medication and lots of sympathy. A very maternal and tender woman, she helped and encouraged him even during their terrible poverty in Paris.

We live in a time when we do not expect marriage to last forever: 50 percent of marriages in America now end in divorce and the other 50 percent end in death. But by the end of the marriage Richard and Minna could not bear to be in the same house together — again, typical of modern marriages.

Despite his search for a sexual partner and a wife, Wagner still had his career as a composer to worry about. Even though he had completed his first opera *Die Feen* by 1835, he could not get anyone to stage it. A man with less self-confidence would have given up on composing and looked for a regular job somewhere. Not Wagner. Instead, he started on a second opera, which became *Das Liebesverbot*, based on Shakespeare's *Measure for Measure*, which proved a flop. This began Wagner's typically Romantic fascination with Shakespeare's plays, the English playwright becoming one of his obsessions. But Wagner was attracted to the characters and plot of Shakespeare's play, especially the situation of the German governor who wants to declare a ban on love while he is governing Sicily. In Wagner's hands the opera would become a contrast between German Puritanism and Sicilian-Italian vivacity and free sexuality. He considerably altered Shakespeare's play to emphasize Wagner's own views of the power of love and sexuality, themes which would continue throughout his operas, especially in his mature works like the Ring, *Tristan*, and *Meistersinger*.

Liebesverbot, unlike *Die Feen*, was actually given a professional production on March 29, 1836, in Magdeburg with Bettmann's company (Wagner was a member at the time). The new opera was a flop after one disastrous performance, though Wagner was using the musical style of the operatic successes of the period, especially Rossini and Donizetti. But Rossini and Donizetti did these things much better. Wagner now started thinking about his third opera, which would become *Rienzi*, his first success as an opera composer.

On November 24, 1836, Wagner married Minna Planer. They were deliriously happy for the first six months, but by the spring of the next year she ran off to Berlin with a Jewish merchant. Wagner was a difficult man to be married to, Minna would keep insisting, because he could be so loving but also so difficult and so demanding. She sometimes compared him to a needy, demanding child like her daughter Nathalie rather than a grown man. Despite Minna's lack of fidelity, Wagner found that he still loved her and also felt that he could not live without her. So when she rejoined him, he forgave her, though he never forgot her infidelity — what husband could? Especially in the 19th century, female infidelity could not be endured by many men, but Wagner did endure this from Minna. Her infidelity tortured him, but he forgave her yet found various ways to get revenge by torturing her.

In the meantime, Bettmann's company went bankrupt so Wagner and Minna moved

4. Minna and Magdeburg: 1833–1840

to Riga, Latvia (then part of Russia) and he got a job as a conductor. There was a large group of Germans living in Riga and they supported a German-language opera company. Wagner had done enough conducting that he became really good at it, in addition to reading and understanding musical scores both operatic and symphonic.

In the same year, 1838, Wagner completed his libretto for *Rienzi*, based on Edward Bulwer-Lytton's novel of the same title. While he was working on his libretto and beginning to compose the music for his third opera, Wagner managed to make some money with his talent as a conductor, conducting both symphony and opera performances in Riga and nearby towns. He developed a real flair for conducting and developed theories about programming symphonic concerts which have influenced our own day. He felt that most concert programs of his period were too long and included too many works which exhausted the audience. His programming clearly reflects modern symphonic programming.

Wagner began to have fantasies about *Rienzi* becoming an international hit and he started spending money like a lunatic, borrowing primarily from Jews who made a living as money-lenders. Borrowing money and not paying it back became the subconscious masochistic and sadistic elements in his personality. He would also borrow from family, friends, theater colleagues, and anyone else he could get money out of. He went around town buying all sorts of things he could not use and did not need, borrowing money from anyone who would lend him anything, especially Jews. Was Wagner turning Jews into sadists to feed his own masochistic needs?

When his conducting contracts were not renewed and the creditors started demanding their money back, based on contracts which Wagner had signed, his financial problems came crashing down around him. The operatic smash hit he had expected failed to materialize and he became suicidally depressed. Minna tried to stop his spending binges but soon found out that she could not. Ultimately, they both had to flee Riga to avoid prison since their creditors were demanding repayment. Wagner and Minna found themselves in Russia, virtually penniless, and facing prison for not repaying their debts. Because of their marriage, Minna was now liable for Wagner's debts. Was this Wagner's sadistic way of punishing Minna for her lack of sexual fidelity?

Such behavior certainly seemed symptomatic of bipolar illness or narcissism or the actions of a needy child who could not act like a responsible adult when it came to money. Wolfgang Amadeus Mozart and his wife Constanze were also capable of this same kind of money lunacy. When Mozart made money, which he often made in big amounts, he and Constanze would spend it as quickly as the composer made it on all sorts of luxuries, and Mozart's father could not stop such irresponsible behavior despite his begging his son to handle money more responsibly and to prepare for periods when he was not making much money. To be a successful freelancer, one has to be able to spend in moderation during the prosperous times in order to be able to survive during the lean times. Wagner seemed unable to understand this. Both Mozart and Wagner wanted to live like aristocrats while they talked about the rights of the poor; had both men lived more modestly, they might well have ended up like Giuseppe Verdi, a wealthy property owner who could live well and had no debts. Wagner was doomed to make the same mistake over and over again and blame Jews or Jesuits or Catholics for his own cyclical demons.

Though Wagner suffered from suicidal depressions, they never prevented him from doing his creative work, whether it be writing music or essays, but that he tended toward cyclical extremes of moods clearly indicates that he suffered as a victims of these mood swings. Thomas Mann's wonderful essay on Wagner, "The Suffering and Greatness of Richard Wagner," indicates that Mann knew that Wagner suffered for much of his life. The depressions that followed Wagner's spending binges drove him very close to taking his own life.

At this point in his life Wagner remained madly in love with Minna and could not live without her and went into a panic when she abandoned him. One can argue that the search for love, especially sexual love, would become a major theme in most of his operas. His second opera, *Das Liebesverbot*, was about the human need for love despite authority figures who try to ban that need and create a forbidden love. The human need for love and the desperate search for love would appear over and over again in Wagnerian opera — from the Flying Dutchman's need for Senta, to Tannhäuser's needs for both Elisabeth and Venus, to Kundry's need for Parsifal. Wagner wrote some of the sexiest music ever written, particularly in his most erotic opera *Tristan und Isolde*, and there that need for love would drive the lovers to murder and suicide. The heart is a lonely hunter, Wagner seems to suggest.

Wagner said that one of the turning points in his life was seeing Wilhelmine Schroeder-Devrient perform in an opera, and he suddenly saw how music and acting could be one and the same thing. What he wanted to do was to put theater and music together as a composer-playwright.

Wagner implied that his own new works would revolutionize opera in Germany and that was pretty startling, but could he produce such a starting and revolutionary new opera? Well, yes and no. But despite the flop of his first operas, he was not ready to give up; instead he was determined to try again. Wagner never seemed to doubt his own genius as a composer and artist and always predicted that within fifty years he would be the most famous composer in Europe — which is what happened. But he had yet to create an operatic success to prove his genius as an operatic composer. The center of opera was Paris. To succeed at composing opera in Paris meant that you were an international figure, and this is what Wagner dreamed of.

How does a genius get along with other people? Despite a basic narcissism about Wagner and a great sense of entitlement typical of narcissists, Wagner had a great many long-lasting friends. So there had to be likableness about him and an ability to get along with people which served him well. He was never the solitary genius like the Byronic hero of Romanticism. He yearned for children and a family, and Minna provided him with some of this since she was his wife and already had a daughter, Nathalie, who was usually living with them. So in a way he had a family, though the child was not his.

But this never seemed enough for him. Perhaps because he himself was from a large family with many children, on some level he yearned for a large family, and this Minna

4. Minna and Magdeburg: 1833–1840

could not provide. (Her age may have been a factor since she was older.) But they both loved pets, and he especially loved large dogs plus parrots. Those animals became the children they never had. Wagner liked to entertain people at his apartment or meet them at restaurants. He liked to live like a Renaissance prince, with the generosity to friends of a Renaissance prince. He also had a genius for friendship since he had so many friends and corresponded with them often. They remained his friends even after he asked them for loans to support his lavish lifestyle and extravagant spending.

Those early years in Madgeburg established a pattern which would control his life for many years to come: the wandering artist, composing operas, married to a mother-figure, and the constant search for subjects for operas and for companies which would stage his new operas.

But Minna never again worked after she married Wagner. She had been a self-supporting, liberated woman, but after the wedding she wanted to be supported as Frau Wagner. One wonders why. Was this part of their marriage agreement, and typical of the 19th century, or was this part of their partly sado-masochistic relationship? They loved each other but also on some level tortured each other.

There was clearly a noble, paternal aspect to Wagner, and a broad-minded attitude towards sexual indiscretions and illegitimate births. His second wife would also be of illegitimate birth, also legally a bastard, whom he would protect for the rest of his life. Wagner, as a man of the theater, was used to being around and working with unconventional people, liberated people, not typically bourgeois people; he was used to being with unusual, creative people, especially since he was one of them.

Wagner seemed to understand the complexities of people and the complexities of the sexual urge. He was non-judgmental of sexual peccadilloes, and perhaps expected others to be forgiving of his own sexual indiscretions. He was hardly the rigid Victorian gentleman of his own nineteenth century era. He did not feel people should be shunned because of their own illegitimacy and their sexual pasts or their sexual tastes. He was not the typical Victorian husband who would only marry a virgin and considered women who had sex before marriage to be prostitutes. Wagner, to his credit, was a liberated 19th century man and not a Victorian hypocrite. The complexities of the human personality, human sexuality, and especially the actions of the subconscious mind would become hallmarks and major themes in his mature operas. But at this point he was only a young man burning with ambition.

5

Russia, England and Paris (First Sojourn): 1837–1842

"Seven years have I wandered."— Flying Dutchman

While in the English-speaking world, opera is considered first of all a branch of music, in continental Europe opera is considered first of all a branch of musical theater. Wagner wanted to create a music drama that combined symphonic music with fascinating characters rather than stereotypes and complex and mesmerizing ideas which would attract thoughtful, intelligent people.

In the spring of 1837 Richard and Minna were in a crisis situation since Wagner's contract as a conductor in Riga was not renewed and his debts were mounting to the point that he was getting threatening letters from creditors. Wagner was faced with the possibility of jail in Riga if he and Minna could not come up with the money that he owed. The only recourse Minna could see was flight and a new attempt to find success in the world of opera. They would flee from czarist Russia, and try to get to Paris, the operatic capital of the world.

So they fled through the Russian border illegally, without documents. The Russian guards at the border crossing spotted them and their coach flipped over in the flight but they escaped. Newman had a theory that this was why she and Richard could never have any children — an injury she suffered on their flight out of Russia. Wagner had more children years later with his lover Cosima, who eventually became his second wife.

After escaping from Russia to nearby Germany, they got on a ship, the *Thetis*, to London, from where they hoped to go to Paris. If one of Wagner's operas could be a success in Paris, it could make him internationally successful, and both Wagner and Minna dreamed of this. So they both wanted to go to Paris, though this of course remained a scary thing to do since they did not have a trust fund and would have to survive by finding some kind of paying job until their dreamed of success finally happened. But operatic success in Paris would only come to Wagner after he was dead, alas. In his own lifetime, Paris became a scene of near-starvation and humiliation and professional embarrassment and failure.

That sea voyage from Russia to London, which was supposed to take about ten days, became one of the legends of Wagner's life. The *Thetis* weathered one storm after another and wound up in the Norwegian fjords, specifically in the town of Sandwike, waiting for

5. Russia, England and Paris (First Sojourn): 1837–1842

the end of the storm and a good wind to take them to London. They were trapped for over a month in Sandwike. Wagner relates in his memoirs how the sounds of the Norwegian sailors singing, and the echo effects of those songs caused by the cliffs along the fjords, helped to inspire him to write *The Flying Dutchman*, which is set in Sandwike. It was the first opera that he felt was in his own musical and dramatic style and not dependent on others, though it clearly borrowed from Weber's popular folk operas.

Wagner describes his sea voyage in his autobiography:

> In cheerful spirits we sailed on past the beautiful castle of Elsinore, the sight of which brought back my youthful impressions of *Hamlet*, and now proceeded hopefully through the Kattegat to Skagerrak, when the wind, which at the outset had been merely adverse and had forced us to a lot of arduous tacking, suddenly on the second day of this leg turned into a storm. For a full twenty-four hours we had to struggle against it, while Minna and I endured sufferings quite outside our previous experience. Cooped up in the captain's pitifully small cabin, without a berth adequate even for one of us, we were a prey to seasickness and every kind of fear.

Wagner had a wonderful ability to turn the major traumas in his life to material for great, revolutionary new operas. Wagner's near-drowning became the basis of his first great opera, *The Flying Dutchman*.

One of Wagner's earliest inspirations was the German composer Carl Maria von Weber. Weber had great success as a composer with his operas *Die Freischütz* and *Oberon*, and then moved to London where both operas again succeeded. He died in London in 1826 and was buried there. Wagner never forgot meeting Weber, arguably the first great German opera composer of Romanticism, a style which Wagner would ultimately bring to its operatic perfection. When Wagner was the director of the opera in Dresden years later, he raised funds to move Weber's body from its burial spot in London to Dresden, where Wagner arranged an elaborate reburial and a monument to the composer near the opera house.

In his memoirs there is more about the *Thetis* voyage, in which Wagner, Minna, and his dog Räuber almost drowned. Wagner describes how he and Minna were clinging to each other during the storms and praying that they would survive. But Wagner had the knack all artists have — of turning his traumas into art. The rest of us just suffer. Wagner may have been pushed into debtor's prison while he was in Paris, but he was still able to compose there, while poor Minna was hysterical and trying to borrow from family and friends to get him out. There was an inner discipline in Wagner so that he could always create no matter what his personal life was like.

Wagner also used in *The Flying Dutchman* a theme that would appear in many of his other operas: redemption through woman. Senta in the *Dutchman* offers to prove her fidelity to the Dutchman through her own death, and by the end they are both dead but both redeemed. Suicide also became a major theme in Wagnerian opera; the Ring cycle ends with the suicide of Brünnhilde, and that suicide redeems the world. *Tristan und Isolde* also uses the theme of suicide repeatedly: Tristan attempts suicide at the end of each act, succeeding at the end of the third act. Does Isolde commit suicide as well? That depends on the production because Wagner's final stage directions are vague on this topic. Suicide was certainly an aspect of Wagner's personality since his correspondence repeatedly mentions the possibility of him killing himself. Wagner would use these kinds of vague or suicidal endings for several of his operas, like *Tristan* and *Tannhäuser*.

Wagner also used the symphonic techniques of Beethoven, his favorite composer, trying to combine Beethoven with Shakespeare. The overtures to many of his early operas like *Rienzi* and *Flying Dutchman* immediately signal to the audience a symphonic use of the orchestra, often reflecting the thematic conflicts, drama, and orchestration of a Beethoven symphony. All these ideas were in Wagner's mind as he was in Sandwike or on board the *Thetis* trying to get to London and then, finally, Paris.

Wagner finally landed in London after six weeks of nautical hell and instantly hated the British capital. He also developed a dread of traveling by sea ever again. He wandered around London in a fog with his wife and large dog. He found London cold and foggy and expensive, and he did not know anyone there, so he soon left for France with wife and his dog. Wagner's dog must have given him feelings of being a Saxon aristocrat who needed his dog as a status symbol — a symbol of the need to guard all his property and his estate in the Saxon countryside. Large dogs were then a real status symbol; they were useful to the aristocracy since they helped to guard the family's property. Wagner did not have any property to guard, but he always liked pets, especially large dogs. Another large dog is buried near him at his grave behind his home, Wahnfried, in Bayreuth.

In the fall of 1839 Wagner got to Boulogne, near Paris, where he accidentally met a woman who knew Giacomo Meyerbeer. Since both composers were Germans, they could converse easily and Wagner hoped to find in Meyerbeer the loving father-figure he was always looking for. Wagner was also desperate for help since he had arrived in Paris with not much money and was looking for some kind of work to sustain him while he was looking for someone to stage his latest operas. Meyerbeer understandably saw Wagner as a competitor and a sponge, a promising young man who was trying to use him to further his own career. Meyerbeer tried to be kind to Wagner and wrote him some useful letters of recommendation but clearly wanted to maintain his distance from the needy, demanding, and desperate young man. Wagner never forgave Meyerbeer for not providing him with the father-figure he so desperately needed. Meyerbeer often told Wagner he was just about to leave town, undoubtedly as a way of getting rid of the needy young man, and Wagner felt this as a rejection of him, which of course it was. Meyerbeer became the most popular opera composer in Paris, thereby triggering profound envy in Wagner since this was exactly what he wanted.

One way that Wagner supported himself in Paris was to write songs for popular singers to get them interested in his work; he did this, though he was never really a master of the salon song unlike other composers like Rossini. Wagner wrote songs for popular opera singers Maria Malibran and Luigi Lablache, but they were not impressed with the songs and the public reaction to them.

A letter of recommendation from Meyerbeer got Wagner an interview with the directors of the Opera di Paris, and he played them some of his music and begged them to

5. Russia, England and Paris (First Sojourn): 1837–1842

stage one or two of his operas. The opera directors were polite but not much impressed with Wagner's music. Given the kind of opera music which was popular in Paris at the time, music by Rossini or Meyerbeer or Halevy, this rejection was understandable. Wagner's music seemed more symphonic than typically operatic and not suited to French taste. Wagner was also in Paris during the bel canto period, and operas by Rossini, Bellini, and Donizetti became very popular in the city. Wagner's early operas tried to reflect the bel canto style but they seemed like pale imitations of operas by Rossini or Bellini.

From the fall of 1839 until the spring of 1842 he lived in Paris, and those three years were in many ways the most horrible and also the most productive of Wagner's life. He hoped to achieve operatic success but how could he have been so naïve? He did not know French very well, and the Parisian capital was a hotbed of artistic rivalries as all the composers of the day were hoping for a great hit at the Paris Opera, where success could lead to their operas being staged all over Europe and even in America. Would Wagner have been better off emigrating to the U.S. or Buenos Aires, where millions of Europeans were escaping the poverty of Europe? Wagner often considered this.

Wagner was a German coming into the capital of France; his French was never very good and most French people had an instinctive phobia of anything German. They probably had trouble understanding him and were innately suspicious of him. Wagner had the narcissism of all artists who feel that what they produce is worth other people's attention. Most Parisians must have been suspicious of him — and ultimately unaware of him. Meyerbeer of course was also German, but his music had more appeal at the time in France, though now his operas are rarely performed in France or anywhere. The German-Jewish composer Meyerbeer succeeded in Paris at a time when Wagner failed, which would have naturally added to Wagner's sense of envy.

Wagner became a freelance journalist and composer and managed to scrape by, but sometimes he and Minna were hungry and desperate. Wagner also spent some time in debtor's prison, though he did not report this in his autobiography. He wrote desperate letters to his family while in debtors' prison in Paris, asking them frantically for help. But instead of killing himself in debtor's prison, which he threatened to do, he composed *The Flying Dutchman*, which would be his first mature opera and his first success as a composer. Poor Minna was trying to feed them plus support her husband's efforts at composition.

Wagner became a freelance journalist and wrote articles and musical reviews about the art scene in Paris. He also wrote a long article on his meeting with Gioacchino Rossini, the famous opera composer then living in Paris. He also wrote an essay for a German newspaper on a German composer in Paris and one on an imaginary trip to Beethoven's grave so he was getting some attention through his essays for German newspapers. Wagner's ability to write journalistic essays helped him and his wife to survive.

In Paris, Wagner worked for the publisher Maurice Schlessinger. He was also facing the copyright laws in Germany, which were terrible for artists. Wagner continued to write songs and tried to get famous singers interested in performing his works, he tried to get opera directors to stage his operas, and he wrote articles about Paris for various German newspapers and journals. Minna was often pawning her jewelry and furniture, getting money where she could. The Wagners had a group of German friends also trying to survive in Paris, mostly gay men, whom they came to adore. The situation was a bit like Murger's *La Boheme,* the basis for Puccini's opera, with a group of struggling young artists trying to keep themselves warm and fed in Paris. Wagner also did musical hack work, like doing piano versions of popular operatic successes in Paris — operas by Donizetti (*La Favorite*) and some French composers. It must have been galling for a man like Wagner, convinced of his own musical genius, to do this musical hack work to survive.

But Wagner, despite the deprivation, continued to compose, working on his newest project, *Rienzi,* based on a novel set in medieval Rome by Bulwer Lytton, and at the same time he was also working on a new opera which became *The Flying Dutchman,* about the curse of wandering at sea and redemption through woman — both themes which would recur in Wagner's forthcoming operas. Wagner was also playing excerpts of his new operas to impresarios, begging them to stage one of his operas. One of those impresarios agreed to stage *The Flying Dutchman* at the Theater de la Renaissance in Paris, but the company went bankrupt before this could happen, though they did buy the libretto from Wagner for 500 francs. Another composer turned that libretto into an opera, but the opera failed. That composer would ultimately conduct Wagner's *Tannhäuser* in Paris — another failure.

In *The Flying Dutchman,* the undulations of the sea, which he experienced first hand on his voyage to London on the *Thetis,* appeared often in the undulating sounds of the orchestra. He would use this technique again in the undulating sounds of the sea in *Tristan und Isolde* twenty years later. Both operas took a great effort on Wagner's part to get onstage, and he wrote hundreds of letters to operas companies in Germany to get them to produce his operas. During these years in Paris, Wagner began to dream of owning his own opera company and staging his own operas there, under his own musical and directorial supervision. He always feared that other conductors and stage directors would ruin his operas, which did indeed happen.

Meanwhile, Wagner experienced hunger and humiliation in Paris, with Minna forced to pawn all their possession so that they could eat. Wagner's sister Rosalie, who was married to Mr. Avenarius, was also living in Paris so he had some family in the town. Wagner was always begging his brother-in-law for loans to pay his and Minna's living expenses. Such relatives as Wagner had at this point in his life were the kind of relatives who avoided Wagner and Minna — since most people saw them as poor and parasitic. Minna was getting panicky and hysterical, but Wagner had an internal strength and ability to survive, perhaps getting this from the example of his uncle Adolf. Both men became notorious for going to pawnbrokers and not always paying their bills.

Wagner developed while in Paris a circle of German-speaking friends, often gay men. Homophobia was so typical in Europe in the 19th century, and it would culminate in the trials and jailing of one of its greatest geniuses, Oscar Wilde. But Wagner liked gay people, especially gay men. As a theater man he was used to dealing with gay people. He must have very quickly figured out that people like Ernst Kietz, Friedrich Pecht, and Samuel

5. Russia, England and Paris (First Sojourn): 1837–1842

Lehrs were gay, but instead of avoiding them or reporting them to the police, Wagner befriended them and encouraged them since most of them were struggling artists like himself. Wagner never said an unkind word about homosexuality in his correspondence and seemed very comfortable with gay men. (The Code Napoleon in France had decriminalized homosexuality, something which Wagner undoubtedly supported since he was not homophobic.) Many of these people must have seen Wagner as always needy, which he was, though when he had money he helped other artists who were equally desperate for money. Ernst Kietz was one of them, a fairly good painter who drew a portrait of Wagner. Kietz had the bad habit of never being able to finish most of his works.

Wagner and Minna had this little group of struggling German artists over for supper when they could afford it, and Wagner wrote musical criticism for several German periodicals. Another German Jew, Maurice Schlesinger, commissioned Wagner to do some musical hack work for his publishing firm — piano arrangements for very popular operas by Rossini, Bellini, and Donizetti. This was the age of bel canto, after all, and bel canto composers were succeeding in Paris at a time when Wagnerian opera was out of tune with the times. Paris seemed to like only third-rate composers in Wagner's view — which posterity has come to agree with Wagner about. The most popular opera composers in Paris at the time — Meyerbeer, Adam, and Halevy — are rarely performed now and their works are not part of opera houses' contemporary standard repertory.

Wagner undoubtedly realized that these were second-rate composers, but such was the taste of the time that these were the composers who succeeded in Paris. Rossini became so rich in Paris that he could afford to stop composing opera and live like a very wealthy man. Bellini died very young and poor Donizetti wound up in an insane asylum in his native Bergamo. You think that would be a warning to Wagner, but he had enough trust in his genius that he plugged away in Paris.

Wagner soon saw that a group of Jewish music critics were helping the careers of Jewish composers — people like Meyerbeer and Halevy — while ignoring German and French Christian composers like him. He came to see this as a Jewish plot to destroy him, though in reality they were helping Jewish composers who happened to be more in tune with the current musical tastes of Paris. While Wagner had some respect for some of the Italian bel canto composers, especially Bellini, and he liked some of the operas of Halevy, especially *La Juive*, he soon developed a hatred of the Jewish cabal which he felt was supporting their own co-religionists despite the fact that (according to Wagner) these were all third-rate composers. Berlioz also felt that the French critics did not like him because he was Christian rather than Jewish. Two of the most important opera composers of the period in France at the time, Wagner and Berlioz, both had nothing but failure in Paris.

Most of those Jewish journalists wanted to help their fellow Jews to succeed in the musical capital of Europe. This was natural enough, but there were hidden agendas everywhere and Wagner was naïve; he and Mozart both were, when it came to other people. But Wagner's naïveté became paranoia as he began to believe that Jewish critics were out to destroy him and his career. Most of them did not know he existed because none of his operas had yet been performed in Paris. Wagner would eventually make enemies of them thanks to his own efforts.

One of those music critics, Hector Berlioz, was a composer as well as a critic, and a Christian, and Wagner liked his compositions which he had heard at concerts. Berlioz, like Wagner, wanted a big success with one of his operas at the Paris Opera, but both men were not to succeed in this regard. Berlioz was working on his epic *Les Troyens*, which he hoped would be a success at the Opera, but like Wagner he too had nothing but failure there, when the Opera noticed him at all.

Wagner introduced himself to Berlioz and tried to develop a friendship with him. Both had revolutionary ideas for opera, especially in terms of orchestration. Wagner greatly admired Berlioz's subtle orchestration and undoubtedly learned from it, but a friendship never really developed between the two great composers. Wagner's French was terrible and Berlioz did not know much German, but the Germans have a word for the special rivalry among people in the same profession. Both men were very competitive and since both were trying to succeed in opera, it is easy to understand that a friendship never really developed between them. They were both arrogant artists and naturally suspicious of each other.

Wagner also introduced himself to Rossini; he wrote a pamphlet about their meeting, which was apparently very cordial (at least according to Wagner). Rossini did attend some Wagnerian performances (in concert) but found the music too long and so alien from the bel canto style of his own period of composition that here too a friendship never really developed. Rossini once said that Wagner's operas had some wonderful moments but terrible half-hours — comic in the way that Rossini could be comic. Professional rivalries undoubtedly were occurring here too. Often poverty and failure create a better environment for friendship than wealth and success. Artists are notoriously competitive people, and Wagner did not seem to realize that these other composers saw him as a competitor rather than a friend. Wagner did not often realize his own competitiveness and his own arrogance when it came to music.

Meanwhile Wagner had his group of German friends, some of them Jews, and they starved together but also helped each other. Wagner was always anti–Semitic in theory but not in practice and had Jewish friends whom he loved. Wagner also liked gay men especially and enjoyed talking with them and encouraging their art. In Paris he developed a circle of such people and together they tried to encourage and entertain and help each other. When he first went to Paris in 1839, he felt like he was leaving provincial Germany for the European capital of art. By the time Wagner left Paris, he was a very chastened man who had a renewed appreciation for his German fatherland — a fatherland which would eventually drive him out. One of his friends was his sister Luise's husband Friedrich Brockhaus, who tried to get some work for him (Friedrich worked for a famous music publisher). Brockhaus got Wagner commissions to write articles on the Parisian musical scene and these articles were published in Germany. Wagner's writing skill was amazing for a composer, most of whom were not also writers, but Wagner also wrote his own libretto for his own (and other people's) operas, so he was clearly a uniquely gifted

5. Russia, England and Paris (First Sojourn): 1837–1842

artist. He was also a theoretician of the art of opera, or music drama as he began to call it. His brother-in-law Avenarius also helped him with money during his lean Paris years.

The gay German artists Kietz and Lehrs were especially kind to Wagner, having the composer and his wife over for dinner and working endlessly on a portrait of the young German composer. Kietz had a sad inability to be satisfied with a work and finish it, but Wagner encouraged him. Still Wagner had to make some money so he did musical arrangements for piano from the great successes of other composers. Wagner also got a job making arrangement for piano and other instruments from the very popular operas of Donizetti, a very popular composer in Paris. Wagner also worked on popular operas by Halevy for Schlessinger, producing piano transcriptions of these popular operas like *La Juive* and Donizetti's *La Favorite*. This must have been very humiliating for Wagner since he felt that he was the better composer. One would have expected Minna to work as well, but she did not speak French so she could hardly act on the Parisian stage.

In *My Life*, Wagner tells of his dog running away from him in Paris — probably because he was not being fed. Wagner relates seeing him in the streets and the dog running away from him. Perhaps this incident is a figment of Wagner's desperate imagination — an image of even animals avoiding him. He certainly often felt unloved and unwanted in his home as a child, though he was always very close to his sisters. Incest became a theme in the Ring cycle with the relationship of Siegmund and Sieglinde, the Wälsung brother and sister. On some level, Wagner liked to shock his audience and realized that shock effect was one of the ways which theater used to entrance audiences. Incest was also a major theme in the Greek tragedies, especially *Oedipus Rex*.

Wagner went from theater to theater begging impresarios to stage *Die Feen*, *Das Liebesverbot*, *Rienzi*, or *The Flying Dutchman*, his most recent work. One company, the Theatre du la Renaissance, agreed to stage *The Flying Dutchman*, but then went bankrupt. Another impresario offered him money for just the libretto of *Flying Dutchman*; another composer, wrote the music for this opera, which eventually failed.

It must have been galling for Wagner to see his libretto given to another composer instead of himself, but these were galling years.

Wagner did have some minor successes. His Columbus Overture was performed under Schlesinger. The full score of *The Flying Dutchman* was completed in 1841. But he always felt like an alien in a foreign country begging people to listen to his music and stage his operas. He even kept writing songs in the hope that some famous singers would perform them and encourage the Paris Opera to stage his operas—a ploy that did not work. These songs were charming but not remarkable and did not succeed in getting any of the famous singers of the day, people like Pauline Viardot, to commission operas from him. As a German composer in France, he was really out of his element despite the quality of some of the music he was producing. People were not out to sabotage his career; they often did not understand him because of his German-accented French pronunciation.

In 1841 the Dresden Court Opera accepted Wagner's *Rienzi* for production and performance in Dresden. Ironically enough, the only opera house to accept one of his works was a German rather than French theater. By the spring of 1842 Wagner and Minna were returning to Dresden, Wagner's own former capital, to stage *Rienzi*'s premiere at the main opera house there. Wagner was also offered the position of Kappelmeister, or conductor, at the Dresden Opera House, even though he was only 29 years old. He must have instantly become the most envied composer in all of Germany since there were many other composers in Germany who wanted the Dresden position even more than he did when he got it. Minna was overjoyed since this was exactly what she had been dreaming of since now she was the Frau Kappelmeisterin, the wife of the court conductor and composer. Wagner had an official position with a very good salary. If only she could control her husband's efforts to spend money manically, their ship had finally arrived.

By the time Wagner left Paris he had developed a hatred for the French capital since it had given him nothing but failure and humiliation. The French had been bombing his hometown of Leipzig when he was an infant in 1813 so his Paris experiences confirmed all his ugliest suspicions about Paris and French culture. There he had seen mediocre composers like Meyerbeer and Halevy and Donizetti succeed while he did nothing but arrange their dreary scores for four hands on the piano or for other instruments. Wagner actually admired some of these composers' operas, but ultimately he decided that Parisian operatic taste was "decadent," which meant it did not recognize his genius. It is interesting to note that Verdi came to the same conclusion since Verdi did not have much success in Paris either. Verdi often called the main opera house in Paris "la boutique," implying that money and marketing were the main concerns there rather than art.

But some of Wagner's musical journalism does indicate some happy memories of Paris. Here he finally got to hear his favorite composer, Beethoven, performed with a great orchestra. He heard model performances of some of the great music of Beethoven, especially his nine symphonies, and other composers. He had never heard performances of Beethoven's symphonies so well as in Paris. Wagner also wrote a story about a religious pilgrimage to Beethoven's grave, indicating his early theory about great art being a substitute for a dead religion, Christianity. He heard first-rate conductors and developed his own theories of conducting and musical preparation.

Geniuses know they are different from other people, and more talented than other people, and Wagner undoubtedly knew he was a genius. While he was making piano arrangements of operas by other composers like Donizetti or Halevy, he knew he had greater talent, and he did. Wagner clearly suffered from envy, which indicates a basic insecurity and perhaps a self-hatred. All of his assertions of his own genius may have been a way of cloaking his insecurities, which were exacerbated by his horrible life in Paris. His life in many ways reflected one of Puccini's greatest operas, *La Boheme*, where the suffering and death of a group of young artists and their friends in Paris at the end of the 19th century accurately reflected Wagner's life in the middle of the same century.

Wagner was always seeking to improve his health in the classic 19th century way, by going to spas all over Europe. Water treatments were very fashionable at the time, especially among the aristocracy; Wagner sought water curses for his skin and digestive problems once he could afford to do this. He sometimes got better and sometimes not, but in many ways he was modeling his life on an aristocratic style even when he could not afford it.

5. *Russia, England and Paris (First Sojourn): 1837–1842*

Wagner continued to write and to compose until things got better and he became the successful composer he always knew he would be. The help came from his own fatherland, Saxony. In his autobiography, Wagner relates his thoughts on his journey from Paris to Dresden, his intense feelings of homesickness as his coach crossed the Rhine, and his seeing the Wartburg on a mountain in the sunlight. That famous old castle would be the setting for his next opera, *Tannhäuser*.

6

Kapellmeister in Dresden — Premieres of *Rienzi, The Flying Dutchman* and *Tannhäuser:* 1840–1849

"Heinrich! What did you do to me!" — Elisabeth in *Tannhäuser*

Just when things were most desperate for Wagner in Paris, a rescue arrived from Saxony, where he had been born. The Dresden royal opera offered him a position as Kappelmeister (conductor) and an offer to stage his third opera, *Rienzi*. At one stroke Wagner, then 29, became the luckiest composer in Germany. He had a court appointment with a very good salary thanks to the Saxon royal family, the Wettin family. What a lucky man Wagner had become — after the horrors of his poverty and his life of begging people to hear his music in Paris, the scene of his greatest failures and humiliations. Wagner was returning to his fatherland with a job, just what his family wanted for him. Minna was particularly delighted to move away from Parisian want and desperation. The architect Gottfried Semper renovated the opera house in Dresden and Wagner got to know him. They would work together on other projects in the future.

This was the kind of success and recognition that Wagner and his wife dreamed of during their hard times in Russia and Paris. Little did Minna know that within eight years Wagner would destroy their comfortable position in Dresden and again reduce them to begging.

Wagner and Minna arrived in Dresden on April 12, 1842, to prepare the court opera for the premiere of *Rienzi*, which would become his first successful opera. Once Wagner and his wife were in Dresden, they immediately went to Teplitz for a holiday and to take the waters. Wagner and Minna clearly wanted to live like aristocrats and spent money freely despite their income. Wagner was now an employee of the court and he and Minna felt they could go to spas. Wagner got a good salary while he was a Kappelmeister in Dresden, but he had developed luxurious tastes (like going to spas) and so was soon going to family and friends for loans and then to Jewish money lenders. But Wagner also had health problems, especially erysipelas, and he was also prone to sometimes painful digestive problems, also triggered by stress. The life of the freelance artist, which was Wagner's life, generated much stress and virtually no stability. But now Wagner was a Saxon court employee, thanks to the king.

6. Kapellmeister in Dresden: 1840–1849

While at the spas, Wagner could be very productive and write librettos for new operas and compose music. He liked soaking in water, where he probably got the idea of water as an operatic symbol. Water, and its musical equivalent in Wagner's leitmotifs, becomes a major symbol in several of his operas, particularly *The Flying Dutchman, Tristan und Isolde,* and the Ring cycle; the first two operas have a first act which takes place on a boat.

Wagner was given a very good salary in Dresden, especially when compared with what most people were living on in Dresden during the same period. There was also a potato famine brewing in the countryside near Dresden since the same blight that was causing starving and emigration in Ireland was also happening in Germany. About eight million Germans left their fatherland during the 19th century, and one of the main reasons was the potato blight that was ruining German farmers and causing starvation there. It is not coincidental

An 1843 portrait of Wagner, touting his operas *Rienzi* and *The Flying Dutchman* (*Der fliegende Holländer*) (Music Division, The New York Public Library for the Performing Arts, Astor, Lenox and Tilden Foundations).

that the theme of hunger and starvation was appearing in many of Grimm's fairy tales, collected at this point, especially in the story of Hansel and Gretel, where the parents abandon the two children in the woods because they could not afford to feed them. In the Walt Disney version of the story the children get lost in the woods but this does not occur in the original Grimm version — grim indeed and realistic given the potato famine in Germany.

In the light of these realities, why was Wagner unable to live on his generous salary in Dresden? This occurred for the same reason that Mozart was never able to live on his income in Vienna sixty years earlier. Both composers wanted to live an aristocratic lifestyle. Wagner, like Mozart, also had problems when dealing with court officials. Wagner had Baron von Lüttichau and Karl Gottlieb Reisinger to deal with; they were in charge of the administration of the arts in Dresden. Wagner got to hate them both. He was not very good at working with authority figures, though both men tried to deal positively with him.

The 19th century developed a whole culture of spas and water treatments for various illnesses. All over Europe there were spas and spa towns, the most famous being Baden-Baden in Germany. The word bath is repeated to emphasize the mineral waters there with allegedly magical properties. Before antibiotics, water and hydrotherapy were important sources for cures. Wealthy people went to these spas for a few weeks every summer to get themselves cured by losing weight and soaking in these supposedly miraculous waters. The ancient Romans believed in this form of treatment as well, and it was the Romans who established the town of Bath in England after finding a well there with supposedly curative water. Richard and Minna went to spas as well — a sign of their status in addition to their search for health.

Minna particularly liked playing the part of the Frau Kappelmeisterin. Now she could go to spas and could even afford to hire servants. They could also afford a lovely apartment in the fashionable part of Dresden. Wagner was very productive in Dresden and subconsciously deciding how to blow up the very wonderful situation he had finally achieved for them. Minna never forgave him for destroying their lives yet again thanks to his subconscious and even conscious neuroses. Maybe the family security he craved never came when he was a child, so when it did arrive as an adult, he became enraged by it. Wagner's life was never logical, but then there are few lives which are. Wagner also found these numerous visits to spas a good place to do research and compose librettos and music for current and future opera projects. Light and dark imagery were also major symbols in Wagner's operas — the composer remained sensitive to lighting on stage before this became fashionable. Wagner's operas now included a leitmotif system reflecting both light and the lack of light.

Wagner's skin disease, which caused painful red eruptions all over his body, but particularly his face, was very painful and disfiguring. This skin disease was often connected with diabetes or alcoholism — was Wagner diabetic or alcoholic? Diabetes is more likely, and in the middle of the 19th century not much could be done for it since insulin was not discovered until the early decades of the 20th century. Both erysipelas and diabetes cause damage to the heart, and Wagner would eventually die of a heart attack in Venice in 1883.

Dresden was a city which Wagner knew very well since he had spent part of his childhood there, and the city was his capital since Dresden was the capital of Saxony. Wagner was born in Leipzig rather than Dresden but Leipzig was the second-largest city in Saxony. Both cities became part of the former East Germany, but since German reunification both have been incorporated in the reunified Germany.

Even in 1842 Dresden would have been considered the most beautiful city in Germany, the Florence on the Elbe as it was often called. It had an opera house which would see some of the most famous Wagner premieres — and fifty years later some of the most famous premieres of Richard Strauss' operas. It had the lovely rococo architecture of the Zwinger and some great art museums, especially the Alte Meister Sammlung and the Gruenegewohlbe. Dresden was heavily bombed during World War II but since then has been rebuilt so that the old part of the city looks much like it did before that war. The Opera was not rebuilt until after Wagner left the city — it had been damaged

6. Kapellmeister in Dresden: 1840–1849

by fire during the uprising of 1849. The opera house was also leveled during the bombing of the city during World War II but was rebuilt again to Semper's original designs. One of the big hits there, while Wagner was still a child, was Weber's *Die Freischütz*, and as a child Wagner idolized both the composer and the opera. Weber was certainly the first opera composer of German Romanticism, and Wagner would become the most famous composer of German Romanticism so there is some justice in the attraction. Wagner became the greatest opera composer of German Romanticism, and indeed the most famous opera composer in the history of the art form in Germany—rivaled only by Mozart and Richard Strauss.

Dresden was almost directly in the middle of Europe and as a result was often at the center of European wars, having been bombed and rebuilt several times. If Dresden was often the victim of European wars and invasions, it also had the energy to rebuild over and over again and to shine again with its artistic treasures. Its ability to survive destruction is truly amazing. It has been leveled five times in its history as the capital of Saxony but it has always been rebuilt. The Zwinger, the opera house, the Frauenkirche, all have been rebuilt and look beautiful these days. Dresden has certainly become a monument to the human ability to survive war and destruction and rebuild after war.

Wagner's life can be summarized at this point as a life of extremes—from fatherless child to Kapellmeister, from time in debtor's prison in Paris and starving artist, to a young composer with a coveted court position. You would think he would finally be happy and be enjoying his new court position. He was naturally worried about whether *Rienzi* would succeed, but at least he was finally assured a fine production of his latest opera so he had much to be happy about and to celebrate.

Wagner also composed at this time *Das Liebesmahl der Apostel—The Love Feast of the Apostle*. This lovely choral work for male chorus was composed for a church in Dresden and was a success; the music sounds like an early version of Wagner's last opera, *Parsifal*. The Wagners lived in some of the most beautiful areas in Dresden and near the opera house, especially in the Marcovici Palace in a lovely apartment.

Wagner did a lot of good work in Dresden, for one thing starting a series of performances of Beethoven, and starting a tradition of performing Beethoven's 9th symphony around the Christmas and New Year holidays, a tradition which continues to this day in many German cities. During his time Beethoven's music, especially his late works, were considered very difficult and peculiar. Wagner felt that Beethoven's 9th was his greatest work and that it, his late symphonies, and even his late string quartets were not appreciated sufficiently. He did everything he could to get these works performed in Dresden. The mover-and-shaker aspect of Wagner's personality was especially apparent during his years in Dresden, and he had a very positive influence on the city's music and opera for someone so young.

A major event in Wagner's Dresden career was the premiere of *Rienzi* on October 20, 1842, at the Hofoper, or royal opera house. The premiere became Wagner's first success as a composer and the opera was schedule for repeated performance. Wagner's favorite soprano, Wilhelmine Schroeder-Devrient, sang Adriano, and her wonderful acting compensated for her loss of some of her vocal splendor due to her age. Karl Reissinger conducted and the orchestra sounded wonderful. Joseph Tichatschek sang the role of Rienzi to great acclaim and the rest of the cast got very good reviews. Wagner finally had achieved the operatic success he and Minna had been dreaming about. He had a hit on his hands and even members of the royal family, including King Friedrich August II, who reigned from 1836 to 1854, attended the performance. Wagner became the most famous member of the opera company, a man who could write a successful opera.

But any opera house is also a political hotbed, and there were political realities in the Dresden theatrical-musical community, just as there were in any arts organization. In addition, the political complications of the court connected with the political complications of the opera house since all its workers were also employees of the king and the court. Wagner, like Mozart, lacked the tact to deal with these political realities. Just as Mozart developed enemies in Vienna during his time there due to his tactlessness in court, Wagner too soon developed a circle of friends but an even wider circle of enemies due to his own lack of tact. He wrote several pamphlets to the king on how to reorganize the administration of all the arts in Dresden. These pamphlets implied that all the current arts administrators were totally incompetent and needed to be replaced. Wagner never understood why these people now became his enemies. His suggestions for improving the arts in Dresden assumed that the current system was corrupt and run by incompetents. In the Dresden court administration, the directors Luttichau and Reisinger eventually became Wagner's enemies. His suggestions for improvements inevitably generated enemies because he seemed totally unaware of the political enemies he himself had made. But despite his widening circle of both friends and enemies, he remained productive and noticed. Wagner's genius made it very difficult for him to work within an arts organization he did not control since he tended to conclude that everyone else was an incompetent. This kind of narcissism made him very ineffective in arts organizations like opera houses, even if he had the king on his side, as he did in Dresden, at least in the beginning. As the king began to reject Wagner's ideas and ignore his suggestions, Wagner became angrier and angrier and sided with the revolutionaries in Dresden, to the detriment of his own career there. Minna saw all this happening and tried to do everything to stop Wagner and save his career there, but to no avail. But in the beginning of his stay in Dresden as Royal Kappelmeister, things went well.

Rienzi was the first successful premiere that Wagner ever had, and the role of Adriano was sung (and acted) by Wilhelmine Schroeder-Devrient, one of his great heroines. He had seen her perform there as a child and he felt that she made him want to compose operas. She had also been lending him money, which put a strain on their relationship. She was coming to the end of her career, but her mesmerizing acting still captivated audiences and they forgave her some vocal deficiencies because of her powerful stage presence. The rest of the acting and singing of the cast got good reviews, and Wagner finally felt like a successful opera composer, and indeed he was.

In his later years, he came to consider *Rienzi* a minor opera which he did not want

6. Kapellmeister in Dresden: 1840–1849

ever performed at Bayreuth, but the overture is still often performed and some of the arias are wonderful. Nietzsche once called the opera Meyerbeer's greatest opera, and in a way it is because it is based on a novel by Bulwer-Lytton concerning a real character from Roman history, Cola di Rienzi. It had Meyerbeer's penchant for using incidents and scenes based on historical events, but scenes often motivated by a desire for theatrical effect rather than dramatic credibility. The opera also uses a large chorus, including a children's chorus, to fine effect. Some other cities in Germany were staging the opera as well, though it did not get the Paris premiere that Wagner had dreamed about. Wagner now had a success and a real career as a composer of operas.

He immediately tried to finish up his new work *The Flying Dutchman,* based on an old sea legend; in fact, ships lost at sea are still called Flying Dutchmen. Now that Wagner had produced an operatic success, his opera company was eager to stage his newest work. The plot of his new opera was based on a European folk legend, and Wagner was indebted to a story of Heinrich Heine's for the plot though Wagner himself wrote the libretto for the new opera. *The Flying Dutchman* premiered on January 2, 1843, at the Royal Opera in Dresden. Wagner wanted to compose new, striking, revolutionary music, and he did — but the opera was a flop at its premiere in Dresden despite the mesmerizing presence of Wilhelmine Schroeder-Devrient as his heroine Senta. Johann Michael Wächter sang the title role of the Dutchman but did not achieve much success in this role. Wagner had already composed the libretto and much of the music while he was still living in Paris. *The Dutchman* was not a total flop in Dresden but the audience did not respond to it as warmly as to the premiere of *Rienzi*. It was the first of Wagner's work which he felt was a significant work, and which he later stated he would want performed at Bayreuth. But the public in Dresden did not agree at the opera's premiere. Wagner first used here his system of leitmotifs, or musical theme connected with particular characters and ideas. From its opening the opera uses the sounds of the sea and the sounds of a storm at sea. The Norwegian sailors' folk-like music is contrasted with the tormented motifs connected with the Dutchman and Senta.

Minna felt she was too old now to act any more, but she did not miss acting much for she enjoyed becoming the Frau Kappelmeisterin, the composer's wife, who was recognized in Dresden and given praise for her husband's works. They could even afford to go to spas and take the waters.

While Wagner and Minna were taking the waters at Teplitz, he developed the idea and a prose draft of the libretto for his next opera, *Tannhäuser*. The more he read of German and Scandinavian history and mythology, the more fascinated he became. Wagner would spend the rest of his career composing operas about medieval and Renaissance Germany with librettos based on German mythology and the history of this period. It is amazing how much of his composing career was planned very early, his attractions to mythology of the Middle Ages especially. He mapped out his whole career as a composer at this time, thinking about operas based on the legends of Tannhäuser, Tristan, the Ring, and Parsifal. Except for the story of Tannhäuser, these projects were all just plans or outlines for operas. But there they were on paper. Clearly Wagner was a mythic artist rather than a realistic one — and here he was typically Romantic with that movement's fascination with medieval mythology.

Wagner must have had an iron constitution to endure all the stress and grief and illnesses he went through — and still he lived until almost seventy. Now he was not a freelancer anymore but actually had a permanent job and a court appointment. Yet he often wondered if he would be better off as a composer living elsewhere, though his wife was very satisfied with her life in Dresden.

Millions of Germans were leaving Germany during this period, and Wagner often wondered if he should do this as well. In the 19th century about eight million Germans immigrated to North and South America, and Wagner sometimes thought of joining this flood of people leaving the fatherland. Maybe the New World would be more attracted to his ideas and finance his operatic and theatrical projects than the Old World of Europe. By the end of his life, he would repeatedly threaten his patron, King Ludwig II, that he was going to go to America instead of remaining in Bavaria. What would have happened to Wagner if he had emigrated to America at a time when millions of Germany were doing exactly that? One wonders if he would have succeeded in the world of 19th century American opera. He had heard of his music being performed in America, and he would eventually be commissioned to compose a march for the American centenary in 1876. (His Centennial March is not considered one of his great compositions.)

Wagner wrote an aria for Bellini's *Norma*, an opera he much admired. He also staged several Gluck reform operas — in fact, his own operas would be often compared to Gluck's operas, though Wagner's did not have happy endings as Gluck's did. Wagner also conducted Handel's *Messiah* and began a tradition of performing Beethoven's ninth symphony annually in Dresden. At the time the symphony was considered bizarre and unperformable, but Wagner got the orchestra, chorus, and soloists together and performed the entire symphony, and thereby started a tradition throughout Germany of annual performances of this perhaps greatest of all the Beethoven symphonies. Wagner also conducted successful performances of Beethoven's 7th and 8th symphonies, then considered Beethoven's failures.

Wagner developed a close friendship with the soprano Wilhelmine Schroeder-Devrient. She had been one of his early inspirations since he immediately admired her performances when he first saw her onstage in Leipzig and Dresden while he was a teenager. Her ability to act impressed him even more than her singing since she was a real acting singer and could make a role theatrically alive. Wagner admired this kind of singer even more than the gorgeous voices of duller singers. The drama always came first for Wagner and Shroeder-Devrient became a dramatic powerhouse onstage. But Wagner also admired the Italian school of bel canto singing and wanted a lovely tone and real legato singing from his singers. Of the bel canto composers, he liked only Bellini, but he did meet Rossini on one occasion when he was living in Paris and wrote an account of this meeting for a German newspaper.

Critics found Schroeder-Devrient's acting much more mesmerizing than her singing, but her enunciation of the words was especially famous. She really presented opera as

6. Kapellmeister in Dresden: 1840–1849

drama with music, and of course Wagner would become famous for the term "music drama"—he called his operas "dramas." He wrote dramatic music and wanted the drama to be primary and the action not stopped for the sake of the music, something which he insisted on in his theory of opera but he did not always fulfill his own theories. Wagner, like other great thinkers, contradicted himself and was not always consistent with his own theories. He also tended to ask the impossible since not many singers could sing the very difficult roles he was writing, let alone maintain a bel canto tone and act with conviction.

Since the beginnings of opera in the 17th century in Florence, there were singers with gorgeous voices and singers who had to act with conviction since they did not have such gorgeous voices. To expect singers to do both was to expect a lot of them. Schroeder-Devrient originated the role of Senta in *The Dutchman* but not even her presence could make a success of the opera with the Dresden public.

Wagner also had a premiere at the famous Frauenkirche with his "Das Libesmahl der Apostel," religious choral music which in some ways prefigures the musical style of his final opera, *Parsifal*. This church, the Frauenkirche in Dresden, was one of the most beautiful churches in Christendom; it was leveled during the horrible bombing of Dresden during World War II but it was completely rebuilt fifty years later. While Wagner was elated over the success of *Rienzi*, he was undoubtedly disappointed by the failure the very next year of his *Dutchman*. But he had much to be happy about — he was finally a success as a composer in one of the most famous and beautiful opera houses in all of the German states.

It was during this period that he worked to move Weber's bones from out of that cemetery in London, where the German composer had died, back to his hometown of Dresden. Wagner succeeded in doing just that. This occurred in December of 1844, and on December 15 Wagner had a ceremony to welcome Weber's remains back to Dresden. There is now a monument to Weber by the side of the Semperoper house, which was built during this period. This gorgeous opera house, after it was rebuilt, was named for the architect who designed it. Semper was a friend of Wagner's.

While Wagner was in beautiful Dresden, he had all sorts of new ideas for revolutioning how classical music functioned. He wrote a proposal to the king on the reorganization of the management of the arts in all of Saxony which, given his age, must have offended most of the other court officials of the time in Dresden. He managed to become an enemy of Luttichau, the man most responsible to the king for the opera in Dresden. Wagner came to believe he was incompetent; most people in Dresden at the time would not agree.

Wagner wanted to revise some of the Gluck operas for performances in Dresden, and this too he managed to do. He also wanted to stage Bellini's *Norma*, one of his favorite operas, and he even added an aria for Oroveso. Wagner was always a big fan of Bellini and all his wonderful melodies. He wanted to mount *Norma* and several of Bellini's other operas, and he immediately thought of Schroeder-Devrient as an ideal Norma. This too he managed to do, at the end of her career.

Wagner was constantly borrowing money from friends in town and at the opera house, members of the orchestra, etc. People were wondering why he could not live on his generous salary from the Saxon king, and why he was making problems for the king by asking for more and more money. He did make very good friends in Dresden, people like Dr. Pusinelli and August Röckel, who would become his friends for the rest of their lives. So clearly there was a pleasant and friendly quality, in addition of course to his genius, which attracted people to him.

The Wagners moved several times while in Dresden, often to more luxurious quarters. They could even afford servants. Dresden and Wagner's position there had become all that she and Richard had dreamed about while they were starving in Paris.

But there was some demon in Wagner which made him want to destroy Walhalla once he had achieved it. Some subconscious forces drove Wagner to create the perfect situation for himself and then blow it all up — and he would do this over and over again in his career. He seemed incapable of humility and gratitude to the king. His motivation was very complicated, but I think there was a rage in Wagner, a rage about not getting the happy, loving childhood which children are entitled to. There was that never-ending rage which made him unhappy even when he was finally achieving success. He also wanted to punish the very people who were helping him — destroy the love which some people were bestowing on him. Why was he so sadistic to the very people who loved him, like Minna? Because he had been treated sadistically as a child, he had a subconscious need to be sadistic to others, which he knew and hated in himself but could not control. His subconscious mind kept sabotaging his efforts to find love and success in his risky career as an opera composer.

Was he on some level a victim of borderline personality disorder, with its accompanying tendency to imagine slights from other people and making enemies based on his own fantasies rather than the reality of the situation? He began to get the reputation of being a genius and an ingrate and a lunatic. Then he discovered politics and began reading Proudhon and his theories of property as theft and the solution in socialism. Wagner, like many idealists of the period, came to believe in socialism and see evil in capitalism and the class system.

In April of 1845 he completed the full score of *Tannhäuser* and submitted it to the Saxon State Opera in Dresden to be staged, and it was accepted and put into production. It was in this same year that he also began working on *Lohengrin*, along with making an initial draft of *Die Meistersinger von Nürnberg*. Lohengrin's father was Parsifal, and he also envisioned as opera based on the Parsifal legend. Wagner's productivity was truly amazing, especially in these years when he had an opera company at his disposal and a sympathetic monarch and a public eager to hear his newest compositions. And he was still in his early 30s at this point.

Tannhäuser had another one of the successful premieres in the history of Wagnerian opera. It was first staged in Dresden on October 19, 1845, conducted by the composer himself. Schroeder-Devrient was the Venus, and his niece Johanna Wagner was the Elisabeth with Joseph Tichatsceck in the title role. By now, the tenor had become Wagner's first Heldentenor, and all three singers got very good reviews. Within four years Wagner had

6. Kapellmeister in Dresden: 1840–1849

produced his first three great operas, an amazing accomplishment. The opera became Wagner's second big success at the Royal Opera, and other opera companies were taking notice. But a conflict soon developed between the two prima donnas. The only thing they had in common is that they had both loaned money to the composer. Schroeder-Devrient was coming to the very end of her singing career while Johanna Wagner was just beginning hers, so of course they hated each other.

Schroeder-Devrient, despite the success she experienced in this latest Wagner opera, went to a lawyer and demanded her money back. Other former friends in Dresden, were also demanding repayment by the composer, who now seemed to them a very wealthy man with two operatic hits to his credit. In the spring of 1846, Wagner submitted plans for changing the way the arts functioned and were funded in Saxony. In this same year he began the musical composition of *Lohengrin*, while continuing to conduct his own operas in Dresden, especially the very popular *Tannhäuser*. He went to the court authorities asking for more money, in addition to his generous salary. He was given a loan by the opera directors, but the arts administration resented his constant pleas for more money.

On January 9, 1848, Wagner's mother Rosine died in Leipzig. This is a traumatic event in any person's life, and it certainly was in Wagner's for his complex feelings of both love and hate came to the surface about his mother. She was a very neglectful mother to Richard but she was the only mother he had. And the death of a parent, particularly a mother, can also have a liberating effect on the grieving son or daughter. He was now a grown-up and could do whatever he wanted. His sister Rosalie died soon afterwards in childbirth, and this was the sibling he was very close to as a child. Did his involvement with the uprising soon to occur in Dresden have something to do with his mother's death and his long-simmering conscious and subconscious anger at her so evident in his autobiography? One wonders.

It was during this period that Wagner first began to read the Nibelungen saga, *Der Nibelungenlied*, written in the medieval period, and he first conceived the idea of turning this long and complicated work into a series of operas. As he was working on *Lohengrin*, now in production, he became aware of the legend of Parsifal, the father of Lohengrin, and also thought of writing operas based on both father and son, which he eventually did. The medieval legend of the Grail began to fascinate him, and he wondered about the operatic possibilities of that subject as well.

With all this productivity on many fronts, one would think Wagner would be too busy to consider becoming involved in politics, but that is to underestimate Richard Wagner. The years 1848 and 1849 were revolutionary in many places in Europe, especially Paris, and Wagner was determined to bring the revolution to his native Dresden as well. It was during this period that Wagner started reading Pierre Proudhon and Karl Marx, and he also met the Russian Michael Bakunin who happened to be living in Dresden. Wagner was especially impressed with Proudhon's essay "What Is Property?" All these thinkers were revolutionaries, especially Bakunin, who became an anarchist, thinking that all government was innately evil. Why were only aristocrats and the wealthy bourgeoisie given any political rights?, these men asked. Why couldn't all men have political rights like the vote and freedom of the press? Wagner felt a desire to fight for political rights for everyone, for the creation of a modern democracy, rights that are now considered basic to democracy. Wagner also wanted the separation of church and state, the basis of modern democracy.

Wagner had been living in an ideal situation in Dresden. While Minna was enjoying the situation and their exalted position in it, Wagner was planning to blow the whole situation up. Subconscious forces were driving him to his own destruction, along with that of much of the rest of Europe during that revolutionary year. In the spring of 1849 Wagner was at the barricades with the revolutionaries, including Bakunin. Wagner clearly resented the class structure at the time, although he modeled much of his behavior on the lifestyle of the European nobility. He too wanted the gorgeous houses full of servants, the travel on first-class trains and coaches, etc.

Wagner's subconscious forces were generating more and more rage, and that would ultimately destroy much that he had achieved in Dresden. His childlike, subconscious needs were endangering the enviable position he had finally achieved. Despite all these subconscious problems, he was still composing. But Wagner was also reading more of Marx, who inspired George Bernard Shaw to write *The Perfect Wagnerite*, a Marxist interpretation of the Ring cycle. Shaw saw Wagner as a Marxist and Socialist, and in many ways Shaw was right. Unfortunately, this side of Wagner's political thinking did not survive his death; his widow Cosima and the circle of Wagnerians at Bayreuth ignored this aspect of Wagner's thinking.

Throughout Europe, there was a new force calling for democracy for all people, and there was a new force calling for an independent and unified Germany and an independent and unified Italy. The German potato famine a few years earlier had driven millions to leave Germany and this crisis had finally produced political repercussions. Revolution and national unity were in the air in Europe in the 1840s. This had already occurred in Greece, and the poet Lord Byron had given his life for this cause, dying in Missolonghi in his effort to free Greece from the Turkish empire. These revolutionary movements were in the air and they were even coming to Saxony and Dresden. The city was soon caught up in revolutionary furor. Hundreds of people died in Dresden during these years, but Wagner managed to escape.

Why did Wagner get involved in revolutionary activities even though his salary was being paid by the Saxon monarch, King Friedrich August? Wagner did this partially for ideological reasons and partially for personal and subconscious reasons. Whenever Wagner found a good position, something self-destructive in his personality drove him to destroy that position. He also hoped that a successful revolution in Dresden could create a state with full democratic rights for all. Wagner was also undoubtedly aware of the potato famine in Germany and saw signs of starvation around him, especially in the countryside in Saxony, and the king did nothing to end the suffering of the poor people on their failing farms. Wagner dreamed of a government that responded to the needs of the common people and not just the aristocrats. Wagner dreamed of a just society obsessed with art and not just obsessed with money.

7

Revolution in Dresden: 1848–1850

"A new age is afoot, a better age." — Wagner, in a letter to a friend

In 1848 and 1849, Paris was in flames, and cities in other countries as well. Italy, Germany, Austria, Poland — they all had revolutions of some sort, though most were ultimately aborted and the powers-that-be regained control, at least for a while. The left was struggling for political rights from monarchy and a rigid aristocracy who had most of the power, although realities changed from country to country. There was no revolution in Great Britain because there was a constitutional monarchy there and a Parliament realizing that the workers (at least the males) had to be given a vote to avert another revolution. A series of laws in Britain extended the franchise to just about all men by the end of the 19th century — and this avoided the revolutionary activities occurring on the Continent. The English had their own revolution in the 17th century when Charles I refused to understand the powers of the English parliament and wanted to reign as a divine right absolute monarch; then the Puritans in parliament, led by Oliver Cromwell, beheaded him. One of the ways Napoleon III came into power as a result of the commune in Paris was by advocating the vote for every Frenchman. Clearly here was a monarch willing to share the power with all men (not women, of course). He declared that he would be a constitutional monarch, bound by the French constitution and consulting with parliament. He was also an imperialist who wanted to spread France's borders by killing many non-white people to show how glorious France was. He was the one who started the war to make Algeria and other parts of Africa colonies of the French. The British were doing the same thing all over the world, the 19th century being the age of imperialism.

While Emperor Napoleon III was trying to present himself as a follower of the principles of the French revolution and he believed in democratic rights for all men, at least all white men, in part saying this just to get the crown, things were very different in Germany. France at least was a unified country in the 19th century. Germany, like Italy, was still a group of often hostile city states. In Germany there was Prussia, Bavaria, Hesse, Saxony, etc., just as in Italy there was Piedmont, Naples, and the Vatican States. By 1871 both Germany and Italy would achieve some kind of unity, so ultimately the revolution succeeded in terms of German and Italian reunification.

These politics were complicated by a great desire for people in Italy, Germany and Greece for a unified government that was free of foreign domination. But there were some enlightened monarchs and the French especially encouraged Italian unification, though certainly not German unification since Germany, especially Prussia, and France were traditional enemies and had fought numerous wars. France even before Napoleon had devastated many parts of Germany, and even Voltaire had made jokes in *Candide* about the backwardness of Germany. But in the face of this, more and more Germans wanted their country to be unified and not a victim of French aggression and invasions. Many Germans felt that a unified Germany would be a safer Germany, especially during the potato famine when people were starving and being forced to emigrate to America.

In the midst of all these political upheavals, 1848 was both a productive and a destructive one for Wagner, though he was very aware of all this political upheaval in both Germany and the rest of Europe. But despite the upheavals all around, Wagner remained very capable of his own artistic productivity, and in fact that productivity may have been a stimulus to Wagner's creativity. By the spring of 1848 he had finished the orchestration of *Lohengrin* and submitted it to the opera house authorities in Dresden for a premiere there. Lüttichau and the other authorities in Dresden had approved it for production.

Wagner thought about and wrote an initial draft of an opera based on the life of Frederick Barbarosa and he also wrote a 52-page draft of a libretto called *Jesus of Nazareth*. He found that his friends were shocked by the idea of turning Jesus' life into an opera, but he had read both Dr. Strauss' *Life of Jesus* and Feuerbach's *The Essence of Christianity*, and both books presented Christ as a historical figure rather than a god. That was undoubtedly the basis of his opera, which he eventually dropped. But Wagner used some of these ideas in his final opera, *Parsifal*, which was loosely based on Christian mythology and religious beliefs. Wagner was suggesting here that all religions were unreasonable and that art could be the new religion for modern man.

In part because of Wagner's anger at the royal rejection of his tactlessly presented suggestions for the organization of a German National Theater for Saxony, he became closer to August Röckel, who had as a boy been in Paris during the revolution there in 1830. Since 1843, Röckel was living in Dresden, and Wagner absorbed many of his revolutionary ideas. Marx's Communist Manifesto appeared that year, and Wagner had already been reading the French socialist Proudhon, who was famous for the phrase "Property Is Theft." So Wagner developed a great interest in and sympathy with the socialist thought of the middle of the 19th century. These social thinkers became convinced that property and money corrupted humanity and that a new social order was possible if the world were free of kings, royal families, and aristocrats, who had most of the wealth and power in Europe at the time. If there were universal suffrage and all men (not women) got the vote, and there was some form of parliamentary government, there would be a more equitable distribution of wealth and a new and more just world order. Wagner was very interested in these ideas and so became one of the revolutionaries in Dresden.

Wagner also wrote an essay at this time about the differences between history and mythology as possible subjects for an opera. He became convinced, as he argued in his essay "Art and Revolution" that history would became limited and dated, but mythology was eternally relevant and fascinating. These ideas would influence all his subsequent

7. Revolution in Dresden: 1848–1850

operas, particularly the Ring cycle and its presentation of the corrupted world of the gods and the hope, at the end, of a new and more equitable and just world order with humanity in charge instead of the gods.

Wagner emphasized in his autobiography that he wanted this new world order because he hoped that it would be better for artists and other creative thinkers. But there was revolution in the air in 1848 and 1849 throughout Europe, and Wagner was one of those revolutionaries, though by the time he was writing his autobiography at the request of King Ludwig II, he deemphasized his revolutionary thinking lest he offend his patron — ironically enough, yet another king, from the royal Bavarian family of Wittelsbach. This socialist point of view, however, would influence Wagner's Ring cycle and its political implications about power, class, property, and money.

Frederick Augustus II of Saxony (the royal family of Wettin) was presented with a new constitution in April of 1849, but he was not this kind of monarch since he basically believed in absolute monarchy with some input from the upper orders so he regally rejected this suggested new constitution. This new constitution would have granted rights to all men, not just aristocrats, but the king was used to absolute power and not sharing power with commoners. Wagner was similar to Karl Marx: Both were in favor of universal rights for all as well by being ill-disposed to the Jews. And Wagner was also sick of dealing with the king and his aristocratic hierarchy and wanted an elected parliament and a constitutional monarchy with little real power. The kings were the ones who were offering him jobs, but this did not endear them to him, ironically enough. Wagner's revolutionary ideas seemed like being on the side of the angels to us — but this was not how it was perceived by the Saxon monarch. One would think that since this was the king who gave Wagner his job, that he would be careful not to offend his biggest and most wealthy fan, but gratitude was never one of Wagner's fortes.

Wagner felt, rather naively, that a new age for the arts would be born if only money, property, and the upper class could be removed and socialism could be the economic system in Saxony. In response, the Saxon monarch felt threatened, called up his military and asked for help from the Prussian monarchy who had the most powerful army in the German federation. The Saxon royal family called in their army and then fled Dresden, their capital, for one of their country estates outside Dresden.

Many of the things Wagner was advocating during this revolutionary period we would fully support: suffrage for all people, a parliament, and a constitutional monarchy with very limited powers which would have to be approved by the parliament. These are basically the principles of modern democracies with monarchs — places like Great Britain, Norway, and Denmark. One of the reasons Bismarck became popular is that he offered Germans not only a unified Germany but also universal suffrage (for all men of all races living there, unlike Israel today where only the Chosen People have full rights of citizenship). Wagner was certainly ahead of his time in demanding rights for all the people living in Saxony, though he also wanted a monarchy — a constitutional monarchy, which is not a very revolutionary idea now but was then in Saxony and the other German city-states.

During these years in Dresden, Wagner developed a group of revolutionary friends like August Röckel, who spent most of the rest of his life in jail because of his activities. Wagner would correspond with Röckel for many years, sympathetic to his revolutionary ideas. He wanted the end of an absolute monarchy and universal suffrage for all men in Saxony, regardless of class and race. In Dresden in 1849 that was treason given the power of the Saxon monarchy and the aristocrats who ran the state. They did not want to give up any of their power so the people (some of them) went to the barricades to get their demands met. Wagner wrote that he did not want the end of monarchy, but he did want a monarch with limited powers.

Also at the Dresden barricades was Wagner's friend Gottfried Semper, the architect, who designed barricades for the revolutionaries. Wagner was in the thick of it — one of the organizers of the attempted revolution. The revolution collapsed in a few weeks, thanks primarily to the Prussian army and its entry into Dresden. Hundreds of revolutionaries were shot and killed, and thousands fled. When the revolution failed, Wagner was a criminal, and a warrant was issued for his arrest.

While Wagner was living in Dresden he was reading Ludwig Feuerbach, whose *The Essence of Christianity* was also being read and translated in London by George Eliot. Wagner would meet Eliot and her lover George Lewes while he was visiting London many years later, and one of the things they talked about was Feuerbach. Eliot translated the book from German into English so she was very interested in this work, and it influenced both the novelist and the composer. According to Feuerbach, you could be a good Christian while still being an atheist since he argued that Christ was not a god but a wise man who said some very good things about how to live one's life. Feuerbach felt that the essence of Christianity was a moral system which presented Christianity as a guide to moral living but which could be used without all the supernatural trappings which Feuerbach felt were silly stuff and not really part of the essence of Christianity. To be a good Christian, he argued, one had to follow the precepts of Christian doctrine and its morality without believing in Christ as a god — or even believing in God period. This was a very revolutionary concept and Wagner found it quite attractive, as did Eliot and many others. Feuerbach became one of the most influential thinkers of the 19th century in his search for the essence of Christianity. The end of a belief in God and religion became a major theme in Wagner's operas, especially the Ring, and a search for moral behavior and redemption without God also became major ideas in his future operas.

Wagner was one of the few composers who was a serious reader and intellectual. He was particularly interested in philosophy and political economy and he read Proudhon, Feuerbach, Marx, and later Schopenhauer, in addition to much of the world's great literature, particularly Shakespeare, Dante, and the ancient Greek dramatists Aeschylus, Sophocles, and Euripides. His reading and his intellectual interests are certainly reflected in his operas, particularly the Ring and *Tristan*.

Mikhail Bakunin wrote about the total destruction of both the monarchy and the state and the total freedom for the citizens in the new government he wanted to form along anarchical lines. Wagner liked all these ideas, though they seem hopelessly naïve to us. But Bakunin was part of a Russian group of intellectuals who could not live in

7. Revolution in Dresden: 1848–1850

Russia — so they lived like Herzen in Paris, advocating radical ideas about the freedom of mankind far away from the czar who would have imprisoned them. Bakunin was clearly an anarchist; Wagner was not this extreme: he wanted Saxony to continue to have a monarchy, but a constutional monarchy with universal suffrage. Wagner's ideas were very consistent with many of the revolutionary principles of the Revolution of 1848. While some of the revolutionaries, especially in Paris, were anarchists, most wanted more reasonable goals. Don't overlook the fact that in the 19th century, millions of Europeans — especially in Britain, Germany, and Italy — were forced to emigrate because of the extreme poverty in their own countries. Poor people were denied all civil rights in Europe at this time, including the vote. One had to own property and be an aristocrat to have any civil rights and the vote in most countries in Europe in the early 19th century.

Wagner remained in many ways an idealist, especially attracted to extreme positions rather than the middle-of-the-road positions. He felt that the destruction of the evil old class system could create a brave new world of human liberation and equality. His extreme positions left him out in the cold in Dresden when his sympathy with the attempted revolution destroyed his career, but maybe that is what he subconsciously wanted.

Wagner published his radical views in the local newspapers and called for a revolution. He was one of the most vocal of the leaders of the Dresden uprising in the spring of 1849. Minna tried to lock him in his bedroom and moderate his views so that he would not lose his job, but Wagner's radicalism would not be restrained thus. He was on the bell tower of one of the churches looking out for Saxon troops and helping the revolutionaries build barricades.

Later the racial side of Wagnerian politics would appear, but only that aspect of his political thinking has gotten much attention for the last fifty years. We need to see both sides of his thinking. After his death, only the racist side has been emphasized, thanks to two women who were not native Germans, Cosima Wagner and Winifred Wagner. Wagner's second wife and daughter-in-law did much damage to his reputation, especially Winifred in connecting Wagner with the Nazis and Adolf Hitler fifty years after Wagner had died. Friedrich Nietzsche's thinking was also distorted by his sister Elizabeth after Friedrich was dead.

The Saxon king never forgave his court composer Wagner for being part of a group that forced him to flee his own capital, and for a while the revolutionaries were celebrating their ousting of the king — forever, they hoped. But once the king was out, general mayhem ensued and many of the people of Dresden were undoubtedly horrified to see their city in flames, including the opera house, and barricades up, and the revolutionaries celebrating but unable to form a successful and stable government. Hundreds had been killed and no one seemed in control.

About thirty people were killed when the Prussian military invaded the barricaded streets in Dresden. The ringleaders of the uprising had to flee immediately to avoid arrest. Wagner was one of them, escaping first to Weimar to visit Liszt, and then to Zurich, Switzerland, where he had friends and where he knew the language.

Richard Wagner

One of his great revolutionary friends, Röckel, wound up spending over twenty years in jail for his revolutionary activities. Wagner never forgot his friend and they corresponded for many years, with Wagner submitting his ideas for operas to Röckel for his opinion. Wagner maintained contact with many of his Dresden friends even after he had to leave. One of his friends was Anton Pusinelli, a physician and fellow revolutionary who took care of Minna in her final years and informed Wagner when his first wife had died. Wagner remained faithful to many of his old Dresden revolutionary friends even though he was not allowed to return to the city for many years after his escape.

Minna remained in Dresden and tried to keep what she could; she was safe since she had not been involved in the failed revolution. But she often wrote to her husband that seeing him as the head of the operatic world in Dresden had been the happiest time in her life, and his revolutionary activities had destroyed her happiness and their financial stability.

Twenty years later Minna would die in Dresden. Her daughter Nathalie continued to live there, though both wound up hating Wagner, along with Cosima and Mathilde Wesendonck. Minna would try to reunite with her husband several times, but these attempts would never succeed and she ended her days in Dresden as a heart patient.

Something very admirable about Wagner was his willingness to fight for democratic principles and to put his own career on the line, but this admirable quality was also going to cause him many problems. All the court opera houses in Germany would be very reluctant to stage operas by a known revolutionary at a time when all those opera houses depended on the local royal family to support them. To become a revolutionary in 19th century Germany was to risk one's life and career, especially in a country were opera especially was dependent on royal and aristocratic patronage. Wagner did a very self-destructive thing to his career by supporting so openly the revolutionaries in Dresden in the spring of 1849. Even now most opera houses are dependent on government funding and the patronage of the wealthy — not a good place to foment revolution since both groups were not going to want major changes in a system which provided so well for them. Opera, the most expensive art form after film, is dependent on government subsidy and wealthy patrons for its survival. Wagner knew these economic realities and dreamed of a new economic system, socialism, which would fund the arts and reflect the desires of all the people and not just the king and the aristocrats. But another reality which Wagner never seemed to understand is that most ordinary people do not like opera but prefer operetta or music for popular singing and dancing. While he dreamed of his operas attracting most of people, they never did.

It is ironic that this revolutionary would be saved by yet another king, Ludwig II of Bavaria, whose munificence to Wagner made his operatic dreams come to life. Without this king, Wagner's Ring cycle and festival at Bayreuth would not have been possible. To want both revolution and money from some king seems incompatible, but Wagner managed to have it both ways.

While Wagner was involved in the Dresden revolution, he was also writing the initial libretto for his Ring cycle, and what he experienced in Dresden from 1848 to 1849 greatly

7. Revolution in Dresden: 1848–1850

influenced the Ring cycle, arguably the greatest masterpiece in the history of musical theater. The Ring cycle remains Wagner's most political work; this vast tetralogy would reflect the complexity of Wagner's political thinking, though this would change over the twenty-five years it took him to complete this work, which had its premiere in Bayreuth in the summer of 1876.

8
Wagner and Liszt — The Premiere of *Lohengrin*: 1849–1850

"Beloved, come visit me here in Zurich." — Wagner to Liszt

Immediately after Wagner fled from Dresden as a result of his involvement in the uprising there, first he went to Paris and then to his friend Franz Liszt in Weimar. Given Wagner's unhappy stays in Paris before, one wonders why he went there of all places. But his friend Gaetano Belloni, who had promoted Liszt's career so successfully, lived in Paris, and Wagner met with him. Since Wagner's career in Germany was now ruined, he hoped that Belloni could develop his career in Paris. But then he went again to Weimar, probably at Belloni's suggestion, to his friend Franz Liszt. Liszt had an appointment as composer in residence for the Grand Duke of Weimar, in charge of the opera house. The Duchy of Weimar had also supported Goethe and Schiller for many years so the town had a rather exalted history of royal patronage for significant artistic figures. Weimar would also become the site of the premiere of *Lohengrin* on August 28, 1850, with Liszt conducting. He had already staged Wagner's *Tannhäuser there* so Wagner could count on Liszt's support. Unlike Wagner, Liszt knew how to flatter wealthy aristocrats and had no interest in radical politics. He was innately tactful and avoided offending people, especially wealthy people.

Liszt loved and supported Wagner. This relationship was one of the most complicated and long-lasting of Wagner's life. They met in Paris while Liszt was mainly a pianist, and the relationship ended with Wagner's death in 1883 in Venice. Liszt and Wagner loved each other, and of course also hated each other. According to Freud, love comes always mixed with hate, even in idyllic Weimar. Liszt greatly admired Wagner's compositions and wrote piano transcriptions of most of Wagner's operas. Piano transcriptions of popular operas became a popular new medium in 19th century Europe thanks to the middle class family's fondness for the pianoforte. Liszt dreamed of being a great composer for orchestra and piano, his instrument, but he also dreamed of writing successful operas. The men loved each other, though not with a sexual dimension — at least from what we know. Liszt wanted someone to help him with orchestration and opera composition, and Wagner desperately needed a wealthy and generous patron given his own desperate situation. Freud argued that all great emotions have a sexual dimension, and this was undoubtedly true of this relationship as well.

8. Wagner and Liszt—The Premiere of Lohengrin: 1849–1850

Both Wagner and Liszt were interested sexually in strong, maternal, aristocratic wives, preferably married to someone else. Both men seemed doomed to marry mother figures, which indicated that both men lacked strong relationships with their own mothers. Liszt especially found aristocratic mother-figures irresistible and he fell in love with two of them, Marie D'Agout and Princess Sayn-Wittgenstein; both women were married to other men.

Liszt by 1847 was living in sin with the Russian princess Caroline von Sayn-Wittgenstein, despite the fact that she was married to a Russian-Polish prince. She was a fiercely maternal woman who had several children but did not want to live any longer with her husband. She now wanted to marry Liszt, who had no objection. Earlier in his career he had been living with Marie D'Agoult, by whom he had three children (Blandina, Cosima, and Daniel); she too was maternal and married. Despite his expressed religiosity, Liszt was willing to commit adultery when it suited him. This did not hurt his career in Weimar since the duke and duchess were very broad-minded about sexual peccadilloes and still admired Liszt the composer and pianist.

Wagner & Liszt by N.C. Wyeth, from *Steinway: The Instrument of the Immortals* (1921). The friendship of these two composers was the most important in both of their lives (Picture Collection, The New York Public Library for the Performing Arts, Astor, Lenox and Tilden Foundations).

Liszt's friend and promoter Gaetano Belloni generated all sorts of publicity and PR for Liszt. Belloni arrived at a town where Liszt was giving a recital and Belloni provided the kind of advance publicity which turned Liszt's recitals into an Event. Belloni helped to make Liszt the most famous pianist and musician in Europe in the 19th century, and Liszt knew this and suggested that Wagner also employ Belloni. Wagner met Belloni in Paris and learned from him about the new science of public relations and marketing and how all publicity was good publicity. The greatest evil was being ignored. Being constantly talked about was the easiest way to further one's career in the arts. Of course, one also had to have a unique talent, and this both Liszt and Wagner had, but talent was not enough.

Weimar was a town with particularly artistic credentials since both Goethe and Schiller had lived there; there is a statue to both men still in the town. The Duke of Weimar was a connoisseur of the arts, especially music and opera, and he employed Liszt to run his opera house. He and his predecessors had created in Weimar an artistic center and an artistic capital, and they supported the arts generously, especially drama and music. For such a small town, there was an important opera company there and lots of orchestral concerts. The Duchy of Weimar and its royal family had supported some of the most important artists of Germany history—Goethe, Schiller, and now Liszt—and perhaps they could be persuaded to support the ever-needy Richard Wagner. Weimar would later develop political implications since it is the town where the ill-fated Weimar Republic was established after World War I. (The hope at that time, in 1920, was that the Weimar republic could bring democracy and peace to Germany after the defeat of World War I, but unfortunately this movement toward democracy lasted only about twelve years due to the rise of National Socialism.)

Since Liszt was a personal friend of Wagner and a Wagner fan as well, Liszt was very eager to stage Wagner's newest opera, *Lohengrin*. Liszt was already known as the most famous pianist of the Romantic era, and he had a reputation as a dazzling, mesmerizing pianist, but Liszt wanted more: He wanted to be a great conductor and composer as well. Liszt knew he needed to learn more about orchestration since he wanted to compose symphonies and operas, and Wagner was already impressive for his use of the orchestra. It was very kind of Liszt to agree to stage Wagner's next opera, especially now that he had become persona non grata in Saxony. Liszt also admired Wagner's abilities to orchestrate and he clearly knew how to use the orchestra in opera in a most interesting way, and Liszt wanted to become a more important composer—to compose for the orchestra and not just for the piano. Liszt felt that Wagner was the greatest composer of his time, and according to legend, his dying word was "Tristan." Liszt also recognized Wagner's sense of drama and his unique ability to connect music with drama to create music theater, the most popular of the musical genres, and Liszt craved attention and popularity.

Liszt by then was a wealthy man living with a very wealthy woman, a Polish princess who owned vast lands in Russia. He was very generous to Wagner at a time when Wagner was penniless, and Liszt tried to help Wagner repeatedly. Wagner often asked Liszt for emotional support and financial support, and Liszt helped Wagner as often as he could. Liszt was a very good friend to Wagner, and Wagner tried to be a good friend to Liszt as well; they both succeeded in their way. This was one of Wagner's longest-lasting friendships.

Wagner, a very lonely man, kept begging Liszt to visit him wherever he was living at the time, primarily in various spots in Switzerland. Liszt sent Wagner large amounts of money and helped to support him in the style that Wagner was accustomed to. Liszt also repeatedly warned Wagner that he had to leave Weimar given its reciprocal agreements with the police department in Saxony.

When Liszt finally staged the premiere of *Lohengrin* in 1850, Wagner was not allowed to be present since he was a criminal in all of Germany because of his involvement in the Dresden uprising. Liszt conducted the premiere at the main opera house in Weimar. This theater was small, as was its orchestra pit, and Liszt's cast was not one of the best available. Cuts had to be made in the score and its orchestral demands, but the opera succeeded

8. Wagner and Liszt—The Premiere of Lohengrin: 1849–1850

and reports of its success spread throughout the German states. Liszt wrote to Wagner about his operatic success in Weimar. Soon other cities in Germany were voicing an interest in staging *Lohengrin*, which soon became Wagner's most popular opera. This riveting tale of the contrast between Elsa and Ortrud, between Christianity and paganism, and between two religious and political forces and two women is the most often staged of Wagner's operas. Wagner knew that conflict was the essence of drama, and internal conflicts remain at the core of *Lohengrin*. And Wagner knew that leaving the audience unsure of who was right added to the opera's mystery and fascination. What Wagner seems to be presenting is the medieval heresy of the Manichean sect—that God is not all-powerful, as the Christians assert, but that God and the Devil are in eternal conflict in the world and that both are equally powerful, an idea which recurs in Wagnerian opera, especially the Ring.

At this point in his life, Wagner was a dangerous man to know and to help since he was considered a dangerous criminal in all of Germany. There were warnings about him in the newspapers and public warrants out for his arrest in all the German states. That Liszt and the Duke of Weimar were receiving him in Weimar was dangerous for them. They could not do this for very long since there was a very real possibility that Weimar could be invaded by Saxon or Prussian troops eager to get their hands on Wagner. Wagner seemed to turn Liszt into the father he never had, despite the fact that Liszt was only two years older.

If one examines the letters between Liszt and Wagner, most of which survived, there is clearly a homoerotic element to them—at least on Wagner's side. He keeps declaring his love for Liszt and keeps begging him to visit him in Zurich, suggesting that they take hikes together in the wonderful Alpine scenery of Switzerland. Wagner developed a real love of Liszt, though Liszt's companion at the time, Princess Sayn-Wittgenstein, did not much like Wagner. Both men were drawn to powerful mother-figures; while Wagner married such women, Liszt lived in sin with them, eventually becoming famous for his religious vocation as an abbe despite the fact that he had never married, and had fathered three bastards. Liszt played many roles in his life, from international celebrity (because of his dazzling performances on the piano) to abbe living in Rome to be near the Pope. Liszt clearly had an eye for role-playing and publicity. He also directed the main musical conservatory in Budapest, which was named after him.

One of the reasons why Wagner fell in love with his second wife, Cosima, was because she reminded him of her father, Franz. Wagner was constantly begging Franz to visit him in Switzerland, and Franz did visit him several times and continued to support him. Liszt would become a great composer and a very influential teacher, mentoring some of the most famous conductors and pianists of his time, including Hans von Bülow, who would ultimately marry Liszt's daughter Cosima, though she would eventually leave him for Richard Wagner. Hans and Cosima's marriage would produce two children but remain very difficult and ended quite bitterly.

Wagner had to endure angry letters from members of his own family. They had helped to support Wagner and Minna during those lean years in Paris, and now they were getting begging letters from him again after he had destroyed his position in Dresden. He had had three operas staged in Dresden while he was there, and two of them had been major successes, and now he was penniless and in debt again. His extravagant spending had especially angered his relatives, in particular his older brother Albert.

Albert Wagner had been helping his kid brother in Paris, and Albert's daughter Johanna was beginning her career as a soprano. She was in Dresden to sing in the premiere of her uncle's *Tannhäuser*; she was the original Elisabeth in that opera at the beginning of her career. Her father Albert, angry with Richard, wrote to him:

> I am used to seeing you respect people only if and as long as they can be useful to you; when the usefulness is over, the person also no longer exists for you. Gratitude for the past is unknown to you: all that is merely an infernal obligation. It has always been so — toward Brockhaus, the King, Lüttichau, Pusinelli, Tichatschek, and everyone else who has helped you in one way or another. Greatly as I value and love your talent, it is just the opposite as regards your character. Since your last letter the first sign of life you give Johanna is — give me 1,000 thalers! A mere trifle!

Wagner must have felt very guilt-ridden and depressed after reading this letter.

Ernest Newman, in his four-volume biography of Wagner, reports on his arrival in Switzerland in May of 1849 at the home of a friend, Alexander Mueller:

> Mueller being at a picnic in the country that day, Wagner had to spend the night of the 28th–29th in the Hotel Schwert, where, by the way, Goethe had more than once stayed. Frau Henriette Hesselbarth, Mueller's daughter, has told us how her father, in answer to the ringing of the house bell on the night of the 29th, put his head out of the window (he had only that evening returned from the picnic), and cried "Who is that so late as this?" "It is I, Richard Wagner: open quickly!" was the reply. Wagner threw his arms around Mueller and said, "Alexander, you must give me shelter. I am safe only here. I have fled from Dresden, leaving my wife and property behind me." As Mueller was out teaching or rehearsing all day, and Wagner felt lonely, he used to invite the two little girls of the house into the room that their father had placed at his disposal: they went rather unwillingly, for they had to sit quite still, not being allowed even to turn the leaves of a book. Wagner would play to them pieces out of his operas, and ask them "Do you like that?" "Like the stupid children we were," said Frau Hesselbarth in later years, "we would say NO!" Then he would say, "In that case you must listen to it until you do." He would often say to us, "When anyone asks you who your teacher was, say Richard Wagner!" [Newman, II, 114–15].

This comic quotation says something of Wagner's rather tyrannical personality, but also his sense of humor. In his autobiography *My Life*, Wagner writes about his arrival in Zurich and his stay with the Muellers:

> I arrived at Mueller's house, requested a room of some kind as my refuge, and handed over to him the rest of my fortune — twenty francs. I was soon obliged to note that my old acquaintance was a bit embarrassed by my open trust in him and became worried at to what to do with me. At once I voluntarily gave up the large room with piano he placed at my disposal in the impulse of the moment, and retired to a modest little bedroom. The only troublesome matter was my participation in his daily meals, not because they were distasteful to me, but because my digestive organs couldn't cope with them. Outside my friend's house, on the other hand, I enjoyed what was by the standard of the locality, the most lavish hospitality.

8. Wagner and Liszt—The Premiere of Lohengrin: 1849–1850

The same young men who had been so kind to me during my former trip to Zurich continued to show great pleasure in my company. Before long Jacob Sulzer emerged as the most imposing member of the group.... Whenever I was asked in later years when I had ever in my life run across what is called, in the moral sense, true character and genuine honesty, I would upon reflection name no other than the friend that I made at this time, Jacob Sulzer.

Despite his new Swiss friends, Wagner was often lonely and missed his wife and many of his friends in Germany, particularly Liszt. Many of Wagner's letters to Liszt during this first Swiss period are quite desperate and even suicidal. On March 30, 1853, Wagner wrote from Switzerland to Liszt:

This cannot go on: I cannot bear life much longer.... Then I shall begin a different life. Then I shall get money how and where I can; I shall borrow and steal, if necessary, in order to travel. The beautiful parts of Italy are closed to me unless I am amnestied. So I shall go to Spain, to Andalusia, and make friends, and try once more to live as well as I can. I should like to fare round the world. If I can get no money, or if the journey does not help me to a new breath of life, there is an end of it, and I shall then seek death by my own hand rather than live on in this manner.

Minna returned to him because of his desperation. She undoubtedly knew about his loneliness and wanted to help him — he brought out the mother in her, even though her only child Nathalie was often in the picture of her marriage to Wagner. Nathalie's presence must have complicated the relationship between Wagner and his wife, especially since Nathalie was his wife's daughter with a previous man.

Wagner was often depressed during these years, and even stopped composing for seven years, though he continued to write essays. Despite his suicidal depressions, Wagner could also write — either music or prose or librettos or all of the above. His depressions were caused by his isolation from Germany and from his friend Liszt. He was unable to realize that his family and friends were still interested in him.

One of the reasons he fell in love with Cosima Von Bülow was because she was the daughter of Liszt. Marrying Cosima was a way for Wagner to keep a part of Liszt with him always. After they were married, Wagner often became jealous of Liszt and any time that Cosima spent with her father. Wagner wanted Cosima to himself and began to see Liszt as a rival for his wife's attention. One wonders how Wagner treated the von Bülow children and his own children given his own needs for a mother-figure. Both he and Liszt were always attracted to mother-figures; Liszt was raised by his father to be a wunderkind since his mother died when he was an infant.

On August 28, 1850, Liszt conducted the premiere of Wagner's newest opera *Lohengrin* at the royal opera house in Weimar. Wagner could not be there because of the warrants out for his arrest all over Germany. The success of that premiere encouraged other opera companies in Germany to stage Wagner's operas even though Wagner was a political exile. It was thanks to Liszt's championing of Wagner's operas that the Wagner vogue finally began in the German states.

While Wagner had had success as a composer before this, especially in Dresden, suddenly he was becoming an international figure; even in America his music was beginning to be performed, in fragments if not total works as yet. The German communities in New York and Chicago were particularly interested in hearing Wagner's music and getting it performed, at this point primarily through military band concerts and performances of Wagner's overtures and piano pieces from the operas.

It was during this time as well that Wagner began to get offers to conduct, especially from Switzerland, Russia, and England. So it was not just his composing abilities that were attracting attention to him, and we have seen how much Wagner liked attention and public recognition.

Liszt, who considered Wagner the greatest composer of his generation, may well have thought of his helping of Wagner as a way of furthering his own career and publicity. Wagner certainly knew how to attract attention to himself and his work. One of the main reasons that Wagner wrote his notorious pamphlet *Jews and Music* was to make his name known throughout Europe and America. Both men wanted publicity and wealth, and both men helped each other to achieve it.

Once Wagner married Liszt's daughter, the relationship between Wagner and his father-in-law cooled down quite a bit. Wagner began to see Liszt as a rival for the affections of Cosima, and clearly Wagner wanted all of Cosima's attentions. Cosima must have felt that on some level Wagner was a needy child who jealously wanted all of her attention, and must have resented her love for her father and her own children.

But Cosima was used to the idea of loving a needy genius since before she married Wagner. She had her father to deal with — another one of those needy musical geniuses. Liszt did not spend much time with his three illegitimate children, but he controlled their destinies and demanded their love. And he was a musical genius. The 19th century developed a cult of the genius as a religious figure who needed to be worshiped and loved. One of the reasons Cosima married Hans von Bülow was because he was the most gifted of her father's pupils. Most people of the period were not interested in such things as needy and demanding egomaniacs, but Cosima certainly was. Her great dream was to be the wife of the greatest musical genius of her time, and she succeeded in this.

There have been several attempts by critics to argue that Wagner was a gay man because of the homoerotic aspects of the relationships between some of his male characters — like Tristan and King Marke and Tristan and Kurvenal and Wotan and Siegfried. But Wagner realized before Sigmund Freud that an erotic element enters most powerful relationships. Eros is everywhere.

The homoerotic was a force that functioned in Wagner's life and in his operatic characters. Kurvenal's love of Tristan, King Marke's love of Tristan, Brangene's love of Isolde, Sieglinde's love of Brunnhilde, Amfortas' love of Gurnemanz — there is a homoerotic element in all these relationships but none of these characters is gay. Wagner realized how complicated human relationships are and that there was an erotic element to all profound human relationships.

Wagner remained very loyal to his friends, writing to them frequently — people like Röckel, Pusinelli, Malwida von Meysenbug, and many others. Wagner did not forget people once he established a friendship; he wrote thousands of letters to his friends, and

8. Wagner and Liszt—The Premiere of Lohengrin: 1849–1850

many of those friends were very loyal to him as well. People seemed to love or hate Wagner, just as their reactions to his music seemed to come in these extreme forms. Wagner's music tended to touch sensitive nerves in people — some people loved this but some people really hated it. This is still the case.

Wagner found friends to support him other than Liszt. While Wagner was traveling in France, he met Jessie Laussot. Her husband's name was Eugene, and they often lived with her mother Mrs. Taylor, who was Scottish. All three of them were Wagner fans and they offered to support Wagner with a stipend of 3000 francs a year. They all liked both Wagner's music and his personality, and they had some very lively dinners together, especially since Eugene spoke very good German. Then all of a sudden Jessie fell in love with Wagner and proposed that they run off together, something which Wagner found very tempting. Wagner never seemed to have any problem attracting women, even when he was married to someone else. He spent part of 1850 in France, especially in Bordeaux, where the Laussot and Taylor families lived. But eventually Eugene got wind of his wife's plans to elope with Wagner so he called the police and forbade his wife to see Wagner ever again, though she did continue to correspond with him.

So Wagner was forced to return to Zurich and persuaded his wife Minna to join him there. But how were they going to survive? Wagner now met two young men who were going to become important parts of his life, Karl Ritter and Hans von Bülow. Both young men wanted a career in music and both were in their early 20s. Ritter also was willing to pay Wagner for composition lessons. Hans was trying to convince his parents to support him while he tried to have a career as a pianist and conductor. He felt he had the talent, and Wagner encouraged him.

Wagner was soon getting offers to conduct at both the opera and symphony in Zurich since Wagner had by now a significant reputation as both a composer and conductor. Wagner had a knack for surrounding himself with loving and generous friends. He attracted such people because of his genius and his kindness to them. Wagner began an affair with Hans' wife Cosima, who had earlier attempted to get into a suicide pact with Karl Ritter. Both Karl and Cosima married within the next few years, and both marriages became very unhappy.

Liszt, his daughter Cosima, Hans, and Wagner were all very good friends, even loving friends, and they were soon involved in very complicated relationships involving marriage, adultery, and loving infidelities on all sides.

9

Refuge in Zurich — The Development of Big Plans: 1850–1857

"We need a new theater for a new work." — Wagner

Wagner was now beginning a twelve-year period when he could not live in the German confederation due to his revolutionary activities in Dresden. As always with Wagner, he kept working and producing both prose and poetry in writing the librettos to his operas. During this next ten years, Wagner wrote very little music but he did write many essays which presented his views on opera, conducting, art, and Jews. Wagner tended to avoid writing about politics since the collapse of the Dresden uprising.

Wagner's hopes for a wonderful new era of human harmony and the end of human exploitation through money and class were now killed thanks to troops from Prussia — and he would never trust Prussia again. The Dresden uprising and his involvement in it made him more realistic about the world of politics and the awesome power of government, especially Prussia. Now his problem was survival for himself and his wife Minna. He had to find a way to survive without a court appointment. The Darwinian concepts of the struggle to survive and the survival of the fittest were once again everyday realities for Wagner.

After a year wandering around France and falling in love with Jessie Laussot, he was forced to return to a safe place until he could return to Germany. He also met Mrs. Ritter and her son Karl, who wanted to be a professional musician and needed a teacher. So his mother hired Wagner. Then there was the Scottish woman Mrs. Taylor, who also provided him with a yearly stipend. At this point in his career, Wagner was able to find financial supporters, but he needed a safe place to live. The most logical place was Zurich, because he had some friends there and German was spoken there.

Switzerland long had a reputation for political and artistic exiles — see Tom Stoppard's play *Travesties*, which is set in Zurich in the 1920s, when revolutionaries and exiles like Lenin, James Joyce, and Tristan Tzara lived there. The Swiss dialect was difficult for Wagner to understand, especially since he himself spoke with a Saxon dialect, but educated people in Zurich spoke Hoch Deutsch so he could live there easily.

But during these years Wagner also developed a very close relationship with Jessie

9. Refuge in Zurich—The Development of Big Plans: 1850–1857

Laussot and her mother, that Scottish lady Mrs. Taylor—both of whom were giving him money. Jessie also wanted to leave her husband for Wagner but her husband, the Bordeau wine merchant, put an end to her relationship with Wagner by going to the local police. Wagner certainly never had a problem attracting women to him.

Wagner also liked to dress up, and once he had money, he could dress up even with fancy underwear and dressing gowns. Was he a cross-dresser? Not exactly, but he was very fond of silks and satin and perfumes, which seems more like female taste than male taste, especially in the 19th century. (Mozart too, a hundred year earlier, liked to wear fancy, colorful costumes and wigs—but that was more typical in the 18th than the 19th century for men.) While in the 19th century there was tremendous poverty in Switzerland, there were also wealthy people who were very interested in the arts, especially music and theater. Wagner soon developed a group of friends and supporters in Zurich who were willing to encourage his creativity, praise his music, and even lend him money. If Wagner had been able to live frugally, he could have been very happy in Zurich, a lovely if rather small city on the shores of a beautiful lake and surrounded by the Alps.

During his years in Switzerland, Wagner wrote essays and made plans for future projects and he conducted more. His essays on aesthetics and opera and music composition are still important and still in print. No other composer has written so much about his theories of theater and musical composition—and also about conducting and programming. Wagner was writing, and his essays would be published within the next years and be noticed and read, and they generated much publicity for him and his operas. Among those essays were "Art and Revolution," "A Communication to My Friends," "Opera and Drama," and "The Artwork of the Future." All of these became widely read among artists and intellectuals of the period.

Once he had a roof over his head, he got lonely for his wife and his homeland. So he started writing to her, begging her to join him in Zurich. The Saxon police were undoubtedly intercepting these letters and now knew where Wagner was hiding. In the fall, Minna came to Zurich, though their relationship as a sexual couple was over at this point. She still liked playing the role of the wife of a famous composer, so she started to occupy the apartment in Zurich which Richard had found and furnished for them. She came with their child substitutes, the dog Peps and the parrot, and eventually they settled into a grumbling kind of middle-aged quarrelsome marriage in Zurich.

Wagner's friend Julie Ritter in Dresden and his friend Jessie Laussot in Bordeaux both offered to support him so that he could continue his composing. Minna must have been annoyed at the idea of women supporting her husband, especially since Jessie Laussot seemed in love with him. At this point Minna must have accepted that their sexual relationship was over and that Wagner would need sexual attention from other women which Minna herself was too angry to give Wagner.

Since he was persona non grata in the German states, and since he did not compose during this period, Wagner was not much in the news. Some of his most important and notorious essays were written then—especially "Opera as Drama" and "Jews in Music." The first essay indicated the best in Wagner, his theories about opera and how it could break away from the old recitative/aria structure and more fully integrate music within the drama. But the worst of Wagner, his anti–Semitism, was also apparent in "Jews in Music." This essay indicated more than anything else his insecurities and his envy of other composers who had achieved international fame at a time when he had not. Wagner particularly envied Meyerbeer and Mendelssohn, two very successful German-Jewish composers, though one could argue that the latter was not Jewish since he had converted to Protestantism, though he was racially Jewish, assuming that this is a race and not a religion. Wagner especially came to hate Meyerbeer because he had success in Paris as an opera composer, something Wagner longed for. Wagner considered Meyerbeer's music third-rate; today's audiences would agree with this, and his operas are rarely staged these days. But in the 19th century, Meyerbeer was considered a major opera composer, much to Wagner's annoyance.

He may have written "Jews in Music" for publicity purposes since Wagner hated to be ignored. He knew that such an inflammatory essay would make him notorious throughout Europe. The essay was originally published under a pseudonym, though later he would unfortunately republish it under his own name. That essay made him notorious and Wagner fans today wish he had not written it, and probably eventually Wagner himself wished he had not written it. But it did attract a lot of attention to him, and rather like a child, Wagner loved attention — which was part of what attracted him to writing for the theater. He never dreamed of being a composer of symphonies or chamber music, though he did write some pieces in these genres. But the popularity of writing operas remained his main focus as a composer. At a time when he was not composing and not having the attention of a premiere of a new opera, "Jews in Music" kept him in the public eye.

One of the most important events of his Swiss exile was the premiere of *Lohengrin* in Weimar in 1850. It came about thanks to Franz Liszt, who staged it and conducted. Wagner could not attend this important and successful premiere because of his political exile in Switzerland — he could have been arrested if he returned to Weimar. Some Germans began to think that it was unfortunate that their greatest composer was banned from his homeland. During this next decade, Wagner's time was finally beginning to come and his operas were performed all over Germany, especially in Munich and Berlin, its two biggest cities. As these operas — especially *Tannhäuser* and *Lohengrin*— were becoming more and more popular, people were wondering what was happening to the composer of those operas. In the aftermath of the revolutionary years, old animosities were dying down, stability was returning, and more and more Germans were yearning for a united Germany, and more and more it seemed that Prussia and Count Bismarck and the Hohernzollern family would be the source of that German reunification. Bismarck's plan for a German Kaiser in Berlin in charge of a group of kingdoms was coming together, and Count Bismarck's shrewd negotiations were working to make this the new reality in a unified Germany. How did Wagner fit into those plans? From Bismarck's point of view, not at all, but from Wagner's point of view there was much planning and plotting occurring. As a united Germany was becoming a much-discussed topic, he began to feel that he could capitalize on this event.

9. Refuge in Zurich—The Development of Big Plans: 1850–1857

It was in Zurich that he began some composition of the Ring and *Tristan*, having already written some of the librettos for these works. He also explained his ideas for these new operas and played excerpts to his friends, which piqued their interest immediately. Wagner was very shrewd at marketing his ideas to others, and he did much of this in Switzerland as he was trying to attract a group of friends and donors to his cause.

In Bordeaux, Wagner visited Jessie Laussot and they even planned to run off and elope together, but then her husband returned and threatened to shoot Wagner. So Wagner fled again back to his wife in Zurich. M. Laussot had contacted the police in Bordeaux so Wagner was now being hunted by the police there too. Wagner's was a messy life especially at this point, caught as he was between extreme emotions and considered a criminal in German and French lands.

The fact that a Scottish widow, Mrs. Taylor, whom he had met in France, would want to support him indicated something about the mesmerizing quality of his personality. And despite his revolutionary activities, he had friends who believed in him and his work. In some people, his operas struck a spark that would keep them fascinated with both him and his operas. There was something unique about Wagnerian opera; both the music and the characters seemed haunting to some people, and distasteful to others.

When Wagner was back in Zurich, being threatened by Minna with ugly accusations (all of which were true), Wagner did what he always did when he was under extreme stress: He wrote. He found that he could not write music for a period, but he did a prose sketch of a new opera based on the life of the young Siegfried. While some men would have slit their throats, Wagner worked on the libretto for the entire Ring cycle instead. He often thought of suicide as a way of getting out of his many personal, artistic, and financial problems. His next opera, *Tristan*, would be about his desire to die with a woman he loved through a joint suicide pact.

He also wrote his nasty essay on "Jews in Music" under an assumed name, but many cognoscenti must have realized who the real author was. The essay clearly indicated his envy of successful Jewish composers Meyerbeer and Mendelssohn. He felt that since they were Jews, the press would promote their works, and he was right about that. Wagner envied money and success, which he did not have at this point in his career. He felt that his Jewish competitors were getting the success he deserved. He did not know at the time that his time would come later. He also underestimated their talents, especially Mendelssohn's.

Actually, he already had success, though he did not see it that way. His opera *Rienzi* had been a success, though he now considered it a very mediocre opera, and his opera *Tannhäuser* was also a success—though here too, its bigger success would come later. Liszt's production of *Lohengrin* in 1850 had also been a hit. But when Wagner got depressed, he felt that all his work had been a string of failures and that only the Jewish composers were having any success. That he failed to see the genius in the great operas of Verdi is astounding given their popularity in the 19th century, but this is clearly yet another example of his narcissism, based on his insecurities.

Wagner was a man who basically was interested in all religions but also suspicious of all religions and was indirectly criticizing all of them—especially in operas like *Lohen-

grin, *Tannhäuser*, and *Parsifal*. These seemingly religious operas were really attacks on the Christian religion, especially Catholicism, and a yearning for religious freedom and secular democracy. He would have undoubtedly agreed with Marx that religion was the opiate of the masses, and felt along with Freud that religion was basically neurosis. As Freud said, religion was the neurosis of mankind, and Freud included the Jewish religion in that statement of condemnation. Wagner dreamed of the death of the gods, which he would put on stage at the end of the Ring. His early disciple Nietzsche would become famous for saying "Gott ist tod," God is dead!

Wagner had inherited from the Enlightenment a fear and suspicion of all religions, and for that reason he was never a church-goer or a follower of any religion. Many of his operas attacked religion on several levels. He knew about what the Christian crusaders had done in the Holy Land — massacred millions of non–Christians.

Wagner believed in separation of Church and State, was suspicious of all organized religions, especially if they were running the government, and so he feared what Jewish Zionists were planning to do to the people of Palestine. He was very interested in Arab culture — Kundry's first line in *Parsifal* describes her getting medicine from Arab lands to try to heal the sick Amfortas. Wagner believed in secular democracy, was always suspicious of religion, did not go to church, and so he saw the Jews and their brutal plans for Palestine and the Palestinian people as threats to secular democracy. The real problem, as Wagner so wisely saw it, was anti–Semitism against the largest Semitic people, Arabs, who were even in the 19th century victims of European imperialism. The Zionist-Jewish determination to have their own apartheid state — with only Jews having political power — would result in a holocaust of the Palestinian Arabs, both Christian and Muslim.

It is interesting to visit Wagner's grave in Bayreuth (right behind his house, Wahnfried, which is now a museum). The tomb contains only the bodies of Wagner and his wife Cosima and is not adorned with any religious symbols as all. Clearly, this is the grave of an atheist, a believer in secular democracy.

Luckily for Wagner, he had some money coming in from Julie Ritter (the Bordeaux money had ceased abruptly). Ritter's son Karl had a great desire to become a great composer, and Wagner must have liked the young man but soon realized that he had little musical talent. Wagner enjoyed socializing with Karl but felt he would never become a significant composer. But he could pretend to teach him and befriend him since he liked the young man, and continued to get money from his mother. Wagner at this point in his life found a mother-figure with a lot of money and an aristocratic title irresistible.

And Wagner found that he could also make money by conducting. He conducted Weber's *Der Fleischütz* at Zurich's main opera house, then called the Aktienstheater. Now Zurich has one of the best opera houses and opera companies in Europe, but in 1850 there was not much operatic activity there — primarily touring opera companies. But Wagner's conducting was popular with the Zurich public, especially its wealthy musical connoisseurs like Otto and Mathilde Wesendonck. They dreamed of turning Zurich into a musical and operatic capital of Europe instead of the musical and operatic backwater it was in 1850. Wagner, a major composer they felt, could help them with their ambitious

9. Refuge in Zurich — The Development of Big Plans: 1850–1857

plans for an operatic and artistic future for Zurich. There was some theatrical and musical activity in Zurich and Wagner quickly became the center of the artistic community there, and his compositions and conducting created a group of friends and fans and supporters for him and his projects. He liked to play excerpts from his forthcoming works for people — something most other composers do not do — and thereby Wagner was marketing his works and creating audiences for them.

While in Zurich, Wagner discovered the writings of German philosopher Arthur Schopenhauer, especially *Studies in Pessemism* and *The World as Will and Idea.* In Schopenhauer's negativism and rejection of all things religious (except for a weakness for Buddhism), and his obsessions with suicide and death, Wagner felt that he had found a soulmate who understood his operas better than he did. Schopenhauer repeatedly emphasized the power of music in his essays. Suicides occur so often in Wagnerian opera, and here was a reason for them, in the writings of Schopenhauer. Wagner became a convert! While the earlier operas of Wagner were more Marxist, the later operas tended more to reflect the world of rejection, pessimism, and death which the composer found in Schopenhauer. This philosopher also emphasized the power of the irrational, especially the sexual, on human life and human motivation. Sexuality and suicide often entered the mind and fantasy world of Wagner, and these two concepts would enter into his new operas — along with images of water, light, and darkness. Those years in Zurich were not wasted years for the composer.

Wagner's famous essay "Opera as Drama" asserted the dramatic essence of opera and that the music always had to serve the drama. He did not want the drama to stop in order to create a lovely aria for the tenor or soprano. Wagner would violate his own rules in his subsequent operas, but his ideals did inform the Wagnerian operas that would come, and his ideals would attract a group of intellectuals who were interested in operatic aesthetics, many of whom would eventually become his fans. Wagner's writing offended some people but it also attracted others to him and made him more popular and kept him in the public eye.

In 1853 he had finished the libretto for all four operas of the Ring of the Nibelung. He had these privately printed and given to his friends in the hope of generating publicity for his vast enterprise of writing and staging this mammoth cycle of operas — based on the *Orestia* and other tragic cycles by the ancient Greek playwrights like Aeschylus, Sophocles, and Euripides. Such a mammoth cycle of four operas would need a lot of publicity and a lot of money so Wagner went about trying to make this happen. He was also arguing that his cycle would need a new kind of opera house instead of the traditional European tier of boxes. He composed parts of the cycle and performed these in public, both on the piano with singers and with a full orchestra when he was conducting. He became a genius at marketing his own operas, especially the Ring.

Wagner was what the Germans called a Macher — a mover and a shaker. He could make things happen: create new operas, create new opera houses, create new operatic movements, create a new kind of art and a new artistic climate. Some of the enlightened leaders in Zurich must have realized that Wagner could be very valuable to the tourist and public relations businesses in Zurich. Wagner, along with his financial backers, could create operas and concerts which would attract the attention of all of Europe. Zurich had not only gorgeous mountain scenery and a lovely lake, it also had tremendous potential as an arts center.

Wagner had a way of talking about his newest operas in a way that would generate tremendous interest. Wagner dreamed at this point of seeing his newest opera, *Lohengrin*, on stage in Zurich, and he described this opera to people who were yearning to see it as well. He also talked about his Ring project. Wagner had already written the text to his project and he read this to his friends. What a magnificent reader Wagner must have been since most of the people who heard the reading wanted to see the four operas on stage. Some people have commented that Wagner's real genius was acting since his skills were such that he himself could mesmerize an audience. At the Fond du Lac hotel in Zurich, Wagner rented a room and invited friends to hear a reading of his proposed Ring cycle. In that audience were Otto and Mathilde Wesendonck, and they and others left the reading fascinated with the new work.

Wagner was also a major conductor and he often used his concerts to market his newest works—like excerpts from *Lohengrin* and his proposed Ring Cycle. This was brilliant marketing since audience members often found these excerpts—for example, "Ride of the Walkyries"—fascinating and yearned to hear more of this new work. In Zurich, Wagner also wrote an important essay, "On Conducting," and this essay, along with Wagner's own practices as a conductor, helped to establish conducting as a force to reckon with in the 19th century. Conductors were not taken all that seriously before then, unless they were also composers, like Handel or Mozart. Wagner emphasized in his essay the power and responsibilities of the conductor to pick a program around a single theme, and shape the music he was conducting into a unified, whole interpretation of the particular score he was conducting. Wagner developed a new approach to conducting which came to define the modern conductor—finding the inner "melos," or internal melody and emphasizing it, but with a unified approach to the whole work so a significant interpretation emerges. Wagner particularly emphasized the importance of conducting Beethoven so that the greatness and force of the music becomes apparent to the audience. Wagner also argued that the 19th century approach to organizing a concert involved playing too many works. A shorter and more unified approach to concert programming would be more effective, he argued. He tried out these ideas first on his wife Minna, and then on his audiences, and many responded favorably.

Otto and Mathilde Wesendonck, an attractive and wealthy young couple with several children, were both very musical, especially Mathilde. Mathilde also wrote poetry of some importance. They had heard some of Wagner's music and became fans. At a time when Wagner felt like an isolated criminal, they entered his life and showered him with encouragement and love. Wagner noticed that Mathilde was surrounded by her children, and he was always susceptible to maternal women. It was inevitable that they fall in love, and in a way Wagner fell in love with both Otto and Mathilde—they must have seemed to him like the loving and wealthy parents he never got. They loved him, they liked his

9. Refuge in Zurich—The Development of Big Plans: 1850–1857

operas, and they encouraged him to write more of them. For a while it seemed like a perfect relationship for all of them. Wagner loved praise and encouragement, something he was not getting from Minna these days, but Otto and Mathilde were giving these things to encourage him to finish *Tristan und Isolde*, the Ring, and the other opera projects he was talking about.

And Wagner had in a way fallen in love with Zurich, despite the horrible local dialect of German spoken there, since people asked him to conduct and they responded well to his music. He programmed some of his new operas, fragments of his forthcoming operas, and the audiences in Zurich by and large responded very favorably. This city could have become the place he spent his whole life looking for—but of course once he found his heaven, he had to blow it up.

His relationship with the Wesendoncks while he lived in Zurich became one of the most important in his life, and particularly his relationship with Mathilde, who became one of the great loves of his life. More than anything else, he wanted to be with Mathilde and die soon—with Mathilde.

10

The Idea of the Ring: Italy: 1857–1858

While Wagner was living in Zurich, he did many things in terms of developing Zurich is musical and operatic life, including conducting the local orchestra and arranging concerts of his own music. He also continued to travel and left Switzerland sometimes to visit its neighbor to the south, Italy.

He met in Zurich with Otto and Mathilde Wesendonck and this became one of the most important relationships in his life. They were both fond of Italy and he visited Italy with them. Goethe in his famous book *Der Italienische Reise* talked about the importance of a trip to Italy for any artist but especially the German artist, and Wagner read this book very carefully. Goethe felt that the German artist can find inspiration for his own art in Italy.

Most of the critics in Germany and Austria hated Wagner and gave his compositions bad reviews. Some of these critics were Jewish, though not all, and they had very good reason to hate him given his essay "Judaism in Music." Wagner earned all of his enemies in the press, but their own sensitivity blinded them to the fact that Wagner's operas were the best German operas around, and truly revolutionary, and the operas themselves were in no way anti–Semitic. So the fact that most of the music critics of the day did not like Wagner's operas made him appear sympathetic to many audiences at the time since they began to see him as the victim of a cabal.

By 1852 and 1853 more and more opera houses in Germany and elsewhere in Europe were staging Wagnerian opera. Towns like Leipzig, Wiesbaden, and Wurzburg were also staging Wagner's operas, proving that even small opera houses could successfully mount a Wagnerian opera. And audiences were giving their approval of these efforts so that Wagner's operas were generating more and more fans who wanted to see more of his operas. A Wagner movement was being generated by these performances and by Wagner's essays and books. Wagner's artwork of the future was becoming a slogan and generating a demand—Wagner's genius at marketing himself and his operas was bearing fruit. Even in Dresden, Wagner's music was again being heard, and in Munich, Franz Lachner was conducting and staging his operas. The revolutionary who was not allowed to live in Germany was becoming Germany's most famous contemporary composer.

Wagner was also promoting the operas he was planning to compose. In Mariafeld in Switzerland, he finished the libretto to his Ring project and read the whole work, over

10. The Idea of the Ring: Italy: 1857–1858

two nights, to a group of friends. Wagner could be a mesmerizing actor, and though he did not have a singing voice, his acting while he read his Nibelung text mesmerized many members of that original Ring audience in Switzerland. Wagner knew how to enchant an audience with his speaking and acting, at least if it was done in German.

In 1853 he was in a hotel on the gulf of La Spezia, a place where the poet Shelley had drowned about twenty years earlier. He describes the vision he had in his autobiography:

> I stretched out dead-tired on a hard couch, awaiting the long-desired onset of sleep. It did not come; instead, I sank into a kind of somnambulistic state, in which I suddenly had the feeling of being immersed in rapidly flowing water. Its rushing soon resolved itself for me into the musical sound of the chord of E flat major, resounding in persistent broken chords; these in turn transformed themselves into melodic figurations of increasing motion, yet the E flat major triad never changed, and seemed by its continuance to import infinite significance to the element in which I was sinking. I awoke in sudden terror from this trance, feeling as though the waves were crashing high above my head. I recognized at once the orchestral prelude to *Das Rheingold*, long dormant within me but up to that moment inchoate, had at last been revealed; I also saw immediately precisely how it was with me: the vital flood would come from within me, and not from without. I immediately decided to return to Zurich and begin setting my vast poem to music.

The dream that enabled him to begin to write the music for his Ring cycle suggests a theory of art which he puts on stage in the third act of *Meistersinger:* that art is a product of the dreaming mind of the artist. The following year, 1854, Wagner wrote the music for *Die Walküre*. After about seven years of not being able to write any music, all of a sudden the music poured out of him for his new masterpiece, the Ring cycle. In the meantime he yearned to hear a performance of his *Lohengrin*. Liszt had successfully conducted the premiere of the work in Weimar in 1850, but Wagner had never had a chance to hear it because he was forbidden to go to Germany.

Wagner later wrote most of *Tristan und Isolde* in Venice, where he lived at the Palazzo Giustianini — Wagner often fled to the nearest palazzo in Italy when he was having problems in Germany. Certainly Wagner was an Italophile, like most German writers and artists, and loved going to Italy for the art, the climate, and Roman ruins. Wagner had a somewhat condescending attitude toward the Italian composers, especially their opera composers. He was a contemporary of Giuseppe Verdi but never said one kind thing about that Italian genius of opera. Certainly Verdi and Wagner were the two greatest geniuses in the history of opera, but Verdi was much kinder to Wagner than the other way round. Yet Wagner was a great fan of Italian art and was constantly going to museums in Italy, especially those in Florence, Venice, and Rome. Titian and Bellini were his favorites, but he could not resist visiting the great museums of Italy — not to mention the ancient Roman architecture or the Renaissance architecture in places in Rome, Sienna, and Venice.

Italy remained a major source of inspiration for Wagner and his operas. He visited Italy as often as he could, mostly to avoid the cold, gray German winters or to flee creditors. Italy had a special attraction for the Germans and English during the Romantic period. Among the English, both Keats and Shelley died there, and Byron visited many times, so in England too the Romantics established a tradition of going to Italy. Among the English Victorians, contemporaries of Wagner, Robert Browning and his wife Elizabeth Barrett were the biggest fans of Italy, which is where they eloped to and got married, and where their son Pen was born. Elizabeth Barrett is buried in the Protestant cemetery in Florence while Keats and Shelley are buried in the Protestant cemetery in Rome. So many of the Romantics were fascinated with Italy and constantly going there and writing music about it. Berlioz's "Harold in Italy" and Tchaikovsky's "Capriccio Italiano" are examples of this.

Part of this grew out of the 18th century fashion for the Grand Tour, the English aristocrat's tour of Italy. Gentlemen students would tour Italy with their tutors to see the great Roman ruins and Italian museums in Florence, Venice, and Rome — some even venturing as far south as Naples and Sicily to see the antiquities there, sites like Pompeii and the wonderful Greek ruins in Taormina and Agrigento. This was only for the very wealthy in the 18th century, but by the 19th century when railroads were built, travel became easier and cheaper so that more middle-class people could do this. But even earlier, Shakespeare's fascination with Italy was clearly indicated by his setting so many of his plays there: *The Merchant of Venice, Romeo and Juliet, Two Gentlemen of Verona, Othello, Julius Caesar,* and many more. In Germany, both Goethe and Schiller set plays and poems in Italy, Goethe's "Kennst du das Land" being a poem about the yearning for Italy. Wagner too placed his first operatic success, *Rienzi,* in ancient Rome. Wagner's political thought would appear in both *Rienzi* and his Ring cycle, the latter work becoming his most political work, which grew out of his experiences in Dresden during the attempted revolution there.

Wagner's first successful opera, *Rienzi,* was based on a character from Roman history. Even earlier, his first opera, *Die Feen,* is based on Carlo Gozzi's *La Donna Serpente*. The watery music of *Tristan* is clearly a reflection of the canals of Venice, where Wagner wrote most of the music. Water is a major symbol in many of Wagner's operas, particularly *The Flying Dutchman, Tristan und Isolde, and* the Ring cycle.

Wagner once said that he got the idea of the Liebestod at the end of *Tristan und Isolde* while viewing Titian's "Assumption of the Virgin" in Venice in the Church of the Frari, where the painting is still displayed to this day. The Immolation scene at the end of *Götterdämmerung* also connects with Titian's "Assumption of the Virgin" in Venice. Wagner also liked Café Florian in the Piazza San Marco in Venice, a café which is still at the same location. Wagner was in many ways a typical product of Romanticism with its love of Italy, landscape, seascapes, sublime experiences, and sublime characters.

Water symbolism was a major element in most of Wagner's operas: Water is a wonderful symbol which suggests both life and death. It reminds us that we are composed mostly of water and can die without water, yet we can also die if we put our heads in water too long. Water can easily symbolize a totality which includes both life and death and has become one of the recurrent symbols of Western literature and art.

It was while Wagner was at La Spezia that he first got the inspiration for the music for what was to become the four operas of the Ring cycle. And that 25-year project would culminate in the staging of the four opera tetralogy in Bayreuth in 1876. Now every opera house in the world dreams of staging a Ring cycle, which is the ultimate test of any opera

10. The Idea of the Ring: Italy: 1857–1858

house. And when one goes to the Ring cycle in Bayreuth, one immediately notices the international nature of the audience — people from Scotland and Japan particularly stand out in this international audience because of the kilts and kimonos. People from around the world are in evidence at the performances at Bayreuth, where all Wagnerians want to go after they die, or perhaps sooner.

While some critics have called that La Spezia story into question, Wagner himself affirms the validity of it in his correspondence and his autobiography *Mein Leben*. The periods of 1850 and 1851 were important for several essays Wagner composed. He wrote "Opera and Drama" and "Jews in Music." His repeated visits to Italy during the 1850s generated many ideas for new operas, but he was forced to return to Zurich and try to develop a career there to support himself and his wife Minna and her daughter Nathalie.

"Opera and Drama" remains one of the most important essays in the history of the art form of opera. In that book he talks about the importance of drama in opera and descries the 18th century format of aria/recitative in which the drama stops and there is a musical number for a soloist or a duet. This format had become increasingly seen as old-fashioned by the middle of the 19th century, and Wagner's essays calls for a more dramatic kind of format in opera. His call for reform reminds many of Gluck's reform operas of the 18th century, though Gluck's reforms often consisted of taking the plots of the Greek tragedies like Orpheus and Euridice and the Oresteia and giving them all happy endings — not most people's idea of good dramatic reform. But Wagner called for a great reform in terms of integrating music with the drama and the action onstage. Clearly his model was what he imagined Greek tragedy was like — with a musical chorus. Many of the scholars of the Greek drama told Wagner that his conceptions of Greek culture and Greek drama were naïve, but Wagner continued to believe that his ideas were valid. Wagner, like Gluck, did not want the action in opera to stop for an aria; he wanted music and drama to be integrated into one unified art form, and he did elevate the importance of the orchestra as a kind of Greek chorus which could comment on the action onstage through Wagner's systems of leitmotifs. Of course leitmotifs themselves were as old as opera — Monteverdi used them in operas like *L' Incornonazione del Poppea* — but Wagner became famous for using his own system of leitmotifs in a much more subtle way and incorporating them into the orchestra and voices to create a unified whole of great power. Wagner's orchestration became one of his trademarks as an opera composer, and one of the things which attracted audiences to him. This subtle use of a large, complex orchestra also added to the expense and difficulty of staging his operas.

Wagner must have been a mesmerizing individual since so many women were attracted to him. He never seemed to lack women, both wives and lovers. His combination of neediness and genius must have been irresistible to many women of his period — and beyond. So after his several trips to Italy, he returned to Switzerland and his friends there. Zurich was part of the German-speaking world and German was the only language Wagner was very comfortable in, though his French was rather good by this time. But he was really most comfortable speaking German, and he could do this in Zurich, despite the local dialect of German used there called Swizzerdeutsch. It was so guttural that it made standard German, or Hochdeutsch, sound like Italian in comparison to the Zurich dialect of German. But educated citizens of Zurich spoke standard German rather than Svizzerdeutsch. Wagner himself had an accent since German speakers could immediately identify his Saxon accent when he spoke. Since he was raised in the two largest cities in Saxony, Leipzig (where he was born) and Dresden, he naturally spoke that dialect of German, though he certainly spoke standard German as well. But when he got excited, he was liable to sound more and more Saxon.

In Zurich, his reputation had preceded him and some people already knew his music. Jacob Sulzer, Francois and Eliza Wille and other musical people invited Wagner to their houses. He was very soon provided with a residency permit so that he could remain in Switzerland and travel to other parts of Europe if he needed to.

In order to survive in Zurich, Wagner did much conducting—sometimes of his own music. The main orchestras in Zurich, then as now, were the Algemeine Musik Gesellschaft and the Tonhalle Orchester, and Wagner conducted these groups many times. The first festival of Wagner's music was in Zurich, and he envisioned staging his Ring cycle and building his festival theater in Zurich, though the thrifty Swiss never provided any financial backing for his mighty project. The Swiss soon got wind of Wagner's mania for spending binges and were often suspicious of this spendthrift operatic genius. And Wagner soon learned that it was wise to separate his German friend from his Swiss friends since they usually did not get along with each other.

Wagner also met the Swiss poet Gottfried Keller in Zurich, and they discussed their concept of art for the people rather than art for the upper classes only. Ultimately, Keller and Wagner disagreed on what kind of folk art could be produced: Keller wanted the folk to produce their own art, but Wagner had a different concept of art for the people. He wanted his art to reflect the common people rather than the aristocracy, a view that had caused him to participate in the Dresden uprising. But Wagner now had an ideological problem here since only the wealthy could afford to contribute to the staging of his revolutionary new operas. He needed the munificence of a king, and eventually found that king in Bavaria's Ludwig II; but in Zurich resided the wealthy Wesendoncks.

It was during these Swiss years that Wagner wrote an article proposing changes in the cultural life of Zurich; they sounded similar to his recommendations for changing the cultural life of Dresden. He also wrote the complete text of his *Der Ring des Nibelungen* and had it privately printed—and he gave copies of this libretto to his friends in Zurich, including the Wesendoncks. He also gave several readings of the four texts on four separate nights—reading all the parts himself. He must have been a mesmerizing reader since most of his audience members reported liking the poems and enjoying his oral interpretation of them. Several contemporaries described Wagner as a born actor and said if he had not been a composer, he could have made a very good living as an actor.

Wagner often wrote to Liszt in Weimar, usually begging him to come to Switzerland for a visit, as in the following letter written by Wagner on May 30, 1853:

> Dearest friend, have you not yet had enough of Weimar? I must own that I frequently grieve to see how you waste your strength there. Was there any truth to the recent rumor of your

10. The Idea of the Ring: Italy: 1857–1858

leaving Weimar? Have they given in? But all this is idle talk. My brain is a wilderness, and I thirst for a long, long sleep, to awake only with my arms around you. Write to me very precisely, also whether you are inclined, after a little stay at Zurich, to go with me to the solitude of the Grisons; St. Moritz might, after all, do you good, dearest friend; we shall there be five thousand feet high, and enjoy the most nerve-strengthening air; together with the mineral water, which is said to be of beneficial effect on the digestive organs. Think this over, consult your health and your circumstances, and let me know very soon what I may hope for. Farewell, best and dearest of friends. Have my eternal thanks for your divine friendship, and be assured of my steadfast and warmest love.

This letter certainly exemplifies Wagner's deep love for Liszt, a love which had a homoerotic element. The letter also indicates Wagner's frequent loneliness in Zurich; he must have missed the many musical discussions he had with the Hungarian composer. Their friendship would last until the very end of both composers' lives—Wagner died in 1883 and Liszt in 1886. This letter also suggests the deep love that Wagner was developing for Switzerland, especially for its fabulous Alpine scenery. The mountains in Switzerland are the tallest in Europe and continue to attract millions of tourists. Wagner wrote most of the Ring while living in Switzerland and its scenery, especially its mountain scenery, certainly appears in the Ring.

Wagner started conducting more and more in Zurich and soon he had a group of fans who liked his ideas and liked his conducting, and especially liked his programming of the Beethoven symphonies. He was one of the earliest advocates for the Beethoven symphonies and felt that they were the greatest classical music composed so far. Wagner's conducting of the Beethoven symphonies was soon attracting comment beyond Switzerland. He conducted parts of his previously composed operas, especially *Lohengrin, The Flying Dutchman,* and *Tannhäuser.* He teased his audience by conducting parts of his forthcoming Ring cycle, which was a clever marketing device which got audiences interested in his Ring and wanting to hear and see the whole tetralogy. Among his many other skills, Wagner was a clever marketer of his own compositions. While in Zurich, he was building an audience for his own forthcoming works, especially the Ring cycle. Zurich could easily have been the place where the Ring had its first performance. Wagner could have built his festival theater in Zurich and begun an annual summer festival there. He even suggested such a thing, though he must have known that the money needed for such an enterprise would have been hard to find in what was then a very small and provincial Swiss city. Had Zurich found the money to fund Wagner, that money would have been repaid many times over in all the Wagnerian tourism which the festival would eventually bring to Bayreuth in Franconia.

Here in Zurich we also see Wagner's genius for marketing himself and his art. He would include excerpts of his former and current musical compositions in his Beethoven concerts, thereby creating a curiosity in the audience for Wagner's past and forthcoming compositions. His excerpts from *The Ring* and *Tristan und Isolde* naturally made audience members curious about these works and wanting to see them on stage right there in Zurich. Wagner's genius for conducting also helped to make the conductor the center of concerts, and he created programs which reflect modern concert programming. While many 19th century concert programs sound like five-hour endurance tests, Wagner's look like the programs we are used to in contemporary concerts. During this time, when Wagner had to conduct to earn a living in Zurich, he wrote essays on conducting and conducted concerts which revolutionized the art of conducting for contemporary audiences and which had a great influence on the important conductors of his period and into our own time, young conductors like Hans von Bülow learning from Wagner's own conducting techniques. Many of these young conductors read Wagner's essays on conducting and went to visit him in Zurich to learn from him. Wagner was a revolutionary on so many fronts. Other people started visiting Wagner while he was living in exile in Zurich.

Minna was with him for most of the period while he was living in Zurich and they tried to resume their married life together, but Minna must have been a very angry woman at that point in her life. They had a lovely apartment in Dresden and even some servants — exactly the kind of life she had dreamed of when they were penniless in Paris and begging relatives for money to feed themselves. This was humiliating for both of them, but for Minna particularly. It must have been very galling to her to lose everything because of her husband's politics and involvement in a revolution which she must have seen as a doomed affair right from the start. How angry she must have been when she moved to Zurich and became again his wife while he was still talking of art and of revolution. He was telling the Swiss how lucky they were not to have a king, but Minna missed the royal stipend they had received in Dresden. Even though Wagner lived with his wife while he was in Zurich, it was becoming clear that they were getting on each other's nerves.

At this point in their lives, Wagner and Minna were a mismatch. They were sick of each other, angry with each other, and needed somebody else in their lives, or in Minna's case, at this point in her life, she would probably have been better off alone or with members of her own family, like her daughter Nathalie, whom she was constantly arguing with but also loved. They had reached the point of often arguing in public with their friends — not a good sign. And Minna frequently had her daughter Nathalie with them in Zurich. Wagner also became more open to Minna about the other women in his life, which added to her anger.

After Minna began to create some ugly scenes with the Wesendoncks and Wagner's other Swiss and German friends in Zurich, he began to avoid her.

Despite the conflicts at home, Wagner wrote a good part of the libretto for *Tristan und Isolde* there. Clearly his first exile in Switzerland had been very productive for him. Wagner's first Swiss period then, from 1849 to 1858, provided political exile but also artistic stimulation since it was here that he met the Wesendoncks and here that he discovered the philosophy of Arthur Schopenhauer. He often discussed Schopenhauer's ideas with the Wesendoncks and his other Swiss friends, though he surely missed his German friends as well. Despite his many personal and financial problems during this first Swiss period, Wagner was always able to write and sometimes to compose as well. As Tamara Evans has summarized:

> His years in Zurich were a productive period. As conductor, Wagner was much sought-after, and he gave the Zurich musical public his very best. He wrote a series of key essays beginning with "Art and Revolution" in 1849, soon to be followed by "The Art-Work of the Future"

10. The Idea of the Ring: Italy: 1857–1858

(1850), "Judaism in Music" (1850), "Opera and Drama" (1851), "A Theater in Zurich" (1851), and "A Communication to My Friends" (1851). Exile did not stifle Wagner's poetic and musical creativity: the texts for *Die Walkure and Das Rheingold* were finished in 1852; in late 1853 and 1854 respectively, he had completed both scores. By 1857, while working on the *Siegfried* score and following the Wagners' move to the "Asylum" adjoining the Wesendonck estate, he devoted his energies in part to the composition of *Tristan und Isolde*, in part to the *Wesendonck Lieder*, and to what was subsequent unseemly encounters between the two women in the summer of 1858 precipitating what had been in the making for quite some time; Wagner fled, some of his belonging were confiscated, and those that were left Minna put up for sale in the local papers. Minna then paid up the debts her husband had accrued with various local merchants and left for Germany [Evans 4].

Wagner was certainly not the only foreigner to find some refuge and inspiration in Zurich. During World Wars I and II, James Joyce would find political refuge there as well, using World War I to write most of his *Ulysses*. Lenin and Tristan Tzara were also in Zurich during this period. During World War II Joyce wrote much of *Finnegans Wake* in Zurich. For Wagner, one of the biggest advances of Zurich is that it was so close to Italy, and as Wagner was getting older, he found the winters in Switzerland and Germany more difficult to endure.

The obsession with visiting Italy became one of the many layers of Wagner's personality, and he visited that country many times, writing most of *Tristan* there, getting the idea for the music of his Ring there, and finally dying there — in Venice in 1883. In many ways Wagner chose to die in Italy since in the final six months of his life he must have realized that the end was near, that his daily heart attacks were clearly telling him that he did not have much time left. He chose to die in Italy, specifically Venice, and perhaps he committed suicide there by not taking his medicine properly, though his end was at hand as he approached his seventieth birthday.

The Romantic artists developed an obsession with Italy, and this was part of Wagner's personality. This grew out of the grand tour concept of the 18th century, the idea that a northern European could not really be a cultivated person unless he spent some time in Italy. The search for Arcadia, as in Stoppard's play *Arcadia*, involved looking for the ancient classical ideal world in the ruins of Italy. Thus in Arcadia, the landscape gardeners were trying to create an ideal world, based on the ancient Roman concept of Arcadia, on the paintings of Salvatore Rosa and the ancient Roman ruins and gardens of Italy. Arcadia was also a part of the Peloponnese in ancient Greece and that too generated pastoral poetry in ancient Greek.

In Southern Italy, Wagner found the gardens of Rapallo, near Naples, and these gardens became the model for the magic garden in the second art of *Parsifal* in Bayreuth in 1882. Wagner was fascinated with the gardens of Italy, especially the tropical vegetation of Southern Italy and Sicily. All the exotic vegetation — palm trees, bougainvillea, cactus flowers, camellias, and azaleas — captured his imagination in his own search for an arcadia. In this way, he was typical of many Romantic artists.

The search for Arcadia, a model world and a tropical paradise, became part of northern European culture in the 19th century and helped to fuel the Italian tourist business from the 19th century to the present. Now people around the world, including China and Japan, want to see the beauties of Italy, which has helped to fuel its billion dollar tourist industry. Most people around the world now want to see Rome, Venice, and Florence before they die, and Richard Wagner was an earlier embodiment of that desire. His last opera, *Parsifal*, was set in Spain, a country he also desired to visit but never did. But Italy remained Wagner's major travel destination. Perhaps he read one of Elizabeth Barrett's short poem:

> Open my heart and you shall see
> engraved in it
> "Italy."

She too died in Italy and was buried in the Protestant cemetery in Florence.

Wagner's career was truly pan–European for he traveled all over Europe, especially Germany, France, and Italy. He also went to London but did not like it much because of all the industrialism and all the fog, though even there he had faithful followers, people who instantly fell in love with his music and saw it as he saw it, as the music of the future. At the time, London was very fond of Mendelssohn's music, and with a sizable Jewish community. But even in London there were intellectuals and musicians who were attracted to Wagner, especially George Eliot and her life's partner George Lewis, both of whom became Wagner fans, and both of whom found Wagner's music very attractive. Queen Victoria invited Wagner to the palace and chatted with him and told him she liked his music, as did other members of the royal family, especially Prince Albert. They all had a particular fondness for German music—Bach, Handel, Mozart, Schubert, Schumann, and now Wagner.

Cycles of nature connect Wagner with Giambattista Vico and his theories of cycles and how cycles control much of our lives. Natural cycles certainly recur in Wagner's operas—cycles of waking and sleeping, cycles of the Earth's revolutions around the sun, cycles of night and day. The water cycles of nature also recur in Wagner's operas, and nature itself is clearly one of his main themes, especially in the Ring cycle.

The Ring cycle begins and ends in the Rhine river. Another major aspect of Wagner's operas is the complexity of characterization. One can never be sure who are the heroes and who are the villains in Wagnerian opera—which adds to their eternal fascination and the opportunities for directors to see the operas in a new and revolutionary way.

11

The Wesendoncks: 1858–1859

"Beloved Mathilde."—R. Wagner

Two of the first people Wagner met in Zurich were Otto Wesendonck and his wife Mathilde. Otto, a wealthy silk merchant, was very interested in the arts, especially music and especially Beethoven. His Villa Wesendonck was one of the most elaborate and beautiful in a suburb of Zurich. This building is now the Rietberg Museum for Oriental and Tibetan art and within the city limits of Zurich. On the villa grounds was a small cottage called the Asyl, and Otto eventually suggested that Wagner move there with Minna. Otto's lovely wife Mathilde was passionately interested in music and opera and was already a fan of Wagner's music, and she also wrote poetry. She wrote the text of the famous Wesendonck lieder which Wagner put to music—to piano accompaniment. (He only orchestrated one of the songs, but the other four songs were also orchestrated by others.) Mathilde quickly became enamored of Wagner's operas.

Wagner liked visiting the villa and he seemed to fall in love with Otto and Mathilde and their children as well. Otto was very receptive to both Wagner's ideas and his music, and Mathilde was utterly entranced with both his person and his music. Did Wagner and Mathilde have an affair right under Otto's nose? One cannot be sure, but their letters are very lover-like. Wagner was always a man who needed a lot of praise for his operas and his ideas. In some strange ways, the Wesendoncks became substitutes for the parents Wagner sought all his life since he did not have them while he was a child, and his relationship with Mathilde became in some way erotic, though we can never be sure how erotic.

Wagner was prone to triangular relationship with a woman and her husband—looking for eroticized parental figures. This occurs in *Tristan* as well—Tristan connects with Isolde and her husband (and his uncle) King Marke. That Mathilde was surrounded by her children added to her motherly quality, just as Minna was surrounded by her daughter Nathalie. Otto could give him large amounts of money, like a beneficent daddy figure, and Mathilde could nurture his art and his compositions with endless flattery like the loving mother he never had. Here again Wagner had the perfect situation for his subconscious needs.

Could Mathilde have had an affair with Wagner while she was still living with her husband and children? Was a *petit ménage* going on between the three of them? I doubt it, but maybe. But the letters between them that survive do indicate that Wagner and Mathilde did love each other passionately.

Richard Wagner

Wagner wrote to Mathilde Wesendonck on April 7, 1858:

> In the morning I regained my senses, and was able to pray to my angel from the very depths of my heart; and this prayer is love! Love! My soul rejoices in this love, which is the wellspring of my redemption.... Be good and forgive me, and forgive my childishness yesterday; you were quite right to call it that! The weather seems quite mild. I shall come into the garden today; as soon as I see you, I hope I may find you alone for a moment! Take my whole soul as a morning salutation! [Wagner, Spencer, *Selected Letters*, 381–85].

And that love was clearly tinged with death and especially suicide, which is apparent in *Tristan und Isolde*. Or was Wagner using this relationship with Otto and Mathilde to help his subconscious mind create *Tristan und Isolde* since the situation so clearly mirrored the situation in his opera? Did Wagner have a subconscious need to mirror in life the dramatic situations in his operas? Did his musical imagination need this kind of real-life stimulus to produce some of the greatest and most erotic music ever written?

Wagner had been friends with the Wesendoncks for several years, and he loved them both, when suddenly love entered into the relationship with Wagner falling in love with Mathilde. Otto suggested that Wagner and his wife move into the cottage on his property, the Asyl, and they did. While Wagner's autobiography does discuss this situation, one must remember that Wagner had been asked by King Ludwig II of Bavaria to write his autobiography for him — and it was dictated to Cosima, his second wife. Was his relationship with Mathilde sexual or platonic? In his autobiography, Wagner writes:

> Upon my return home I had to discover more precisely the unpleasant outcome of my wife's conduct toward our neighbor [Mathilde Wesendonck]. In her crude misinterpretation of my purely friendly relationship to the young lady, who was always deeply concerned for my well-being and my tranquility, Minna had gone so far as to threaten to tell her husband and by this had so profoundly insulted her, being really unaware of having done wrong in any way, and she even began to have doubts about me, as she did not understand how I could have permitted my wife to nurture such a misconception. The upshot of this disturbance was that, thanks to the discreet mediation of our good friend Frau Wille, I was eventually absolved of any responsibility for my wife's conduct. Yet, I was given to understand that henceforth it would be impossible for the insulted lady to set foot in my house, or to continue any association with my wife. They did not seem to realize clearly enough, or want to admit, that I could only respond to this by giving up my dwelling and leaving Zurich.

So while he was visiting the Villa Wesendonck, his complex mind was both enjoying the attention and wondering how to destroy the family life he was not a part of it. Wagner's subconscious mind often sabotaged what he was consciously seeking — killing the love of the people he loved the most. Wagner was reflecting some of Freud's theories, which would start appearing within ten years after Wagner died. It is sad that Freud really did not like opera because he would have found a gold mine of material to support his theories in Wagnerian opera. We see this appearing when Otto offered Wagner, rent-free, a cottage on his property called the Asyl, the Asylum, as a refuge for Wagner and his wife Minna where he would be safe from the German police and most of his financial problems and he would be free to compose. The name of this cottage soon became very ironic given all

11. The Wesendoncks: 1858–1859

the feuding that was going on there. The cottage did not become an asylum in the literal sense, though it did become an asylum in the more modern sense of a lunatic asylum.

Otto and Mathilde were very wealthy people and their home was really a palace on a hill overlooking Zurich, with wonderful views of the surrounding mountains. Otto was very interested in music and opera, and he liked Wagner's leitmotific approach to opera. He became a big fan of Wagner's operas, particularly for their symphonic use of the orchestra, and Wagner outlined his plans for future operas, particularly *Tristan* and the complete Ring. Otto also found Wagner's theories of opera and the connections between text and music to be fascinating and revolutionary, and he was willing to support Wagner. Otto generously offered to give Wagner a monthly subsidy to complete his current opera projects, in addition to letting him and his wife live rent-free in his cottage.

Honeymooner Hans von Bülow and his new wife Cosima visited the Wagners and stayed for about a month. You would think this couple would want to be alone on their honeymoon, but Hans was fascinated by Wagner's genius and was also trying to develop a career as a professional pianist and conductor, and Wagner could certainly help him. There they got to see first-hand what a horror Wagner's marriage had become, how jealous Minna was of Frau Wesendonck and her relationship with her husband. But while Minna was filled with anger at Wagner, Mathilde provided him with the motherly love and affection that he desperately needed. Mathilde was also convinced that Wagner was the greatest musical genius of the time and she told Wagner this, while Minna remained angry with Wagner and skeptical of his new musical developments and operatic theories. She felt he should use the same musical style as *Rienzi* and *Tannhäuser* since they had become successful, but Wagner was constantly changing musical styles to reflect his new interests and the musical needs of the libretto he was working on and planning to turn into a "music drama," or opera as we now call them. Minna was also becoming increasingly suspicious of Wagner's friendship with Mathilde.

During this period, Minna, Mathilde, and Cosima were sometimes all in the same room with Wagner—and they were arguably the three most important women in Wagner's adult life, other than his mother. And somehow they all seemed to get along though this would become an explosive situation which would help to end Wagner's first marriage and ultimately lead to his second (and more successful) marriage to Cosima.

Were Wagner and Mathilde having an affair, as Minna accused them of having? Their letters, the few that survived, were certainly passionate enough. Minna thought so and publicly accused them of that. Minna came to feel that Mathilde had destroyed her marriage. She wrote to friends painful details of Wagner's duplicity and infidelity and her bitterness pained her for years afterwards. Was most of this in her imagination or did this infidelity really happen? We can not be sure.

Frau Mathilde had pretensions of being a writer herself and wrote the lovely Wesendonck poems, which Wagner set to music; these became the *Wesendonck Lieder*. Wagner himself wrote piano music for these songs, all to texts by Mathilde. He orchestrated only one of the songs, but they became so popular that someone else orchestrated the songs and they have become staples of orchestral concerts ever since. Wagner meant these songs to be sung by a soprano, but they have been transposed so that other voices can sing them. They are glorious songs, and Mathilde's words match Wagner's music wonderfully. The songs are all about love and death, and these two themes were the main desires of Wagner's life, as they are of many people. Some people yearn for death as an escape from their suffering, and as a way of coping with the ever-present fear of dying. One can pretend to long for what one dreads as a way of escaping the fear. Some of the music in the Wesendonck songs is clearly in the style of Wagner's next opera, *Tristan und Isolde*. The songs seem like a rough draft of the opera, with their chromatic sounds undulating under the songs, and some of the melodies would appear in the score of *Tristan*. There are little love notes in the autograph of the score which seem to be addressed to Mathilde—and certainly this opera is the story of a frustrated, adulterous love affair, which seemed to be the case with Richard and Mathilde.

Wagner had the ability to turn personal trauma into art—like any great artist—but for the other people involved, the situation must have been hell. Minna felt betrayed and Otto must have felt embarrassed by a man he had been so generous to, gratitude not being one of Wagner's fortes. These complex feelings of love and betrayal exactly mirrored the situation and personalities in *Tristan und Isolde*. But despite the emotional uproar, they all maintained some sort of relationship—though Minna and Mathilde never had any contact after this incident. But the Wesendoncks visited Bayreuth for the premiere of the Ring so Wagner did have an ability to hold onto relationships while at the same time testing them. Wagner remained very fond of them, and apparently the feeling was mutual.

Finally Wagner left Minna and went by himself to Venice, where he wrote most of *Tristan und Isolde* near the Grand Canal. The undulating sounds of the tides and waters of Venice became central symbols in the most erotic opera music ever written. It is such sexy music, especially the second act, and mixed with longing. While most men would have been beside themselves with love or grief or remorse or guilt as a result of the emotional mess he had just been through, Wagner could experience all these emotions and still write both the text and music for perhaps the greatest opera about love every written, *Tristan und Isolde*. He had to go through hell to try to get it staged, begging all the major opera houses to stage it. He came closest in Vienna, where the opera was put into rehearsal, but finally rejected as unperformable. But all those rehearsals did not go to waste, for a few years later in Munich, the National Theater staged the premiere of *Tristan* in 1865. The opera would not be staged again for about twenty years, and then become wildly popular. *Tristan* can now be called Wagner's most influential work, but that was certainly not evident to most people at its premiere in Munich, when it must have seemed a very long and weird opera. King Ludwig II and some members of the audience immediately loved it. There is certainly something undulating and fascinating about Wagner's unique musical style in that opera.

The Wesendoncks were in on Wagner's Ring project from its inception when Wagner told them he was working on the text and the music, and thought that Zurich would be a great place for the premiere of this work. Wagner's plan was to build a special theater

11. The Wesendoncks: 1858–1859

for the premiere, do the entire tetralogy, and then burn down the theater. Why burn down the theater after the premiere? This is part of Wagner's recurrent patterns of creating a perfect new home for himself and his art, and then destroying it.

After the scandal, Otto and Mathilde Wesendonck left their home in Zurich and went to visit his family in Frankfurt where he was born. Mathilde's family was from Frankfurt as well. Wagner left Minna and went to Venice. In many ways, this scandal ended the marriage of Richard and Minna since they never really lived together for any length of time after that. There was too much anger and animosity between them.

Minna returned to Dresden where she could live with her daughter Nathalie. She wrote to one of her lady friends about the situation on the Asyl cottage:

> Mme. Wesendonck used to visit my husband secretly, as he did her, and forbade my servant, when he opened the door for her, to tell me that she was above. I calmly let it all go on. Men so often have an affair; why should I not tolerate it in the case of my husband? I did not know jealousy. Only the commonesses, the mortifications, might have been spared me, and my ludicrously vain husband should have concealed it from me [Newman, 2, 549].

Mathilde Wesendonck was Wagner's Isolde, his Sieglinde. He developed a passion for her which may or may not have been reciprocated. Most of her correspondence to him has been destroyed, and not much of his to her has survived either. Who destroyed their correspondence? Maybe Wagner and Mathilde did, maybe Cosima, maybe Otto. They certainly wrote many letters to each other, even though they were living on the same property in Zurich. Was their love just an excuse to write an epistolary novel to each other? Was the situation really just a literary exercise? Did Wagner need to fall in love with a new woman to generate within himself the most erotic music ever written — in *Tristan und Isolde*? Maybe.

Ernest Newman reports that one of Liszt's students, Kellerman, told him that:

> Richard Wagner was a man who was absolutely dependent on his moods: what he was turning into poetry or music reflected itself instantly in his daily life. If he was dealing with some great conflict, he came into conflict and quarreled with the people around him. If he was working at something beautiful and winning, he was exceptionally friendly and enchantingly sweet. His art was to him the highest and weightiest thing on earth: everything had to be subordinated to it [Newman, II, 553].

When one looks at the books in Wagner's various libraries, one realizes that Wagner was an intellectual who liked to read and thought about what he read. He also liked talking about ideas and he read many of the great thinkers of his time. The nineteenth century was one of the great periods of German philosophy, and Wagner read these thinkers, especially Schopenhauer and Nietzsche, the latter of whom became a personal friend. Wagner was also a man who had ideas about the theories of opera and the theories of art, in other words, aesthetics, and he wrote about his theories in various important essays which he wrote during the seven years when he was not composing an opera.

This very ability to be verbal remains one of his most unusual characteristics as a composer. Here Wagner is similar to Hector Berlioz, who was a music critic in addition to being a composer. He too wrote thousands of letters and hundreds of reviews of music performances, though not as much as Wagner. This ability to be articulate and literary is very unusual in composers since they are mostly auditory in their abilities. Wagner's essays eventually became much more influential than Berlioz's, as were Wagner's musical compositions. Not one of Berlioz's operas has entered the standard repertory of most opera houses — not even in France.

Wagner wanted an international reputation for his musical and literary compositions, and he developed such a reputation. Perhaps like a narcissistic child, he was determined to be the center of attention, and if his music could not attract much attention, his writing would do that. Years later, Cosima Wagner told a guest at Wahnfried to let Wagner be the center of attention in their discussions since that made him so happy. She understood him better than anyone else. Despite his sometimes infantile needs, Wagner was able to compose arguably the ten greatest operas in the history of the genre. Those ten operas, all part of the standard repertory of most major opera companies, are unique works — and only Verdi has given so much opera to the opera houses of the world. Wagner insisted on calling his works dramas rather than operas, but that term has fallen out of fashion now for opera and was a marketing tool even in Wagner's own lifetime — and Wagner was always a clever marketer. Wagner's use of the term "music drama" was his way of trying to present his operas as totally different from all other operas, but were they? In some ways yes, but in most ways not really. Verdi liked to call his operas "melodramas," which means virtually the same thing. Wagner and Verdi were great rivals in 19th century opera, and their respective fans could get into very heated arguments about their respective operas. Now we can easily enjoy them both despite their various theories of art.

Some musicologists have called *Tristan und Isolde* the most influential of his operas because of its chromaticism and its subsequent influence on 20th century composers. Wagner's genius had a profound effect on modern composers like Strauss, Debussy, Bruckner, and Mahler. Wagnerian opera has haunted some people as no other composer's music has ever been able to do. Now Wagner's operas, especially his Ring cycle, are being performed more than ever before.

12

Venice, Switzerland and Paris: 1859–1861

"Do you know the land where the oranges bloom?" — Goethe

After all the drama at the Asyl and the Wesendonck villa, Wagner had the pressing need to flee. The safe asylum he thought he had there became a complicated horror of angry feelings. His obsession with Mathilde Wesendonck and Minna's fury over the relationship (whatever it was) and Otto's increasing jealousy made Der Asyl a prison for Wagner. He traveled all over Europe and visited some of the most glorious scenery and villas in Venice. Generally he fled to the first villa, palazzo, or first-class hotel he could find and then wrote letters to his friends complaining of his poverty and begging them for money. Wagner pledged his support of the working classes in his speeches and actions during the Dresden uprising of 1849, but he continued to live like a prince rather than like one of the workers. But it seems that what he wanted more than anything else was to commit suicide, and this became the subject of his work in progress, *Tristan und Isolde*, though he combined suicide with love and sexuality.

In January 1859, the Venetian police department, under the control of Austria, which then controlled all of Venice and the Veneto, was being pressured by the Saxon government to expel Wagner. But the Venetian police chief, a fan of Wagner's music since it had been played in several spots in Venice, promised to protect Wagner if he did not cause any political problems while in Venice. Wagner asserted that he only wanted to compose his opera and promised to avoid all political activities while in Italy.

Wagner stayed at the Palazzo Giustiniani, right on the Grand Canal, and immediately started work on the music of the last two acts of *Tristan und Isolde*. We can see something of his state of mind in a letter he wrote from Geneva to Mathilde Wesendonck on August 21, 1858:

> On my last night in the Asyl I retired to bed after 11 o'clock: I was due to depart at 5 o'clock the next morning. Before I closed my eyes, the same thought flashed through my mind that had always done each time I wanted to lull myself to sleep with the idea that, one day, I would die here: this is how I would lie when you came to me for the last time, when, openly and before the whole world, you enfolded my head in your arms, and received my soul with a final kiss! To die this way was the fairest of my imaginings, and it had taken shape entirely within the locality of my bedroom: the door leading to the stairs was closed, you enter through the study curtains; thus you wrapped your arms around me: thus I died, gazing at

you — And what now? Has even this chance of dying been snatched away from me? Coldly, like some hunted animal, I left the house in which I had been entombed with a demon which I could no longer exorcise except by flight. Where — where now shall I die? [Wagner, *Selected Letters*, 416].

This was exactly the death Tristan would have at the end of the last act of *Tristan und Isolde*, dying in Isolde's arms. He had attempted suicide at the end of each of the acts of that opera, succeeding at the end of the third act. *Tristan* was clearly intended to be Wagner's most suicidal opera, though ironically enough it contains his most erotic music.

While he was working on *Tristan*, Wagner complained of his loneliness, so friends started visiting him, and he played them excerpts of his new opera on the piano. Karl Ritter, his student, was one of the first visitors. The watery city of Venice must have permeated Wagner's thoughts since the chromaticism of the score gives the music a watery, undulating sound, and of course water became one of the main symbols in the opera, climactically repeated in Isolde's Liebestod. In addition, light and darkness also became major symbols in the opera, especially in its second act. In the first act, the action takes place on a boat, a voyage from Ireland to Cornwall with Isolde under the command of the loyal knight Tristan; he is taking her to his uncle to be married, a move which undoubtedly will end all the hostilities between England and Ireland. Then as now, the relationship between England and Ireland remains very complicated and the two countries were often disagreeing and in a warlike state. Water became a major symbol in this opera, as it does in several other operas by Wagner, particularly *The Flying Dutchman* and the Ring cycle. Light and darkness become the other major symbols in this opera, in which Wagner wrote the most erotic music ever written for these two lovers — lots of fast rhythms and musical climaxes for Tristan and Isolde. In the prelude to the first act, Wagner presents all the major leitmotifs he will use in this opera, cleverly connected and always suggesting love, death, and frustration in this prelude.

The opera dramatizes clearly a political marriage since Isolde had never met King Marke — she is a political trophy and a pawn in the continuing conflicts between England and Ireland. Tristan, a knight famous for his loyalty to his uncle King Marke, has murdered Isolde's fiancé Morold in the continuing conflicts between the two countries. Wagner set all of *Tristan* in Celtic-speaking lands like Cornwall, Ireland, and Brittany. The situation of his love of Mathilde Wesendonck and her husband Otto, whom he also loved, is clearly mirrored in the situation of Tristan and Isolde. Did Wagner need to create a situation similar to the opera he was working on to drive his subconscious mind into musical creativity? Here we can see yet again how Wagner could use the trauma and pain in his own life and turn them into great art. But was some of that suffering self-generating, Wagner needing to mirror in his own life the actions of his characters? This is what the great artist can do — also the mediocre ones, to less effect. And the combination of sexuality and the belief that only death can solve the problem of their adulterous love makes *Tristan* an interesting work in terms of an original approach to the problem of desperate love and adultery.

Venice soon became one of Wagner's favorite cities in Italy. He may have even thought

12. Venice, Switzerland and Paris: 1859–1861

that this dying city would be a good place to die himself. He loved the beauty of the art and architecture and he loved floating around the city in a gondola. The lapping waters of the city, floating through all the little canals, enjoying the interplay of stone and water that the architecture creates — it all fascinated him. He also liked Florian, his favorite café in the main square, the Piazza San Marco. At Florian he could have coffee, cappuccino, Venetian pastries, and the pleasant conversation of friends. He could wander around the churches and museums in Venice and he could visit Torcello, Burano, and Murano — islands and small towns near Venice. He could also wander around the beautiful tombs of San Michele, the cemetery island in Venice. He could go to the Lido and sit on the warm sandy beach there and enjoy the warmth of the sunshine instead of the cold winters in Germany. How he came to love Venice — and who can resist this city? Thomas Mann would place his famous novella *Death in Venice* on this same Lido in this same city about fifty years later. The very title of this novella was an allusion to Wagner since Wagner himself would die in Venice in 1883. While he was there, he wrote tormented letters to Mathilde Wesendonck. He was also writing more rational and life-asserting letters to Minna, despite their recent trauma caused by his infatuation with Mathilde.

Certainly *Tristan und Isolde* is the most sexual and suicidal of his operas, an interesting oxymoron, and indeed the text of the opera contains many contradictions, right from the sailor's song at the very beginning of the opera. The adulterous affair of Tristan and Isolde generates fabulous love music but also the theme of suicide. Tristan is suicidal throughout the opera, probably a reflection of Wagner's mood after the breakup of his relationship with Mathilde. Wagner's relationship with Mathilde was one of the most important in his life; some of Wagner's biographers feel it was sexual, others feel it was not. Wagner's combination of erotic love and suicide and attempted murder connects Wagner's opera with some of the great love stories in Western literature, especially Shakespeare's *Romeo and Juliet*. While suicide was a great taboo in Western religious thought, this taboo recurred in the love stories of Western literature, especially in plays like *Othello*, *Romeo and Juliet*, and *Phedre*.

Wagner frequently visited his favorite Venetian church, the Frari, to see his favorite painting in Venice, "The Assumption of the Virgin" by Titian. Titian's great painting gave him the idea for the ending of *Tristan* and the ending of the Ring cycle. For the hall of the Grail in *Parsifal*, Wagner used the Cathedral in Sienna, one of the greatest cathedrals in all of Europe. Wagner was often affected and influenced by Italy and its arts. The gardens at Rapallo, near Naples, were the basis of the magic garden in *Parsifal*. Even in art, Wagner found himself repeatedly attracted to mother figures in Italian paintings.

Wagner's student Karl Ritter came to visit him and helped him with some money. Wagner was very fond of this young man and they enjoyed eating together and wandering around Venice together. As Ernest Newman describes Wagner in Venice during this period:

> As usual with him, he organized his time on routine lines — till two in the afternoon, work; then down the Grand Canal in a gondola to the Piazzetta, for a meal in the Piazza San Marco; then a walk, either alone or with Karl, along the Riva to the Giardino Pubblico; at

nightfall back to the Palazzo Giustiniani by gondola; then a little more work and a chat over tea with Karl. Occasionally he would go to a theater, taking especial pleasure in the Goldoni performances at the Camploi.... The opera did not attract him often. If he wanted music, there were excellent Austrian military bands playing in the evenings on the Piazza San Marco: he made the acquaintance of some of the bandsmen and officers, who treated him with great respect; and the overtures to *Rienzi* and *Tannhäuser* frequently figured in the programs [Newman, II, 561].

In March of 1859 Wagner moved to Lucerne, Switzerland, where he noticed how nice the small city was and that a little villa called Triebschen was on a finger of land which jutted out into Lake Lucerne. He would move into that villa within ten years after he had to flee Munich as a result of his personal, financial, and political complications there. It was during this period that Wagner developed a real love of Switzerland, primarily because of its fabulous mountain scenery and also because most of the people speak his native tongue, German. Also, the Swiss were quickly building railroads to connect all their cities and also to connect their country with the countries around them. This meant that there were soon railroad connections between Switzerland and Germany and Italy and France so travel became much easier. Wagner became a big fan of this new industrial wonder of his period, the railroad — and he hated boat travel, understandable after his voyage on the *Thetis*, though this resulted in *The Flying Dutchman*. Throughout his travels, Wagner remained a genius at turning his own impressions and experiences into operas.

One of the first railroads in Germany connected Dresden to Leipzig, and this new mode of travel was soon seen as one of the great inventions of the Industrial Revolution. Some Europeans were very suspicious of the new railroad tracks appearing all over the country, and some were even afraid to use these new trains, but not Wagner. He loved this new invention and was very eager to take trains all over Europe. Wagner became a fan of this modern invention, as did his friend Franz Liszt. In his later years, Liszt spent his time between Weimar, Rome, and Budapest — all possible thanks to train travel, which seemed a miracle to Europeans of the 19th century.

While in Lucerne, Wagner finished the score for *Tristan und Isolde,* sent it to his publisher, and undoubtedly wondered if he would ever be able to stage it. He originally envisioned the work as a short little money-maker, though now that the whole opera was finished he must have realized that what he finally came up with in *Tristan* was a long, complicated, highly original work. It was one of the most difficult of operas to cast given the difficulties in the two title roles. Tristan remains an especially difficult role to cast even today. Where are the great Tristans? There was clearly a naïve, idealistic quality to Wagner's personality since he never seemed to realize the difficulty of casting and staging his operas, which even now are considered the most difficult operas in the standard repertory to stage because they require a large orchestra, important soloists, often a chorus, and make great demands on the scenery and costumes departments. They also require a major conductor to control and give shape to all these forces.

Wagnerian operas remain very expensive to stage, especially when contrasted to many of the Italian operas by Verdi and Puccini which are much more realistic in their demands

12. Venice, Switzerland and Paris: 1859–1861

on orchestra, voices, and production requirements. Wagner would not be able to stage *Tristan und Isolde* until 1865, over twelve years after its composition. When Wagner began this opera, he imagined it would be easy to stage with a small cast which would make him a lot of money, but he was gradually realizing that *Tristan* would become his most difficult opera to put on stage. Wagner also realized that this was his most personal opera. As he wrote to Liszt:

> Since I have never in my whole life enjoyed the true happiness of love, I intend to erect a monument to this most beautiful of dreams, a monument where this love will be properly sated from first to last. I have planned in my head a *Tristan und Isolde*, the simplest, but most full-blooded musical concept; with the "black flag" which will flutter in the end. I shall then cover myself over in order to die.

Meanwhile he began to suffer from his chronic loneliness and even missed, of all people, Minna, whom he begged to visit him. So they decided to meet in Paris in September of 1859. Why did he move to Paris? He had earlier concluded that Paris was the city he most detested and the city which had given him nothing but poverty, rejection, and defeat. Well, he could not move to Germany since his involvement with the Dresden uprising of 1849. It was ten years later but the German states had declared him a criminal and persona non grata in all of the German states. Switzerland was a backwater without any major opera companies, just theater where traveling companies sometimes staged operas. He considered it a cultural backwater, though if he had known about all the singing festivals in Switzerland he would have undoubtedly reconsidered his opinion. At least Paris was still the European capital of opera with several opera companies, the most famous being the main Opera and the Italian Theater, which did Italian opera. Paris then had more professional opera companies than any other European city so naturally Wagner was attracted to it for professional reasons.

Wagner had a knack for developing fans and admirers, in addition to people who loathed his music, and there was a French conductor called Guadaloupe who was putting on concerts of Wagner's music in Paris despite the failure of *Tannhäuser*. Military band concerts and band concerts in general had become very popular aspects of the musical scene in both America and Europe throughout the 19th century and even early into the 20th century, and these concerts introduced audiences to new music — not just John Philip Sousa — and Wagner's music got heard throughout much of Europe and America through these concerts. Especially in America and England and France, but also Italy, these concerts, often open-air events in public parks, became very popular and in their turn made new music very popular, especially airs from new operas. Wagnerian music became more popular or at least known to the public through these events and encouraged local opera companies to stage complete versions of these new operas. Such events also served to bring Wagner money. For example, the American government commissioned Wagner to write a march to celebrate the centennial of the country's founding in 1776 — so 1876 brought Wagner some American commissions.

It was during this period that Wagner's operas began to get more and more popular within Germany, and were being staged more frequently. The Wagner craze was finally beginning and Wagner's operas were finally getting popular and staged all over Europe — first in Germany but then elsewhere. Wagner was slowly being recognized as a major composer of opera, despite the continuing success of Meyerbeer and Mendelssohn. Meyerbeer had real success as an opera composer, especially in Paris, and soon all around Europe while Mendelssohn did not succeed in opera. By the end of his life Wagner himself became a fan of Mendelssohn's music, and it was often played in Wahnfried, his home in Bayreuth.

But now Wagner again was in Paris and trying to generate success for himself and his music. Since 1852, France had been ruled by Emperor Napoleon III, France's last king, the nephew of Napoleon I, who had been bombing Leipzig when Wagner was born. Clearly Wagner had developed a love-hate relationship with France, and by now his French was much improved and he could both speak and write it, though with a heavy German accent.

Napoleon III had a fairly long reign as France's final monarch — from 1852 to 1870 — and he employed the most famous town planner in France's history, Baron Eugene Haussmann. Baron Haussmann is credited with turning the medieval city of Paris into the beautiful modern capital we now known. Baron Haussmann himself in his memoirs always said that he was only following the orders of his emperor, Napoleon III, who had a vision of Paris with city lights and modern amenities like sewers and clean water running into each apartment — and most important of all, wide, beautiful, tree-lined boulevards which made it possible for Parisians to move easily from section to section of the city. Also Baron Haussmann and the emperor had a vision of public transportation which would enable Parisians to move easily and cheaply by horses, public omnibuses, and eventually subways. But some lovely buildings were destroyed in Paris to create the modern city of Napoleon III's dreams — and which we can all enjoy now by visiting it.

As Baron Haussmann continued to modernize Paris, it remained a European capital for opera, though by the end of the 19th century Berlin, Munich, London, and Milan had become major sources for operas as well. The sign of having "arrived" was having a major opera house — this was becoming increasingly so around the world as American and South American cities (even Brazil's Manaus) built opera houses. *Fitzcarraldo* is a wonderful film by Herzog about a lunatic who wanted to build an opera house in the middle of the Amazon in the town of Manaus, which he did, and the Ring cycle has been staged there.

Wagner was a victim of Baron Haussmann's plans when a house he rented was slated for demolition and he lost his money. Wagner saw both the old Paris and the new Paris — before and after Baron Haussmann — and he must have wondered at the miraculous changes as the baron turned Paris into a modern city, destroying many of its old buildings, though also destroying some lovely architecture in the process. But Haussmann also created a water and sewer system for the city so that diseases like typhoid and cholera, which Wagner's father had died of, began to disappear thanks to Paris's modern sanitation and water systems.

Napoleon III made a fatal mistake in 1869 by deciding to attack and invade Prussia. His defeat at Sedan by the Prussian army and the Prussian invasion of Paris, and the

12. Venice, Switzerland and Paris: 1859–1861

Commune which followed the collapse of the Napoleonic regime, ended Napoleon III's regime most ingloriously, much to Wagner's delight — he was living in Switzerland again by then. In Paris, of all places, a united Germany was declared in 1870, in the hall of mirrors in Versailles. By January of 1871, Germany was finally a united country under a Prussian emperor, Kaiser William I. And that united Germany would get mixed reactions from Wagner — mostly he hated it, as he hated most politicians and empires. He came to hate the unified German empire under Bismarck and Wilhelm I — but that will come later.

Though Bismarck and the Hohenzollerns had finally managed to unify Germany, Napoleon III's desire to humiliate and defeat the Prussians resulted in the reverse of what he had anticipated and he lost his throne and France never again had an emperor. Emperor Napoleon III and Empress Eugenie fled to England, and their only son died fighting for Britain in Africa. This was the end of not only the Napoleonic regime but the end of the monarchy altogether in France.

Meyerbeer would have seen Wagner as both an anti–Semite and a competitor in Paris. According to Ernest Newman, Meyerbeer now controlled the Parisian music critics:

> Even before [Wagner] had made an open attempt to interest the French public in his music Wagner had to contend with the enmity of the corrupt Paris Press, which, it is no secret today, was handsomely taken care of by the rich Meyerbeer. So far had the campaign of calumny already gone by December 1859 that in that month Wagner was compelled to publish a protest [Newman, III, 3–4].

Even before any of Wagner's music had been performed in Paris that year, the music critics were already attacking him. But this time Wagner tried a different approach. Rather than begging any of the opera houses in Paris to perform one of his operas, many of which had already been successes in Germany, Wagner decided to try to conduct concerts of his music in Paris. If he could perform his music successfully in concert format, maybe the Paris opera houses would be tempted to stage one of his operas. This approach had worked very well in Zurich, where he and his music had become famous thanks to the concerts he conducted there. The Zurich audiences had responded to hearing excerpts of his music very favorably, and they had wanted to see complete performances of his operas staged in their city.

Wagner announced a series of three concerts in Paris on three Wednesdays: January 25, February 1, and February 8 in 1860. In these three concerts Wagner conducted and performed excerpts from those of his operas which had succeeded in Germany: the overture to *The Flying Dutchman* and excerpts from both *Tannhäuser and Lohengrin*. The halls were full and there was much applause, which indicated that most people in the audience enjoyed the performances.

Then came the reviews of the French press, which were almost all very negative. The critics just did not want to give the music a fair hearing; instead, they wanted to sabotage all three concerts because of their dislike of the composer. They had undoubtedly read Wagner's anti–Semitic essay, which had been published under a pseudonym, but they knew who had foolishly written it, Wagner. But the concerts did succeed in letting the

Richard Wagner

French hear Wagner's latest music, and many of them really enjoyed the experience and became life-long fans of Wagner's music and wanted to hear the complete operas. Two Frenchmen, Perrin and Champfleury, wrote a pamphlet defending Wagner and his music. He also got a very kind and appreciative letter from the great writer Charles Baudelaire:

> I am a Frenchman — that is to say, a man scarcely constructed for enthusiasm, and born in a country where poetry and painting are hardly better understood than music is. I am of an age at which one no longer amuses oneself by writing to eminent men; and I should have hesitated for a long time to send you a letter expressive of my admiration if my eyes did not light, day after day, on absurd and shameful articles in which every possible attempt is made to defame your genius. You, sir, are not the first man in connection with whom I have had to suffer and blush for my country. In the end, my indignation has driven me to testify to you my gratitude: I said to myself, "I want to mark myself off from all those imbeciles!"

The French composer Camille Saint-Saëns was only twenty-five years old when he came to Wagner's concerts in 1860 and he immediately became a Wagnerian, feeling that Wagner was the greatest composer alive. This French composer would also visit Wagner in Bayreuth. The Italian composer Rossini was living in Paris then, and a friend urged Wagner to visit him. They had a very pleasant conversation, and Wagner was particularly intrigued by Rossini's description of his visit to Beethoven many years earlier. Beethoven had urged Rossini to write more operas like *The Barber of Seville,* which Beethoven considered Rossini's greatest opera. Wagner had also been a friend of Berlioz when Wagner had lived in Paris twenty years earlier. The German composer tried to meet with Berlioz but felt rebuffed by the rather bitter and highly competitive French composer.

Ultimately many French people came to love Wagnerian opera, and one French fan started the journal *La Revue Wagnerienne* to help promote Wagner's music in France. Wagner's traveling and conducting throughout Europe ultimately attracted to him an international following of Wagner enthusiasts. At the Bayreuth Festival, one hears many languages spoken and various costumes in evidence, from Scottish kilts to Japanese kimonos. Wagnerian opera has in some ways became an obsession around the world, as more and more opera companies are staging Wagnerian operas, especially the Ring.

The wider Parisian public was not much interested in his music, with a few exceptions. After the *Tannhäuser* fiasco, he did develop a group of French admirers — people like Theophile Gautier and his lovely daughter Judith, Flaubert, and Camille Saint-Saëns — who visited him both in Triebschen and Bayreuth once he had moved there. His French admirers were not only musicians but also writers and poets who started *La Revue Wagnerienne* and become the foundation of the Symbolist and Decadent movements in the arts by the end of the 19th century.

Wagner's influence on art has certainly been profound and widespread. Among the artists Wagner influenced were James Joyce, Joseph Conrad, Virginia Woolf, E.M. Forster, and D.H. Lawrence, and that is only among the modern British novelists. The French, Italian, and German writers and artists of the early 20th century were all influenced by Wagner and his operas.

These years of wandering from Germany to Switzerland to Paris and then back to

12. Venice, Switzerland and Paris: 1859–1861

Switzerland generated much sorrow and loneliness in Wagner but also generated some wonderful music and some wonderful plans for the future. He was able to write essays on the nature of opera and music, and he was also able to work on two projects at once: the Ring cycle and *Parsifal*. He also had an idea for the greatest comedy in German opera, *Meistersinger von Nüremberg*. He was a busy and productive man in the French capital despite all his grief. In the meantime, his promoter Gaetano Belloni told him that his music was being performed at concerts and salons around town and becoming increasingly popular. Belloni also told Wagner that there was a rumor going around musical Paris that the Opera de Paris was interested in staging his *Tannhäuser*—this, the most beautiful and important opera house in Europe at the time. Paris was beckoning—at least that was the rumor.

13

Paris and *Tannhäuser*: 1860–1861

"Goddess, let me flee!"—*Tannhäuser*

Every opera composer in the 19th century dreamed of a successful premiere in Paris. Since it was the operatic capital of the world at the time, Wagner had yearned for a premiere there as well. A successful premiere there would be followed by offers from all the other opera companies in Europe and around the world, especially in North and South America. Ironically enough, he got his wish but it became one of the most notorious flops in opera history. Be careful what you wish for, as the philosophers say, because you may get it.

Wagner wanted what all composers want, money and fame, and Paris was then the center of the world of opera, and a success there could ensure a success on both sides of the Atlantic. *Tannhäuser* was already a success since it had been staged in several opera houses in Germany after its successful premiere in Dresden in 1845, but the work had never been staged outside Germany and Wagner hoped that the Paris premiere would turn the opera into an international success. The composer failed to reckon with the political and artistic complexities of a premiere in Paris, always a tricky proposition.

Princess Metternich, the wife of the Austrian ambassador to France, pressured the French emperor to order the premiere of Wagner's *Tannhäuser* for the Paris Opera in March of 1861, and the emperor Napoleon III acceded to her request. She had been a Wagnerian fan for a while, and she wanted Wagnerian opera performed in Paris. Wagner's dreams were answered — or so he thought — when he was informed of this. Rumors circulated in Paris that Wagner was a republican and a revolutionary, but nevertheless the imperial order for the staging of *Tannhäuser* went to the Paris Opera.

The opera had first to be translated into French; the rule back then was that all opera had to be given in French at the Opera in Paris. This was pretty much a European-wide tradition since most audiences in the 19th century were accustomed to hearing an opera in their native tongue. (But there were exceptions in England, Germany, and Austria, where opera audiences were used to hearing Italian opera in Italian rather than their own languages.) Back in the 18th century, some audience members in England attacked Handel's operas because they were sung in Italian rather than English — one of the points of satire of Gay's *The Beggar's Opera*. So Handel started writing operas in English, which did not please many of the operatic connoisseurs there, who preferred opera in Italian, opera's original language back in the 17th century.

13. Paris and Tannhäuser: 1860–1861

For Wagner, and for other opera composers, there were special problems with having premieres in Paris. First, the operas had to be given in French, by law. Then there had to be a ballet in the second act to please the powerful Jockey Club, who bought a bloc of expensive tickets and who came to see the ballet (primarily) and the dancers' legs. Also, the French critics were expected to be given complimentary tickets and gifts to insure good reviews. Then there was the French tradition of the Claque, a group of paid audience members who were hired to applaud particular operas and particular singers. If the Claque was not paid off, they would threaten to boo for free in revenge. Wagner (and Verdi) did not want to butter up or pay off the French critics, and they certainly did not want to pay off the Claque to insure success for their operas. They were used to their operas succeeding or failing on their own merits and not through the machinations of a paid claque and bribed reviewers. But this became part of the reality of success in the opera houses of Paris, especially the Paris Opera.

Wagner became adamant on this point and refused to bribe either the claque or the reviewers to insure the success of his opera. But other people were willing to bribe them to insure the failure of *Tannhäuser* in Paris. Why? Some audience members would have hated Wagner simply because he was German and consequently an enemy of France. Even in the 18th century, Voltaire had repeatedly made fun of anything German and especially in *Candide*, which was a spoof of all aspects of German culture, which was seen as provincial, comic, and revolting—starting with the German language and the people who spoke it. The Prussian king, Friedrich the Great, also disliked the German language, and in the 18th century there was a tradition of the aristocracy all over Europe speaking only French, especially in Russia where some aristocrats prided themselves on not knowing the Russian language. But by the 19th century, things were changing on this topic and even the aristocrats were speaking in their native tongues. However, the French prejudice against all things German remained a part of the reality of Paris at the time. The French were used to thinking of Germany as a group of powerless little city-states or duchies, but the Prussian army had become successful and this too added to the annoyance of some of the French at the changing political realities in the German provinces.

There was also the requirement of a ballet in the opera, preferably in the second act, in time for the entrance of the Jockey Club and the other aristocrats. Wagner had never put a ballet in any of his operas, but here he had no choice, and he thought a ballet in the first scene in the grotto of Venus might be a good idea. He had to be persuaded on this point by the opera management, who actually wanted a ballet in the second act. To Wagner a ballet in the second act made no dramatic sense at all, but in the first act this was possible. That involved composing new music for the Paris version of *Tannhäuser*, but since he had matured as a composer, this posed stylistic problems since his current compositional style was certainly different from his musical style of twenty years earlier. But Wagner was nothing if not flexible when it came to the staging of his operas, particularly if this involved a premiere at the Opera de Paris, the richest and most important opera house in Europe. The Paris Opera also had a very fine orchestra so Wagner could change the opera to take advance of the fine orchestra available to him.

Richard Wagner

Wagner's new optimism as a result of the commission of this premiere generated a mania of spending on Wagner's part, something that had frequently occurred in his past. Some good news, particularly in regard to his operas, sent him into a manic spending binge so that he moved to one of the most expensive areas of Paris and commissioned new clothes for himself and Minna. He hired more musical assistants and more furniture and drapery for his Paris apartment as he rewrote the first act of his opera to increase the role of Venus and to add ballet music for the Venusberg scene in the opening. The Paris version of this opera is now considered much better than the Dresden version, and the Paris version has become standard at most opera houses. Most audiences like the ballet music in the first scene of the first act, though there is some stylistic inconsistency with the rest of the music, some of which Wagner also changed. Most audience members prefer the Paris version and enjoy the highly erotic ballet music Wagner added, certainly consistent with the setting in the grotto of Venus.

There were political intrigues going on as well. A segment of the French were suspicious of anything German—after all they had guillotined the Austrian queen Marie Antoinette, wife of King Louis XVI. The German faction in the French court had both friends and enemies in Paris, but there was a popular French antipathy to anything German going back for centuries. This faction did not want to see a German opera succeed in Paris.

Then there were the Jewish faction in the press, some of whom wanted only Jewish composers to do well in Paris and who hated Wagner thanks to his essay "Jews in Music." Wagner earned all of these enemies thanks to his own anti–Semitism. He probably wrote this ugly pamphlet for publicity purposes but did not foresee all the hatred it would cause him. Ernest Newman suggested that Meyerbeer was also responsible for this Wagnerian flop since he had great influence on the Paris musical press. Some have suggested that Princess Metternich herself had engineered this flop for the sake of Austrian politics back in Vienna. Wagner could not have foreseen the dire and long-term consequences of his own racism and stupidity.

The 19th century became the great era of imperialism and colonialism, especially in Britain and France. Both countries wanted empires, and this imperialism was usually justified with racism—the idea that non-white people were inferior to white people. Some imperialists also involved the deity, arguing that God wanted all the land on the face of the earth to be owned by white people from Europe. Some racists still feel this way, often using their holy scriptures to justify this.

As a result of these special demands of the Paris Opera, often only third-rate composers got much success there. If one looks at the composers who really succeeded in this house, they were people like Meyerbeer, Adam, Massenet, Halevy, etc.—composers who are now considered minor figures. Rossini had great success in Paris and stayed in Paris when he retired from opera composition. Wagner and Verdi, now considered the greatest of opera composers, had little success in Paris. Even Bizet did not have much success in Paris, his death hastened perhaps by all the bad reviews he got in Paris for his *Carmen*. But the Opera de Paris also had a reputation for staging the most

13. Paris and Tannhäuser: 1860–1861

beautiful and impressive productions in Europe, and this too added to its attractions for Wagner.

Given these operatic realities, Wagner's *Tannhäuser* was doomed from the start in Paris. There is a very comic film called *Meeting Venus*, about a modern attempt to stage this opera in Paris which is also doomed to failure due to the special demands of that house. But the reality is that from the end of the 19th century and through most of the 20th century *Tannhäuser* has been frequently staged in Paris and to great success, but not while Wagner himself was alive since he did not address some of the then unique problems with the Paris Opera.

Lucien Petipas was in charge of the choreography for *Tannhäuser*. He had been a great dancer and now he choreographed for the company. But he had classic French ballet in mind for this opera, though Wagner had his mind on Nordic Stromkerl, a primitive god of fertility. They were clearly at cross purposes in terms of what choreography would be suitable for the first scene of the opera. Edouard Desplechin designed the sets and Wagner was very pleased with the results. As the rehearsal process continued, from Wagner's point of view the big problems were the tenor, Albert Nieman, and the conductor, Dietsch. Wagner considered them not up to their tasks in *Tannhäuser*: He found the tenor arrogant and unwilling to take direction and the conductor unable to control the orchestra and shape the music.

So *Tannhäuser* joined the long list of operas which are now considered great works which flopped at their premieres in Paris. The list of Parisian flops in the 19th century includes *Carmen, Don Carlo, I Vespri Siciliani,* and many others. And the flop caused Wagner to lose a lot of money which he did not have. He spent much money on hiring new copyists, new assistants, new apartments, new furnishings. He spent on the assumption that the Paris premiere of *Tannhäuser* would become a major success and the source for much revenue in the future.

Tannhäuser's problems began with the conductor in charge of the staging: Pierre Louis Philippe Dietsch, a Frenchman despite his German-sounding last name. He was also the man who used Wagner's libretto for *The Flying Dutchman* to write music for what became his own operatic flop twenty years earlier. Wagner considered Dietsch incompetent to conduct his score; Wagner and his assistant Hans von Bülow conducted some of the rehearsals but were not allowed to conduct the premiere. Opera of course is a living art with living people performing, and a bad singer or a bad set or a nasty audience or a stuffy auditorium — all of these elements can produce a flop, even when the work itself is considered a great work now. Mozart's *The Marriage of Figaro* failed at its premiere in Vienna in 1786. Success and failure in the theater all depend on many elements, all of them living elements — that is the nature of the beast. Opera, a branch of theater, demands the cooperation of many different kinds of artists, and also the sympathetic response of the audience. This cooperation of course does not always happen despite the genius of the work being performed.

The Paris Opera did provide Wagner with an excellent cast for its staging of *Tannhäuser*. Albert Nieman sang the title role and Wagner was somewhat pleased with his singing but not his acting. Wagner and von Bülow found him very vain and unwilling to take any direction from them. Fortunata Tedesco sang Venus and the composer and his assistant were happy with her. Marie Saxe, as Elisabeth, also satisfied Wagner and von Bülow. The Italian baritone Morelli sang the part of Wolfram very well. So except for the arrogant Nieman, Wagner was happy with his cast.

Wagner also struggled with the French text of his opera and the version provided by the Opera. Wagner wanted changes in the translation and he himself worked to improve the French translation of his opera. Von Bülow did some of the conducting at the rehearsals, but only a French conductor could conduct in the theater itself. Wagner and the cast felt that the sets by Edouard Desplechin were beautiful and impressive.

So after countless rehearsals and what seemed like the impossible demands of both Wagner and the French public, *Tannhäuser* got its notorious premiere on March 13, 1861, and was booed and whistled off the stage. It survived for three performances and then was withdrawn. Some people admired the opera very much, including some composers and poets like Baudelaire. Saint-Saëns commented, "Would that I could write such a flop." Some of the French musicians and intellectuals who attended one of those few performances liked the music and the text very much, but the Jockey club and the claque were determined to create a flop and a public scandal at the premiere by blowing whistles, horns, drums, and rattles and booing — and they succeeded despite the efforts of some audience members to keep quiet and actually hear the music.

Wagner undoubtedly knew there would be problems with staging his opera in Paris and he tried to be flexible and predict the problems. He helped with the French translations and he wrote ballet music for the first act. He knew he had enemies in Paris, but he had not been able to predict that some of those enemies would not allow the audience to hear his music. After three attempted performances, Wagner withdrew his score. He had friends there, including his wife and Malwida von Meysenbug, a very liberated woman of the period and a friend of Wagner and his music. But the forces against Wagner in Paris were too much for him.

In 1861 Wagner had to deal with a French conductor, a French choreographer, French designers — all of whom had a radically different set of priorities and a different taste. Wagner even had theories of choreography and how dance could be used in opera, but these were new to opera and not in vogue in Paris at the time. Wagner develop the theory of the Stromkerl and the Bacchanalian concept of dance in opera — which connected very well with the first scene of the opera in the grotto of Venus. So with his fractured French, Wagner was driven to distraction by the demands and tastes of the French opera and the Parisian taste of the time. Verdi was too during the Paris premieres of his own operas — *I Lombardi*, *Don Carlos*, *Les Vepres Sicilians*, etc. Verdi lived in Paris for several years but was never very fond of the city. Wagner lived in Paris even longer and got to hate the place, though he still had some fond memories of his friends there. He developed French friends there at the time, people like Catules Mendes and Judith Gauthier, who would remain faithful friends throughout his life. Baudelaire too was at the flop and became a great admirer of Wagner and wrote essays to defend Wagner and his operas. So even at

13. Paris and Tannhäuser: 1860–1861

the flop there were people who liked the opera and felt that the composer was not being treated fairly. Even French composers like Hector Berlioz had failure and rejection at the Paris Opera. Berlioz himself spent much of his life trying to get the Paris Opera to stage his works, so naturally he saw Wagner as competition, not as his old friend. Wagner's work was being staged at the Opera before any of Berlioz's operas were staged there.

Wagner's writings and personality had created enemies already who were determined to destroy his premiere regardless of the quality of the music they were presented with. Some of them were undoubtedly Jews offended by his anti–Semitic essay. Also, not paying off the critics and the claque would have horrendous consequences on the possible success of any new opera. Meyerbeer was very clever to these ways of insuring success in Paris, and one wonders why Wagner was so inflexible on this topic. Wagner was very rigid on this subject and felt the work would have to depend on the honest reactions of the audience — but when parts of that audience were out to get him and his opera, he should have foreseen what the reaction would be. As a result, there developed a group of Wagner fans in Paris, people like Baudelaire, who were embarrassed by the ridiculous reaction to the opera by goons determined to cause a scandal. They came to love Wagner and his works even more, and they ultimately insured that this Wagnerian opera would become very popular in Paris.

Wagner certainly had a wonderful cast for that Paris premiere of *Tannhäuser*, except for the hostile tenor Niemann. Given the elaborate productions which the Paris Opera was famous for, and the production which *Tannhäuser* received, this should have been a wonderful and successful premiere, but there were political forces at work which doomed the opera. Nonetheless, the Paris version of *Tannhäuser* remains the one that is usually staged these days, with the added music for Venus, including the ballet, not the original Dresden version. Wagner's glorious, dramatic music for this opera, plus the fascinating characters of Tannhäuser, Venus, and Elisabeth, entranced audiences and the opera is now considered one of the greatest works in the standard operatic repertory. Great conductors remain fond of this work because of Wagner's superb orchestration, so that French audience at the work's Paris premiere has been proved wrong over and over again.

Tannhäuser was hardly an opera typical of the period but a revolutionary opera without the usual set numbers, though it did include the "Aberdstern" aria. But the music was through-composed and without the usual division into arias and recitative. Also, the ideas in the opera were complicated because of Wagner's interest in cycles. On the surface the opera seemed about the sexual love of the Roman goddess Venus and the spiritual love of St. Elisabeth, but looking more carefully at the opera indicates that Venus has a spiritual interest in Tannhäuser's art and St. Elisabeth has a clearly sexual interest in the poet's body. These complications present the poet as a man who is always fleeing women. When he is with Venus in the first act, he yearns for Elisabeth, and when he is with Elisabeth in the second act, he is yearning for Venus. These psychological complications mark Wagner's art — with psychological and self-contradictory complexities like the fear of intimacy which fascinate modern viewers.

Wagner here indicates the complex psychological responses which modern audiences are fond of—like Tannhäuser as a man who always wants what he can not have, and when he gets it, does not want that either. The problems of intimacy and people who fear intimacy, which Sondheim used over and over in his own music dramas, can first be seen here in the character of Tannhäuser. But given the modernity of the theme and the modernity of Wagner's music, many people who came to the premiere in Paris must have been confused and bored by it, even if they did not come with horns to play during the performance. But the opera had been a big success in Dresden, where it has been performed many times. The Paris Opera probably thought they were staging a proven hit when they staged *Tannhäuser*, but they had not counted on the cumulative effect of the anti–Wagner and anti–German feelings among members of that 1861 audience. Ten years later the French, led by their Emperor Napoleon III, would make war on Prussia and invade it, but Napoleon III's error in attacking Prussia became the occasion for a German invasion of France, the declaration of a unified Germany at the hall of mirrors in Versailles in 1870, and Napoleon III's loss of his crown. The French would never again have a monarchy after this famous defeat, and Wagner's glorification of that defeat, in his oafish pamphlet "Eine Kapitulation," did not add to his reputation in France. Wagner in that pamphlet glorified in the French defeat during the Franco-Prussian War, but then he was born right before the French occupation of Leipzig.

One of Wagner's fans who was at the premiere was the French composer Camille Saint-Saëns, whose own opera *Samson et Dalila*, which premiered in 1877 in Weimar, Germany in German (ironically enough), owed much to Wagner's *Tannhäuser*. Saint-Saëns later visited Wagner in Switzerland and told the German composer how much he liked his music. Clearly Wagner had a positive effect on many French people through that Parisian premiere.

But Wagner's dream of an operatic success in the operatic capital of Europe, Paris, was turned into a farce and a nightmare, and it fuelled his basic Francophobia. It was the French, after all, who were bombing his hometown of Leipzig when he was born, a child of the Napoleonic invasion of Germany. That many of Wagner's enemies were of his own making did not occur to him, but then few people have any insight into the consequences of their own self-defeating behavior. Wagner created many of his own enemies due to his own tactlessness and his sometimes tactless writing. But the poet Theophile Gautier and his daughter Judith became friends. The French were divided on Wagner and his operas, as were the Germans. Wagner's music as well as his person were always getting mixed reviews—either love or hate. People were rarely neutral about Wagnerian opera, which is also true now.

But *Tannhäuser*'s fascinating ideas and compelling music would insure that twenty years later the opera would become a staple of the operatic repertory in Paris—long after the "successful" composers of Wagner's own day would sink to the periphery of the operatic repertory. During Wagner's attempts to insure the success of his French premiere, he also developed a new vocabulary of musical development for his operas. The most erotic of all operas, *Tristan und Isolde*, would grow from the musical vocabulary of the first scene of the first act of the ballet music he added to *Tannhäuser* for its Paris premiere.

13. Paris and Tannhäuser: 1860–1861

Ultimately, Wagner not only had a fiasco at his French premiere, but he also was inundated with bills because of his own self-destructive spending. He and Minna had to flee Paris to avoid his creditors, and Minna was undoubtedly sick of being subjected to the embarrassing consequences of his spending binges, especially the public embarrassment. She was also undoubtedly sick of seeing bailiffs at the door threatening to evict them if they did not pay their bills. Minna clearly remembered when Wagner was in debtors' prison in Paris; he was working on a new opera there, but Minna was dying of embarrassment. She yearned for the comfortable life and high status they had when they were living in lovely Dresden, where she did not have to struggle to make herself understood by the locals. She had usually followed him when he fled from his creditors, but she was getting old and weary and sick of being the victim of his mood swings. When they left France (again fleeing from creditors), they were both getting sick of each other's company. Wagner wanted emotional support and adulation from his wife, but Minna wanted financial security from her husband and she did not understand why he could not control himself and provide her (and her pets) with financial stability. Their sex life must have been non-existent at this point, but there was still some love in the relationship.

It was during this time, 1861, that Wagner was allowed to return to the German states and to his native Saxony. The Saxon edict disallowing him to enter Saxony had been rescinded, and he could return to his native country. While Minna had been living in Dresden without him, she had repeatedly been petitioning the Saxon court to forgive her husband's ingratitude and his involvement in the Dresden uprising of 1849. After twelve years he could finally return to his homeland and visit his family there. He could also enter the other German states since the ban against him had also been rescinded by them. While he had been a victim in Paris, his German friends had been reading about his humiliation and wanting his own country to help him.

So many of Wagner's complex characters and complex themes would become popular only in the 20th century. In his *Tannhäuser*, Wagner had contrasted the sensuous man (Tannhäuser) with the caste man (Wolfram). Which was he in 1861? Life is nothing if not ironic and Wagner is hardly the only artist who was not understood in his own time, at least not in France, though he always had his fans even in France. But in the meantime, how was Wagner going to survive? He had to flee his creditors in France, as he had had to do so often. If only he could live within his income. One of the places he sought refuge was the Prussian embassy in Paris, where there were two black swans in the garden pond, and in gratitude he wrote a piece of music about them. This was a form of gratitude Wagner was capable of. And the big flop in Paris was widely reported by the German press so this generated a lot of sympathy of Wagner there — many Germans felt that this was another example of a great German artist victimized by French prejudice against Germans and German culture.

As Germany was approaching an imperial unity under Bismarck and the Hohenzollerns, Wagner's time would come. He would become the German national composer when Germany was finally unified in 1871, ten years after his Parisian flop. But even before then, Wagnerian opera had become increasingly popular in Germany, and indeed across Europe and America. By the beginning of the 20th century, major opera houses in both Europe and America were staging more and more of Wagner's operas. Within thirty years of its premiere in Paris, *Tannhäuser* would become one of Wagner's most frequently performed works, though the controversial composer would be dead by then. But despite the fiasco that was the premiere of *Tannhäuser* in Paris, he had a group of French friends and admirers who maintained a correspondence with him and visited him in Triebschen and Bayreuth. They were all Wagnerians who found in Wagner's operas inspirations for their works in poetry, painting, etc. Camille Renoir painted a portrait of Wagner in the final year of the composer's life.

Wagner impressed many in Paris despite the immensity of his failure with *Tannhäuser*. He wrote the text and music of his operas, and he also revised them and staged them himself, in addition to conducting of course — though he was not allowed to do this at the Opera de Paris. He was a one-man opera company who specialized in brand new operas which people actually wanted to hear. He revolutionized the art form of opera and his theories of art, the artwork of the future, and the Gesamtkunstwerk revolutionized all the arts, especially the literary arts. Wagner was also a workaholic who kept working on essays and new operas despite this failure at the most important opera house in Europe. The revolutionary concept of Wagnerian opera inevitably attracted avant-garde artists to him. By the end of the 19th century even Oscar Wilde and Bernard Shaw considered themselves Wagnerians. Shaw's famous essay "The Perfect Wagnerite" presented a Marxist interpretation of the Ring which many people still consider valid.

More and more Germans were asking if the time to forgive Wagner had finally come despite his republican activities in Dresden. German opera companies were now more interested in staging Wagner's operas and giving him the fame which he deserved and which the French denied him. Among German opera house managers, Wagner's operas had a reputation for being too long and complex and ultimately unperformable, but these judgments were beginning to be questioned. Maybe Wagner's operas could attract an audience after all and actually were performable. His operas were on their way to becoming popular in Germany and around the world, and Wagner would survive the greatest flop in his life.

14

Vienna, Russia and Matrimonial Crisis: 1861–1864

"Let me die!" — Tristan

As a result of the fiasco in Paris and his mounting debts, the Wagners had to flee Paris to avoid debtor's prison, where he had already spent some time twenty years earlier. They first went to Mainz to visit his publisher Schott, who kindly housed the couple. Wagner was suicidally depressed at this point, which is indicated in some of his correspondence.

As Wagner wrote in his autobiography:

Replete with pleasant and agreeable impressions, which constituted the only gain of any real worth extracted from my arduous Paris undertaking, I left the beneficent refuge provided by my Prussian friends during the first week in August [1861], proceeding first via Cologne to Bad Soden. Here I found Minna in the company of the aforementioned Mathilde Schiffner, who seemed to have become indispensable to her as an easy person to tyrannize. I spent two extremely painful days devoted to the task of making the poor woman understand that she would have to settle in Dresden, where I was not yet allowed to stay, whereas I would have to look around in Germany, but first in Vienna, to find a new base of operations. Upon hearing of my plans and my promise to make certain that in any event she would receive one thousand talers a year from me, she glanced at her friend in strange satisfaction. This bargain set the standard of my relationship with her for the rest of her life. As I was now turning to Weimar for the moment, she accompanied me as far as Frankfurt, where we parted. Schopenhauer had died there a short time before.

It is surely significant that as he was parting from Minna in Frankfurt, his thoughts were of Schopenhauer. The philosopher had died in 1860, the year before Wagner's Parisian disaster, but Schopenhauer's vision of the world as a sea of conflicting desires with happiness only possible in a rejection of desire must have been comforting to the composer at this point. His marriage was breaking up and his career seemed like a total failure. First he must visit Weimar to consult with Liszt and then try his luck in Vienna. But Wagner and Liszt developed a breech in their friendship. Liszt and Princess Carolyne had been in Paris while Wagner was there for his *Tannhäuser* flop, and they had avoided him. Princess Carolyne developed a dislike of Wagner because she felt he was always trying to get money out of Liszt, and she also saw Wagner as a competitor to Liszt in terms of musical composition.

Richard Wagner

Wagner's friends, especially Liszt, saw the many good qualities in Wagner and understood his suffering, usually caused by his own psychological problems. Other things which complicated his life were his ambition to become the most famous and the greatest opera composer in Europe, and his desire to conduct and stage his own operas all over Europe. At this point in his life he was traveling all across Europe to conduct, primarily but not exclusively his own operas. At he was approaching his fiftieth birthday, he must have wondered what he had accomplished and whether to go on with his operatic endeavors, but there were signs of hope on the horizon.

During this period Wagner's operas were becoming increasingly popular in Germany and some of the major opera companies there were staging his works. This was partially for political reasons, and more and more Germans wanted to hear German operas rather than French or Italian operas since this was a period of increasing German nationalism as Germany, by 1871, would finally become a unified country — as did Italy at about the same time. A unified country demands its own art; the Germans had been used to importing musicians, artists, and composers from Italy and France, but now German artists became the vogue. Germans increasingly felt that as a unified country they could generate their own art, not having to depend on their neighboring countries for original art. It was becoming a matter of pride for Germans to support their own artists. The music of Wagner and Beethoven was now performed more often in Germany.

In 1862, after the flop of *Tannhäuser* in Paris, Wagner wrote most of the text for *Meistersinger*. He even wrote the overture for this opera, which had a successful premiere in his hometown of Leipzig with the famous Gewandhaus Orchestra. Wagner had the ability to compose through his mental problems or perhaps because of them. Hans von Bülow once said that Wagner was actually a master of finance, and he was able to finance his many artistic projects, somehow getting backers and followers despite all the grief he could cause. This too is a kind of genius.

For a while Wagner moved to Biebrich in Prussia since it was near several important opera houses. While there he met Friederike Meyer, a sister of soprano Frau Meyer-Dustmann of the Vienna Opera. Both women were interested in Wagner's music and Friederike introduced him to several important Wagnerians in the area. Wagner also met Mathilde Maier, another Wagnerian who encouraged him in his work. While living in this area, he met Ludwig and Malvina Schnorr von Carolsfeld. They were interested in singing the title roles in *Tristan und Isolde*; both were professional singers singing in the opera in Dresden. Wagner summoned Hans and Cosima von Bülow to listen to them. With Hans at the piano, the two singers sang excerpts from the score of *Tristan*. Both Wagner and Hans felt that they could sing these roles for the premiere of the opera, though there was still no opera house willing to stage it.

Wagner began doing what he had spent a lifetime doing — begging various opera companies in Germany and elsewhere in Europe to stage his works. Now that *Tristan und Isolde* was in print, he was sending the score to many opera companies with pleading letters. The opera companies of both Karlruhe and Vienna voiced an interest in staging the premiere of *Tristan*. Vienna was certainly the more important opera company with a

14. Vienna, Russia and Matrimonial Crisis: 1861–1864

much better orchestra and more famous soloists. So Wagner moved to Vienna in the hope of having an operatic success there and even finding a home and a refuge in Vienna. Most of Mozart's operas had been staged in Vienna with some success, and Wagner was hoping he too could find operatic success and a permanent home in Vienna since Dresden and Paris did not work for him.

Wagner was also getting offers to conduct in Russia, especially St. Petersburg, and so he went there to conduct and introduce new audiences to excerpts from his former works and works in progress—Wagner really became a genius at marketing his art to audiences all over Europe to generate a desire to hear his complete operas. His expert conducting, often of excerpts from his own operas, generated real enthusiasm in the audience and a curiosity about hearing the complete opera. He found he really loved touring in Russia and conducting the orchestras there, and he found very good orchestras. Verdi had a similar experience there and both men made money in Russia. In fact, on November 10, 1862, Verdi's *La Forza del Destino* had a very successful premiere in St. Petersburg and the overture of that opera became especially famous thanks to Verdi's wonderful orchestration for the fine orchestra in that opera house.

An oval portrait of Wagner (date and artist unknown) (Music Division, The New York Public Library for the Performing Arts, Astor, Lenox and Tilden Foundations).

Wagner moved to Vienna in May of 1861 and conducted a series of concerts of his own works, and Beethoven's, and these concerts actually made some money for him. It was also during this time that Wagner developed a reputation as one of the great conductors of his age. Wagner's revolutionary ideas about conducting and programming for both symphonic concerts and operas had a great effect on modern performances. His programs were much shorter than the typical concerts of the 19th century, which included so many works and often excerpts of works. Wagner's programs tended to be shorter and primarily to include complete symphonies—much closer to modern practice for symphonic programming.

Wagner's reputation was growing and he was making the conductor and his approach to a score more and more important. Wagner had ideas about conducting and he wrote essays on this topic. Ever the clever marketer, Wagner's reputation as a conductor grew as he discussed his theories in print. He was also often conducting excerpts of his new works, thereby marketing them and whetting the audience's appetite for hearing these forthcoming operas, thereby creating pressure on opera companies to stage them. Wagner was very clever at promoting and marketing himself and his works, something he learned from Franz Liszt, who always had advance men and publicity men when he was on tour as a pianist. Liszt too was clever at marketing himself as the greatest pianist in the world, and that is what he became thanks to both his talents and his marketing skills. But now Liszt was marketing himself as a major composer rather than just a pianist, which caused conflicts with Wagner despite their many years of friendship.

Wagner's programming looks just like modern programming for concerts — as opposed to earlier programs in the 19th century which seems exhausting to us. These often included several symphonies, several songs, and a few concertos — they must have lasted four or five hours and would be considered too long for most modern audiences. But Wagner's programming was short but more logically put together and included more complete works. His programming undoubtedly had its effect because more and more conductors were following his lead. Wagner helped to establish modern programming for classical musical by realizing that a concert should have a thematic whole and not exhaust the audience with too many pieces. Wagner certainly influenced music conducting and musical programming in the 19th century, and that influence continued into the 20th century. His essay on conducting had an enormous influence and he helped to make conductors an important aspect of any opera performance. Before his time, a conductor was considered someone who kept the beat and accommodated the singers and kept the orchestra from drowning out the singers, but Wagner argued that the shaping and interpretation of a musical composition, the search for its inner melos, or dominate melody, were the real jobs of a conductors. Wagner insisted that the conductor remained central to the success of any musical performance. Wagner also emphasized the interpretative power of the great conductor — a person who interpreted the music and helped the audience to see it in a new light.

Wagnerian opera became the inspiration for many other arts. Writers and composers of the late nineteenth and early 20th century all considered Wagnerian opera an inspiration. People like Flaubert, Joseph Conrad, Oscar Wilde, and E.M. Forster were influenced by Wagner and his theories of art. Wagner was now considered part of the avant-garde and so avant-garde artists, especially French ones, became increasingly attracted to him and his work, and his music was often performed in orchestra excerpts around the world. Wagner was developing a popular audience now, even in America, where bands especially were making his music popular. This generated curiosity about productions of Wagner's complete operas, which more opera companies were doing now, particularly in Germany. Wagner's music — especially the overtures of *Rienzi, The Flying Dutchman,* and *Lohengrin*— were being frequently performed and even entering popular culture.

Wagner also emphasized the conductor's concept of a musical work so that his perception of that work would give the work a stylistic unity and interpretative approach. Rather than just banging out the time or keeping the beat in a mechanical way, the con-

14. Vienna, Russia and Matrimonial Crisis: 1861–1864

ductor must have a subjective concept of the work's internal construction and melos, or basic melody, and the conductor must conduct so that the performance becomes a stylistically unified interpretation of the work. We now understand how Wagner's theories influenced modern conductors since they now follow many of Wagner's then-revolutionary ideas. It is a shame that William Ashton Ellis' translations are still being used for Wagner's many prose works since Wagner's German is often rendered by Ashton Ellis into confusing Victorian prose with Germanisms rather than proper English equivalents. Often Wagner's prose is clear and to the point but has not been properly translated. Someone needs to write new translations of Wagner's prose works.

While Wagner was living in Vienna, the Vienna opera decided to stage his newest work, *Tristan und Isolde*. Perhaps because of the *Tannhäuser* fiasco in Paris, Vienna wanted to give a Wagnerian opera a sympathetic premiere. This was a German-speaking land, after all, with a wonderful musical and operatic tradition, and the main Royal Opera in Vienna had offered Wagner a contract to stage the premiere of *Tristan und Isolde*. The rehearsals began with a lot of enthusiasm; the orchestra was especially fascinated with this entirely new score, difficult though it was. One of the reasons the management wanted to stage this Wagner premiere is the success they had had with his *Lohengrin* twelve years earlier. The orchestra players had never been confronted with such unusual but captivating music as the prelude to that opera, and many of the players found the prelude to *Tristan* even more interesting.

Vienna's main opera company was now under the direction of a new manager, Matteo Salvi, who was interested in Wagner and sympathetic to his music. The main conductor was now Heinrich Esser. Since the opera was currently staging Wagner's *Lohengrin*, he could finally hear his own score being performed. He was very pleased with what he heard at the opera in Vienna. The orchestra was already famous as one of the best in Europe and it delighted Wagner to be able finally to hear his score in performance. Wagner gave a short speech to the audience after that performance of *Lohengrin* at the Vienna Opera: "Tonight I have heard my work for the first time, performed by an ensemble of artists the equal of whom I do not know, and received by the public in a way that well-nigh overwhelms me. What can I say? Let me bear in all humility the burden you have thus laid on me; let me go on striving towards the goal of my art. I beg you to support me in doing so, by continuing in your good will toward me."

Three days later the Vienna opera performed *The Flying Dutchman* and he was in the audience. That opera was also a great success and he was brought onstage after the performance to a thunderous ovation. These Viennese successes must have been particularly sweet for Wagner after all the booing and whistling he endured in Paris.

Wagner also became quite enthusiastic about the soloists at his disposal for the premiere of *Tristan und Isolde* in Vienna. He had proposed Ludwig and Malvina Schnorr von Carolsfeld in the title roles, but the Vienna Opera already had singers under contract. The company had proposed Luise Meyer-Dustmann as Isolde (Wagner had already met her sister) and Aloys Ander as Tristan. The first rehearsal with the orchestra went very well, and Wagner concluded that the Karlruhe opera had to be told that Vienna would have the honor of staging the first production of *Tristan und Isolde.* Wagner and his assistant Hans von Bülow were at the first few rehearsals and, especially after the trauma in Paris, they both felt that the opera would be a major success in Vienna. Wagner at this point in his career was depending more and more on von Bülow to conduct and to advise him since he did not have his former energy.

Backstage rumors spread that the opera was so difficult, especially for the tenor, that the opera was essentially unperformable and unlikable and would never please a contemporary audience in Vienna and indeed never even be staged. The gossipers called *Tristan und Isolde* a voice killer, especially for the tenor. The orchestra music was so loud and so complex that it drowned out the singers. Then the tenor Aloys Ander lost his voice in the middle of the rehearsal period and asked to be relieved of the role. He announced that the role of Tristan was beyond his capacities. Wagner started looking for a replacement.

Eduard Hanslick, a very conservative critic, was suspicious of Wagner and soon came to be a great advocate of Brahms. Hanslick wrote some very negative articles on the new opera by Wagner, and Wagner's operas in general, and they became enemies. The Wagner people and the Brahms people now became great rivals in Vienna, with the Wagnerian music of the future versus the new conservatism of the Brahms faction. After these negative articles by Hanslick, the opera house decided not to stage the premiere of Wagner's *Tristan und Isolde.* One can only imagine Wagner's profound disappointment and fury at another aborted premiere of his newest opera, and he undoubtedly blamed Hanslick for this.

It was in 1863 that he continued his life as a wandering conductor, going primarily to St. Petersburg, Moscow, Prague, and again Vienna. Some of these concerts made money, some lost money, but Wagner was having real success as a conductor. Many of the musical cognoscenti in those cities recognized the revolutionary nature of his conducting approach and the kind of music he was championing — primarily his own and Beethoven's. He made a lot of money in those concerts, but could never handle money rationally. He was a great man, he felt, and was entitled to his luxuries — and so he told his friend Nietzsche, who based his Superman in his *Thus Spoke Zarathustra* on the narcissistic qualities of Wagner. Ernest Newman quotes one of Wagner's friends, Peter Cornelius, on how Wagner spent money on Christmas gifts for him:

> The mad Wagner has fixed up a big Christmas tree, and underneath it a royally rich table for me. Just imagine: a marvelous heavy overcoat — an elegant grey dressing gown — a red scarf, a blue cigar-case and tinder-box — lovely silk handkerchiefs, splendid gold shirt stud ... in short, all sorts of things that only an Oriental imagination could think of. It made my heart heavy, and the next day I gave half of them away [Newman III, 207].

With the huge amounts of money Wagner gained through his conducting, he rented a house in Penzing, a suburb of Vienna, and hired a Putzmacherin, a seamstress who made him silk costumes and silk curtains in all sorts of outlandish colors. He was also buying colognes in Paris to fulfill his olfactory needs. These scents and colors and fancy fabrics seemed to fulfill some sort of primitive luxury need in him. Wagner always defended these luxury items by arguing that they were not for him but for his art, and these luxurious

14. Vienna, Russia and Matrimonial Crisis: 1861–1864

fabrics helped him to compose his operas and work on his Ring cycle. Were they really an artistic necessity? The letters between Wagner and his Viennese Putmacherin (a seamstress named Mrs. Maretschek) have suggested to some that Wagner was really a transvestite who wanted to dress up like a woman rather than in the sober black outfits which most men wore in the 19th century. Wagner certainly liked to dress up in silks and satins and furs.

The 19th century became famous for black, somber clothing for men, unlike male attire of the previous century, but Wagner's portraits seem atypical. He seemed more like a clothes horse of the 18th century, when wealthy men were in colorful and elaborate attire, silks and satins in bright colors with powdered wigs. He liked luxurious fabrics, especially silks and satins, and colorful apparel. He also liked to redecorate the rooms he lived in with colorful and bright silk curtains. This is typical of the period since 19th century interiors tended to use oriental rugs and elaborately patterned and colorful curtains and furniture. After looking at a lot of 19th century interiors, one can see why modern and art deco minimalism came into fashion early in the 20th century — a reaction against the elaborate patterning of the 19th century. Victorian interiors make one begin to yearn for 20th century modernism and minimalism. Minna seemed much less interested in fabrics, scents, and interior décor than her husband. He wanted to be surrounded with luxury like an Oriental pasha.

The voluminous correspondence between Wagner and Minna makes for painful reading since it indicates the depth of Wagner's needs and the insanity of his demands on people. Though he feared isolation, he never really lacked company since he could be so funny and charming and that attracted people to him, especially homosexual men. Wagner was certainly not homophobic and enjoyed the company of gay men and women now that he was living in a suburb of Vienna. Some people have argued that Wagner himself was gay, but there is no real evidence of that, though he certainly liked fancy dress or dressing up in outlandish attire. He was fastidious about his dress and liked bright colors in his apparel. He was a real dandy in his way, rather like Oscar Wilde in London. Wagner too had an element of the peacock in him and dressed to attract as much attention as possible.

Liszt was still safely ensconced in Weimar with a generous patron and now with Princess Carolyne, who was getting to dislike Wagner. Wagner was still begging his friends to visit him, especially Liszt, since Wagner apparently feared that he lost his friend if he was absent for any length of time. One of the main attractions of Cosima was undoubtedly the fact that she was the daughter of his dear friend Liszt.

While Wagner was moving around so much to conduct, going so far as Russia, he was also working on his compositions since he kept telling friends about his plans for his Ring cycle of four operas telling the story of the young Siegfried and Siegfried's death. He seemed obsessed with this story. It began as one opera about Siegfried's death and was eventually expanded into four operas telling about the gods, Alberich, the ring of the Nibelung, and the death of the gods and the destruction of the whole world, and the hope of a new and better world after the death of the gods.

Minna and Wagner were not living together any more. An added complexity in their marriage was the constant presence of Nathalie, whom Minna described as her younger sister. As Wagner undoubtedly soon discovered, Nathalie was actually Minna's illegitimate young daughter. Nathalie's father was some actor friend of Minna's who had an affair with Minna, impregnated her, and then refused to marry her. Wagner never told people the truth about the relationship between his wife and Nathalie, and he continued to support them both for many years after the marriage was over in all but the legalities — in fact, until Minna's death in 1866. Wagner in many ways was a very honorable man and kept Minna's secret. Eventually Minna moved to her favorite German city, Dresden, and established herself and Nathalie there.

Wagner began falling apart physically and emotionally, and to think that suicide was his only way out. Perhaps Tristan was right, that suicide and death were preferable to life. This was also the suggestion of the philosopher Schopenhauer, whose *Studies in Pessemism* was arguing that life was eternal struggle and frustration and suicide was sometimes better. Wagner was now entering one of the most suicidal periods of his life when he felt anything he produced would inevitably be a failure. Maybe he should follow the example of his Tristan and terminate his painful, failure-prone life. He was wandering around Munich in the spring of 1864 when he came upon a death notice in the shop windows. The king of Bavaria, Maximilian II, had died suddenly and he would be succeeded by his teenage son, who would become Ludwig II. Wagner must have wondered why the king had died so suddenly and how this young man could take over the Bavarian crown during this complex period in German history.

15

The Rescue by King Ludwig II of Bavaria: 1864–1865

"Is there no king who will support me?"— Wagner

One of the most important dates in Wagner's life, and a great turning point, was May 3, 1864, when Wagner received a Count Pfeistermeister at the hotel Marquart in Stuttgart, where he was avoiding his creditors; he was there for a performance of *Don Giovanni*. Count Pfeistermeister, a court advisor to the new king, Ludwig II of Bavaria, gave Wagner a portrait of the king accompanied by a ring. The count told him that the king was a great admirer of his operas, wanted to see him immediately in Munich, and would help him stage his Ring cycle. At first Wagner feared that this was a hoax or a practical joke, but he got assurances that this was not the case.

The Bavarian monarch, on his throne only two months and a mere 18 years old, was at the Residenz, the royal seat of government in the capital of Bavaria, Munich. This message from the king would certainly change Wagner's life and fortunes forever for now he became a royal employee (again, but a different monarch, Bavarian rather than Saxon) by a man who declared his love of Wagnerian opera, a fan who promised to free him from all his financial worries so that he could concentrate on his musical compositions. The king's father, Maximilian II, had died suddenly and so Ludwig came to the throne much earlier than he had planned and certainly without enough experience. But he had already seen several of Wagner's operas in Munich's royal opera house and these operas had changed his life.

Wagner had been writing about looking for a royal savior, and that savior had arrived! The situation was rather like Elsa's in the first act of *Lohengrin*: She was desperate, had been accused of murder, and was helpless when her savior suddenly arrived. Finally, the longed-for and generous king had arrived and would help him to complete his work, and then he could commit suicide with a peace that passeth all understanding, as the Buddhists say. The European tradition of a monarch supporting a great artist became true for Wagner — actually a second time, since he was a royal employee in Dresden as well. Given how the Dresden situation ended, one would think that King Ludwig II would be more cautious, but he was only 18 years old when he ascended the throne, and he was already a Wagner fan who was determined to help the composer. But one cannot help wondering how this new opportunity from a king was going to end up, given how the Saxon king's generosity to Wagner in Dresden ended. Wagner clearly had a problem with authority figures, especially ones who were rich and generous. He both yearned for them and made problems for them once he found them — rather like the yearning and anger directed at a phantom father-figure.

The day after Count Pfeistermeister arrived, Wagner wrote a very emotional letter to the king:

> These tears of the heavenliest emotion I send to you, to tell you that now the marvels of poetry have come as a divine reality into my poor, love-lacking life. And that life, its last poetry, its last tones, belong henceforth to you, my gracious young King: dispose of them as your own property.

This short letter sounds like the love letter of a loveless young virgin to her generous rescuer. The letter is filled with metaphors of art, of poetry and music. One wonders why Wagner used such a tone in his first letter to the king. Wagner seemed to be establishing some sort of erotic bond with the king — or was this tone merely a product of the composer's own desperation?

Ludwig had a brother, Otto, who had mental problems, and was hidden away by the family in one of its many castles, Schloss Hohenschwangau. Ludwig was the older son and heir to the throne, but the family — like so many royal families in Europe — had a history of profound mental problems. Ludwig II's grandfather King Ludwig I, had been forced to abdicate due to his obsession and adulterous affair with the Spanish dancer Lola Montez. (She was actually Irish and was named Eliza Gilbert, and she died in Brooklyn and is buried in Green-Wood cemetery there under her real name. But she used the name Lola Montez and presented herself as a Spanish dancer.) The old king Ludwig I became obsessed with her and lost his crown as a result of the scandal of his adulterous affair. His grandson was about to fall into a similar trap due to his obsession with the composer Wagner. It cost the Bavarian treasury millions of dollars and made both Wagner and King Ludwig II very unpopular in both Munich and Bavaria in general due to the local newspapers and their reporting on the nature and cost of the king's obsession with Wagner.

Count Pfeistermeister would become one of Wagner's enemies in Munich because this prime minister came to fear the influence that Wagner had on the young king and what Wagner and what his ambitious plans were costing the Bavarian state. Wagner's political naïveté and excessive demands for money, plus the scandal of his life in Munich, would end his career there rather abruptly, but now all looked rosy and the king obviously adored him as the composer of the age and the savior of Germany. The young king's interest in art rather than politics and the military struck many people in the court at Munich as inappropriate, and reminded many older people of the career of King Ludwig I. The years between 1864 and 1871 became crucial years for both Bavaria and all of the German states. There would be several wars culminating in the Franco-Prussian war when France's Emperor Napoleon III attacked Prussia. Due to their alliances, Bavaria was forced to be on the side of Prussia. This would lead to the unification of Germany in 1871 under a Prussian emperor, Wilhelm I. During these crucial years, Bavaria needed a king obsessed

15. The Rescue by King Ludwig II of Bavaria: 1864–1865

with Bavaria and its future in the unified German state, not a king obsessed with Wagner and his operas.

When Wagner first met King Ludwig II at the royal Residenz in Munich, Wagner must have been astounded. The king was a very tall and handsome young man, only 18 years old, and he seemed madly in love with both Wagner and his operas, many of which had already been staged at the royal opera house in Munich. Within ten minutes Wagner must have realized that the king was very naïve, madly in love with him, and gay. Wagner responded very kindly to the king since the king could do wonderful things for the composer's career. But Wagner must have realized that this was going to be a difficult situation for him. The king had heard of the failed attempt to stage *Tristan und Isolde* in Vienna so he immediately ordered the Bavarian State Opera to stage the opera. He also wanted to have the Ring cycle finished and staged for him at the royal opera house in Munich.

The king enjoyed meeting Wagner frequently and discussing his artistic plans, which the king was fully engaged in and fascinated by. The king wanted Wagner to live very near him so he could see him every day and they could discuss their artistic plans, which must have made Wagner a bit nervous. Wagner talked about other plans, like a new opera house to stage the Ring in Munich, the founding of a new music school to prepare singers to sing in the revolutionary new operas of Wagner, etc. The king was totally fascinated by Wagner and his operas, and he encouraged Wagner to plan all sorts of new projects for Munich and its opera house. The king was suddenly Wagner's biggest fan, and he wanted the composer to work with him on these projects. The king did not seem so interested in Bavaria and its future, and he came to dislike his capital city, Munich, and prefer the fabulous scenery of the Bavarian Alps in the southern part of the province. The king also wanted to build fantastic new castles in that wonderful alpine scenery. But while Wagner and the king were making big plans, the king wanted Wagner close to him. He moved him to some of the royal properties in the Bavarian Alps, and he wanted Wagner to live near him in Munich as well so he asked him to move into the Villa Pellet in one of the most beautiful and fashionable parts of town, which was near the king's royal residence in Munich.

As Wagner demanded more and more money from the king's generosity, he developed enemies who began to see him as a narcissistic ingrate who could never be given enough money. Wagner's demands for money became Wagnerian. In addition to all this was the developing scandal in Wagner's household, with the composer having an affair and fathering children with his student Hans von Bülow's wife Cosima, daughter of his closest friend Franz Liszt. The town of Munich was soon buzzing with rumors about Wagner's life. It was no wonder that Wagner was becoming unpopular in Munich. People were calling for his exile from the city. Many citizens saw him as someone who was corrupting the king, a situation which could result in the king being forced to abdicate.

Many people in the 19th century had a theory of homosexuality which most people now would consider very naïve: that homosexuality was caused by a young teenage boy corrupted by an older gay man. Some people still have this theory, though there is no evidence for it from psychiatrists. The young men at court in Munich hired a prostitute to be at the winter garden in the royal palace in Munich, but when the king was confronted with a sexually available woman, he rang for a servant and fled the garden. As the king's homosexuality became obvious, especially after his engagement to his cousin Sophie fell apart, people began to see Wagner as a corrupting influence on the life of the handsome, young monarch.

Wagner was yet again in a large royal arts organization, like the royal opera in Saxony, and similar problems soon arose with Wagner making heavy demands on the royal treasury and suggesting changes in the administration in the arts. Wagner talked to the king about the incompetence of the people currently in charge; as in Saxony, Wagner was too naïve and too arrogant to survive in any large arts organization, especially one connected with a king and royal court. Like Mozart, Wagner made enemies without realizing how — his position at the king's favorite meant that he was resented by the non-favorites at court who were also trying to develop their careers under royal patronage.

To be gay in the 19th century and to be a king, thus living in a goldfish bowl, must have generated wonderful opportunities for Ludwig and horrendous guilt since he must have realized that it was his Catholic duty as a Wittelsbach monarch to marry and produce at least two children — an heir and a spare. On some level, the king was a very religious man who took his Catholic religion very seriously, but being homosexual put him in an impossible situation since his very sexuality was a mortal sin (and unmentionable). Since the thought of sexual intercourse with a woman clearly repelled him, he must have realized what an impossible situation he was in. For the king, Wagner perhaps became the loving father interested in the arts which he had never had. He had rarely seen his real father, King Maximilian II, and had been raised by servants — typical of royal families in Europe at the time.

Soon after they met, Wagner received the following letter from the king:

> Rest assured that I will do everything in my power to make up to you for what you have suffered in the past. The mean cares of everyday life I will banish from you forever; I will procure for you the peace you have longed for in order that you may be free to spread the mighty wings of your genius in the pure ether of rapturous art. Though you were unconscious of it, you were the sole source of my delight from my tenderest youth onwards, my friend who spoke to my heart as no other did, my best teacher and educator. I will repay you everything to the best of my ability. O how I have looked forward to the time when I could do this! I hardly dared indulge myself in the hope so soon to be able to prove my love to you.

This first letter from the king would eventually become thousands of letters which the men wrote to each other over the twenty years of their relationship. The king's first letter sounds like a love letter, or a letter from a very lonely teenager to his first love. The letter also suggests a boy looking for a loving father figure — something which both Wagner and the king never had. The two men had many similarities in terms of terrible, unloving childhoods and constant loneliness.

As Wagner wrote to his friend Mathilde Maier soon after he met the king, "He has the profoundest understanding of my nature and my needs, he offers me everything I want for my life, for my creative activity, for the production of my works. I am

15. The Rescue by King Ludwig II of Bavaria: 1864–1865

to be simply his friend: no appointment, no functions. He is the ideal fulfillment of my desires."

But Wagner must have also realized that this wonderful situation brought with it special problems. The young king ruled Bavaria at a particularly perilous time when there was a movement toward German unification, and the Prussian royal family and its prime minister in Berlin, Count Otto von Bismarck, were going to try to unify all of Germany under the Prussian monarchy (Hohenzollern). The religion of Bavaria, Catholicism, made homosexual acts a mortal sin, which meant the king would have to lead a double life and be threatened with hell and public exposure and the loss of his throne. The king was not an absolute monarch, though he dreamed of being one, and he remained very vulnerable to how his parliament, the press, and the public viewed him. He also had a lot of duties and was already indicating that he did not love to have to march in parades or give medals to his soldiers and citizens when he could have been going to the opera. He also had to have his requests for money approved by the Munich parliament so he could not spend money as he wished but had to request funds — which made him angry since his requests were sometimes rejected by his court ministers.

The king also loathed his capital city, Munich, and that also earned him some enemies. His brother Otto was certifiably insane so Ludwig had no choice about becoming king since he was the only Wittelsbach and only son of his father who was available. A reign that began with so much hope — a handsome young man who was only 18 and interested in the arts — ended with such tragedy, the probable suicide of the king in 1886, occurring three years after the death of Wagner. King Ludwig II never was capable of being a good king for Bavaria because politics bored him. In the beginning he diligently tried to do his duty and attended hundreds of meetings and signed thousands of documents. But the reality remained that he was very interested in the arts but not much interested in the political, social, and economic problems of his people.

The fact that the king was obviously in love with the composer must have immediately generated the rumor that the king was gay, which he was. And the amounts of money he was spending on the composer must have also generated rumors about the Bavarian treasury being sacked so that the king could cater to his royal favorite's every whim. The king was dreaming about luxuriating in his new palaces and having performances of Wagnerian opera just for him. There were several such performances at the Bavarian Royal Opera in Munich — for only the king and his circle of handsome and probably gay men.

One of the people who became most suspicious of the king's new protégé (Wagner) was his mother Queen Marie. Since her husband's death she had depended on Ludwig to continue the Wittelsbach reign in Bavaria. Queen Marie suspected that her son was being corrupted by a disreputable older man and a Protestant republican, Richard Wagner. When he moved to Munich at her son's invitation and was demanding and getting money from her son, and also engaging in an unsavory relationship with Hans von Bülow and his wife Cosima, Queen Marie warned her son about the composer. She began to fear that her son's obsession with the composer would result in his sexual corruption, the loss of his crown, and the end of the Wittelsbach dynasty.

Queen Marie was also trying to persuade her son to marry the Archduchess Sophie Charlotte, an aristocratic cousin, and was delighted when they became engaged in 1863. Queen Marie undoubtedly hoped that marriage would cure her son of his obsession with Wagner and end the rumors of his homosexuality. But when Ludwig II broke off the engagement after repeatedly delaying the marriage, she became convinced that Wagner was both fleecing and corrupting her son. When she pointed this out to the king, he became enraged and pushed her out of his life, much to her horror. She began to fear that both her darling sons, Ludwig and Otto, were clinically insane — and she was right.

Wagner was presented with the Villa Pellet on the Briennerstrasse in Munich, a gorgeous villa. The house (in the neo–Gothic style popular in the 19th century) was within walking distance of Ludwig's royal residence in the center of town. The king bought the villa and allowed Wagner to live in it without charge. Wagner wanted to live on an aristocratic style and the king wanted to provide him with this. Such a house demanded a large staff of servants, and Wagner was now used to having servants. Wagner was not satisfied with the villa as it was since he loved to decorate in his own lavish and typically Victorian style. He furnished his new house lavishly — with all the silks and satins and perfumes he demanded. Cosima and her children soon moved into the Villa Pellet, with her husband visiting occasionally. The Bavarians were probably used to the image of a composer as a quasi-religious, monk-like figure who wrote music for the church and lived a chaste, humble life. They were not used to a composer who lived like an Oriental potentate surrounded by luxuries and mistresses.

There were all sorts of ugly rumors, which turned out to be true. Why was this narcissistic Protestant composer who wrote these weird operas (which few other than the king liked) being supported on such a royal level while Bavarian artists were being ignored? And why was his arrogant young protégé, Hans von Bülow, being given high royal positions and making rude remarks about Bavarians at the Bavarian Royal Opera? Where there was public interest, there were journalists who were going to supply the public with the information they were curious about. Wagner was soon covered in the Munich newspapers, all of whom wanted to get Wagner out of Bavaria because of his own mistakes. There were some musical connoisseurs who began to love Wagner's music, but most Bavarians would have found his operas too long and boring. It was during this period that Wagner developed his hatred of the Jesuits, who were a powerful political force in Munich and who had many churches and many friends in the capital. Michaelskirche, on the Kaufingerstrasse, was a Jesuit church and it would ultimately house the tombs of both Ludwig I and Ludwig II.

But the immediate problem for the king and the composer was getting his new opera *Tristan und Isolde* staged in Munich. There were rumors that the work was musically ugly, unperformable, and had almost ruined the voice of the star tenor at the royal opera house in Vienna. But the king and the composer were determined to overcome any obstacles. They would stage *Tristan und Isolde* despite the problems and of course all the costs would be absorbed by the monarchy. Von Bülow was made conductor of this production; it was

15. The Rescue by King Ludwig II of Bavaria: 1864–1865

reported in the newspapers that he was saying rude things about the Bavarian people, though they were paying for this expensive new production.

While Wagner was the king's favorite in Munich, he produced illegitimate children with Cosima von Bülow. Meanwhile her husband Hans was offering to duel anyone who suggested what was obviously going on. Many people in Munich chalked his actions up to careerism since conducting this premiere would make him the most famous conductor in Germany.

Eventually even Ludwig began to dislike Wagner despite all his talent because of the stream of letters he received from the composer which were clearly lies about the exact nature of his relationship with Cosima von Bülow. The repeated lies that Wagner and Cosima told the king and the press, that theirs was an innocent, platonic relationship, added to the king's eventual rage at them when the truth finally became apparent.

Part of what attracted Wagner to Cosima was that she was a baroness because of her marriage to von Bülow. The fact that she used this title, and the fact that Wagner often referred to her as "the baroness," added to the complexity of their relationship, and also indicated something of Wagner's desire to be part of the aristocracy. In part, Wagner was a snob who wanted to be a part of the very upper classes which he often mocked in his operas, especially in the Ring and Meistersinger. This he probably learned from his friend Liszt, who was always developing relationships with aristocratic mother figures.

Good things were happening with the premiere of *Tristan* and the composition of the Ring cycle forging ahead. This was a complicated Wagnerian situation, but the good news was that Wagner had found another wealthy patron who was anxious to see Wagner's operas being performed by the National Theater — or the Royal Bavarian National Opera, as it was called during the time when Munich had a king — though those days were clearly numbered since their neighbor to the north in Protestant Prussia was developing plans to swallow up Bavaria and create a united Germany. By 1871 Germany was united thanks to Bismarck and Wilhelm I, but Bavaria was technically still an independent country. After World War I, Bavaria became part of the united Germany — a movement which would cause much grief in Bavaria thanks to what happened in the '30s in Germany and the subsequent developments culminating in World War II.

The Wagner-Ludwig relationship came at a crucial point in the history of Bavaria. There was a movement to unify Germany under a Kaiser — just as Italy had been unified about this same time. Many people wondered if this would be a good thing for Bavaria. Would they be better off united to Catholic Austria or remain independent, like Switzerland? Many Bavarians were suspicious of anything Prussian, especially its army, and feared that their state would suffer under Prussian domination. If ever there was a time when Bavaria needed a shrewd king, now was the time. Instead, the king was getting large sums of money from Bismarck's secret Guelph Fund to support Prussia. King Ludwig II was the man who urged King Wilhelm I of Prussia to become the new Kaiser in 1870, when the German states were all gathered in Versailles as a result of the German victory after the Franco-

Prussian war. King Ludwig II later said he did not want to offer the Prussian king that throne but felt forced to — probably because of the money Bismarck offered him. Many Bavarian historians have argued that as a result of King Ludwig II, Bavaria lost its independence, and would later be dragged into World War I and World War II by Prussia. If King Ludwig II had been as concerned with the Bavarian people and their needs as he was with Wagner, millions of Bavarian lives would have been saved.

16

Tristan in Munich: 1864–1865

"Let me die."—Isolde

One of the first items on the agenda of the team of Wagner and King Ludwig II was to stage the premiere of *Tristan und Isolde* in the spring of 1865. The king was very eager to see Wagner's newest work, especially since Wagner had been playing excerpts to him. Hans von Bülow, who now had a job as court musician to the king, was also playing excerpts for the king. Wagner was always a very clever marketer.

Wagner was now living at the Villa Pallet thanks to the king, but a complication arose in November 1863. Wagner himself explains this complication in his autobiography when describing his brief stay in Berlin:

> As my only remaining source of profit was now the concert at Loewenberg, I turned my steps in that direction, but in order to avoid Dresden made a little detour to Berlin, where I arrived, utterly exhausted after traveling through the night, early on November 28. I was met, as I had requested, by the Bülows, but they at once persuaded me to postpone my immediate departure for Silesia for a day and devote this time to them. Hans probably wanted me above all to attend a concert to be given that evening under his direction, and of course this then induced me to stay. In cold, raw and dank weather we spent our time as cheerfully as possible conversing about my miserable situation. To augment my funds, it was decided to hand over the Grand Duke of Baden's gold box to our friend, the worthy Weitzmann, to be sold. The proceeds of this transaction, amounting to about ninety talers, were brought to me at the Hotel Brandenburg, where I was dining with Bülow, and there was no lack of jokes concerning this buttressing of my existence. As Bülow had to make some preparation for his concert I again went for a drive in a handsome carriage alone with Cosima. This time we fell silent and all joking ceased. We gazed mutely into each other's eyes and an intense longing for the fullest avowal of the truth forced us to a confession, requiring no words whatever, of the incommensurable misfortune that weighed upon us. With tears and sobs we sealed a vow to belong to each other alone. It lifted a great weight from our hearts. The profound tranquility which ensued gave us the serenity to attend the concert without any sense of oppression. As a matter of fact, a sensitive and buoyant performance of Beethoven's small concert overture (in C major) together with the very clever arrangement by Hans of Gluck's overture to *Paris and Helen*, even managed to attract my close attention [*My Life*, 728–29].

This remains one of the most remarkable passages in Wagner's autobiography. Wagner describes here the beginning of his love and adulterous affair with Cosima von Bülow, without an iota of guilt over the fact that they were both married to someone else. And the start of this affair is described in terms of a triangular relationship: Wagner is still a very good friend of Hans, and Hans and his conducting talents surround the declaration of love. The new lovers seal their new honesty by going to a concert with Hans on the podium. The subtext here, in a way, reflects a child who has finally found his parents, despite the fact that both Hans and Cosima were twenty-five years younger than Wagner. The situation, to coin a term which Freud would describe within fifty years, became Oedipal. This situation is exactly reflected in Tristan's love for Isolde, his beloved uncle King Marke's wife.

But with or without Freud's theories, the immediate problem for Wagner was staging his *Tristan*. The composer had originally envisioned *Tristan und Isolde* as a short, popular opera which would make him a lot of money, but he was being more realistic now about the vocal demands of the two title roles, not to mention the orchestral demands. He often played excerpts of his newest works to friends and that got them eager to hear the whole opera. Wagner also of course used this technique to get impresarios in other opera companies to stage his works — he spent much of his life begging impresarios to stage his works at various opera companies in Paris and Germany. But now that Wagner had King Ludwig II as one of his fans, the realities he had to face were much altered.

Wagner also wrote essays for Ludwig on the reform of the state, religion, and musical education and performance in Bavaria, and the contents of these essays must have made the local musical establishment and religious establishment in Bavaria very nervous. Some of Wagner's musical reform ideas made some sense, and if he had presented them tactfully to the local musical and artistic establishment and showed them that the new plans would involve them and not threaten their livelihoods, Wagner might had done some good work in Bavaria. But tact was not his forte, and his concept of reform implied that the local musical establishment needed to be replaced. Wagner generally started his reform essays by saying that the people in the current positions of power were totally incompetent and he had a new ways of administering the arts, thereby making enemies of all those people. Was this Freud's repetition compulsion, with Wagner making the very same mistakes he had made in Saxony?

Wagner also suggested a brand new opera house for the performance of only his works and a brand new musical conservatory to train a new type of opera singer to sing in his operas. Such plans would have involved millions of dollars, in addition to the money he was already getting from the king to live in Wagner's usual palatial style. Where was the money to come from? From the Bavarian treasury, of course, and that needed the approval of the government. King Ludwig liked to act like a monarch with absolute powers, and his favorite historical figure was Louis XIV, but in reality Ludwig was living as the king of a constitutional monarchy and had to have his plans approved by the parliament since he himself did not have unlimited funds. His projects were already straining his own Wittelsbach family funds, and he needed approval from the Bavarian parliament to get government funds — and the parliament was increasingly reluctant to give Ludwig any more money since that would raise taxes on the people.

With King Ludwig's personal encouragement, and the promise of a special theater to be built for the express purpose of staging the premiere of Wagner's current project,

16. Tristan *in Munich: 1864–1865*

the Ring cycle, Wagner went back to work on the Ring. He had left that work in the middle of the second act of *Siegfried*, but he resumed work on his great tetralogy, arguably his masterpiece. Wagner wanted his works, especially his proposed new Ring cycle, staged in a special new opera house designed to his specifications. Wagner had fantasies of building a special theater, staging his Ring cycle, and then burning the new opera house down and destroying all the scores. This revolutionary new theater would be used to stage only one performance of only his works. These ideas must have struck most people as appallingly narcissistic — the current opera houses in Munich had been used to stage operas by Mozart, Beethoven, Bellini, Rossini, Donizetti, Verdi, and Weber, but now a brand new opera house had to be built (and paid for by the Bavarian taxpayers) only for the works of Richard Wagner. Meanwhile, Wagner's friend the architect Gottfried Semper was commissioned by the king to draw up plans for a new opera house in Munich — the old one had been there for about twenty years. Was a new opera house really needed for the needs of just one composer, many people in Munich wondered. And how was this new theater going to be paid for? By the king or the taxes of the citizens of Bavaria?

In the midst of all this uproar, in April of 1865, Wagner's mistress Cosima had a child called Isolde. The press was suggesting that the child was really the product of Wagner's adulterous affair with Cosima rather than the efforts of Hans. Wagner was making more and more enemies in Munich, and some people in court were calling him Lola Montez II, after the courtesan who forced Ludwig I to abdicate.

At first Wagner wanted *Tristan und Isolde* staged at the little Cuvilles theater in the Residenz, but his huge orchestra would have probably blown the roof off the little rococo theater that only seats about 500 people and was designed for Mozartian Baroque opera. Eventually Wagner agreed that the new National Opera House would have to be used. He seemed to become more demanding with each rehearsal. King Ludwig II must have been a very patient man but that patience had a limit. Hans von Bülow also became known as a difficult man to deal with, subject to saying nasty things about Bavaria which soon got into the Munich newspapers.

The king was also making plans to build three new royal castles — Neuschwanstein, Linderhof, and Herrencheimsee. Neuschwanstein was a neo–Gothic fantasy, left incomplete by the king's death. Linderhof was a rococo-style fantasy, also incomplete. Herrencheimsee, in a Baroque-style based on Versailles, is also incomplete. King Ludwig would have one castle commissioned, and after a few rooms were finished, he would lose interest in it and start another. It is easy to dismiss all three of these castles as Victorian kitsch, but the 19th century was particularly fond of historicism in architecture, or building in an older style rather than trying to develop a completely new style. The king himself could not afford to support all his artistic projects and was dependent on his government and parliament for funds, but they were resistant to his plans because that meant raising taxes.

One of the members of the court, the minister Ludwig von Pfordten, had now become one of Wagner's enemies. He had dealt with Wagner while he was a minister of the royal court in Saxony and had predicted what would happen. He became the center of the anti–Wagner faction in Munich, and they wanted Wagner driven out of Munich as soon as possible.

Wagner had worked with Ludwig Schnorr von Carolsfeld in Heldentenor roles and decided that he and his wife Malvina would be the perfect Tristan und Isolde. They were both delighted to be cast and felt that they could handle these very difficult roles. Hans von Bülow was a young pianist who had no previous experience conducting opera, and the public and the king naturally wondered why this greenhorn was chosen by Wagner to conduct. They suspected that this was Wagner's way of keeping his mistress, Cosima von Bülow, near him. Was this the real reason for Wagner's insistence on Hans' conducting — so he would ignore his wife's affair with the composer?

On the morning of the scheduled premiere, May 15, 1865, the soprano singing Isolde, Malvina, got sick and had to call off the performance — and there was obviously no cover available. After a month, the premiere finally took place on June 10, and both Wagner and Ludwig II were enthralled with the performance, though the reviews were mixed and some of the audience was somewhat bewildered and bored by this strange, revolutionary opera. But all the performances were sold out and applauded. There were several more performances, and then the great Heldentenor, Ludwig Schnorr von Carolsfeld, got sick and died on July 21, 1865, thus establishing the tradition that the tenor role was a killer for the tenor, literally. *Tristan* was soon seen as a jinxed opera, having killed the first tenor to sing the role within six weeks — rather like Shakespeare's *Macbeth*. Malvina was showing signs of insanity within a few years of the premiere.

One of the things which alarmed people in Munich must have been the murder-suicide pact in the first act of the opera, and the combination of love and death through suicide which repelled many but fascinated both Wagner and the king since both men were often suicidal. The opera concerned Isolde's plan to murder Tristan in the first act and then commit suicide. Many people in that original performance must have been shocked by the drama and confused and bored by the music — which was hardly typical 19th century music for opera.

But the good news was that the opera had finally been staged successfully, and many in the audience enjoyed it, especially Wagner's biggest fan, Ludwig II, and this enjoyment encouraged him to continue favoring Wagner and giving him money to complete the Ring, *Meistersinger*, and *Parsifal*.

Angelo Quaglio, from a long line of Italian designers for the theater, was chosen as the set designer and lighting man for the premiere. His grandfather had designed the famous rococo Margrave's opera house in Bayreuth. Hans von Bülow had a hard time with the orchestra, getting them used to playing this difficult score. Richard Strauss's father was in that orchestra, by the way, and he never was very fond of this opera. The father of the future composer was a Mozart fan and very suspicious of Wagner and the music of the future. That his own son, the composer Richard Strauss, would eventually become a Wagner fan and in many ways a follower of Wagner's theories about opera, especially the leitmotif and the symphonic use of the orchestra, must have been a bitter irony for the old orchestra player his father.

16. Tristan *in Munich: 1864–1865*

Mark Twain would later become notorious for asserting that Wagner's music was better than it sounded, which was in some ways true for *Tristan*. The musical architecture and the use of the Tristan chord and the chromaticism of the score gave the opera a liquid, undulating quality which reflected one of its main symbols, water, and much of the score had been composed on that most watery of cities, Venice, where Wagner was surrounded by its lagoons.

The opera also indicated Wagner's increasing fascination with the philosophy of Arthur Schopenhauer, particularly his book *The World as Will and Representation,* which had appeared 20 years earlier. Wagner read the book several times and was fascinated with its eroticism and its pessimism, its belief that we are doomed to unhappiness and despair and are often consciously suicidal, which Wagner certainly was, but find relief for our suffering in art and in love, that sex is when we are most purely human and when we can escape the inevitable suffering that we must endure. Schopenhauer was also a great defender of the arts as the medium which can offer help and relief for suffering humanity. In sex and in the arts, man can find relief from his frustrations and suffering. Schopenhauer described theories which Freud would later present in Vienna at the end of the 19th century. Wagner greatly admired Schopenhauer and sent him a copy of his *Nibelung* libretto, the text for his Ring cycle, but never got a response from the irascible and difficult old man. *Tristan* certainly reflects Schopenhauer's view of life as frustration and suffering, which is certainly the case for both Tristan and Isolde. Their suffering finds relief primarily in sex, dreams, and death, with Tristan attempting suicide at the end of each act, finally finding death at the end of the opera. Isolde's ending is more mysterious since whether she dies at the end depends on the production — Wagner's stage directions say only that she falls on Tristan's corpse at the end of the opera. Right before then, she relates a dream she has in the Liebestod: She is standing over the corpse of Tristan but she fantasizes him alive, in the water, and beckoning to her. To drown with him in that water, she says, would be the greatest bliss.

This is arguably Wagner's greatest opera. It is a unique opera which has influenced much of the development of 20th century classical music and opera. Its undulating chromaticism suggests the end of the European diatonic key system, upon which much of the development of Western music has depended. What a wonderful, complex, and haunting opera *Tristan und Isolde* has remained since its premiere in Munich in 1865, and how strange it must have seemed to its original audience in Munich. Luckily Ludwig II loved it immediately and wanted it performed again and again.

Meanwhile Wagner's finances were again in a mess and his creditors were gathering. Now he was considered a very wealthy man because of his royal patron and so they felt he should pay his debts, though Wagner thought that his creditors were a cabal of Jews and Jesuits who were out to ruin him. He did not seem to understand that he himself had spent vast amounts he did not have on curtains and furniture and perfumes and rugs. He went to moneylenders, they did not go to him. All the deliveries of luxury goods were noticed by the Bavarian servants in the house on Briennerstrasse in Munich where the king had allowed Wagner and his entourage to live rent-free.

Given all the creditors demanding payment on notes that Wagner had signed, and given the many enemies Wagner had earned in Munich, a public scandal was occurring. The Jesuits had a large presence in Munich, with some of the most important churches and schools under their control, so Wagner undoubtedly felt that the Jesuits (and the Jews of course) were determined to persecute him.

The king once again provided another allotment to Wagner to pay off his most pressing debts and a public scandal was avoided, but the press got wind of the affair and there was a scandal despite the king's generosity. In one case, the king's money to Wagner was presented to Cosima in sacks of coins — probably to embarrass her. Why was she, and not Wagner, picking up the money, the press wondered? And why did she arrive with a baby carriage? Why the baby was called Isolde, and exactly who was the father of this Isolde?

Gottfried Semper was employed to design a new opera house for Munich and the king liked Semper's design very much. But Bavarian politicians balked at the huge cost. Court ministers like Count Pfordten were lecturing the king about the immorality of his favorite composer. Ultimately the ministers of Munich gave Ludwig an ultimatum: He had to give up either his throne or Richard Wagner. On December 10, 1865, just six months after the *Tristan* premiere, Wagner was ordered by the king to leave Munich. Wagner looked at the south of France but ultimately settled in a villa in Luzern to be in Switzerland but still very near the King in Munich or his royal castles in southern Bavaria.

Tristan was a great love story but it ends with suicide, and that must have been how King Ludwig came to feel about love and his own sexuality. His death in 1886 was most probably a suicide (after he murdered his doctor), and the suicidal theme in Wagner's operas must have attracted him to the composer's operas in the first place. Both the king and the composer were in many ways suicidal personalities who often fantasized about committing suicide when they were frustrated. In 1886, when Ludwig was forced to abdicate, there were rumors that he had murdered one of his servants, and there is evidence that he murdered his physician when he tried to prevent the king from committing suicide.

The desire for death and the temptation to commit suicide was an enduring aspect of Wagner's own personality — as was the combination of love and death. This is a very paradoxical combination since love is usually combined with sex and new life, but in Wagner's *Tristan*, love and sex are combined with death. In so many of Wagner's letters suicide is mentioned, especially in his letters to his greatest friend, Franz Liszt.

The fear of death can be comforted with the desire to commit suicide, a fantasy of being able to control an event which we must all face even though we never know when it will happen. This layer of Wagner's personality was prominent in many of Wagner's works since suicide occurs so often in Wagnerian operas: Senta's suicide at the end of *Dutchman*, Tristan's at the end of *Tristan*, Brunnhilde's at the end of the Ring.

17

The Triangle in Triebschen: 1865–1870

"This little word, and." — *Tristan und Isolde*

Wagner's relationship with King Ludwig continued even though Wagner was now living in Switzerland. As the years went by, the king became less and less tactful about his male relationships.

Wagner had now become the most famous composer in Germany and people were talking about him and his music. He had been driven out of Munich, just as he had been driven out of Dresden, but he was now internationally famous thanks to the successful premiere of *Tristan*. One of the rumors circulating around Munich was that Wagner was the king's lover, and that the king's obsession with the composer was physical rather than artistic. A look at their correspondence would suggest this to the casual observer. Clearly there were many people both in the court and in Munich who wanted Wagner out of the country since they suspected Wagner of corrupting their naïve young king. What they did not seem to want to accept was that the king was gay with or without Wagner.

Wagner, both embarrassed and infuriated, began wandering around Switzerland — his usual place of refuge when he was in trouble, as after the Dresden uprising — but without his wife, his lover Cosima, or any followers, though he soon attracted people in his search for a safe place and a home. He found the Villa Triebschen and he thought this large villa, now a Wagner museum, would be a wonderful place to live. Wagner was now living on the shores of Lake Luzern and surrounded by high mountains — a truly beautiful spot. The king granted him money to be able to rent the villa. Minna refused to leave lovely Dresden, where her daughter lived. By this point Minna was a sick woman, suffering from heart disease, and would soon die. Wagner loved Cosima, Hans' wife, and their daughter Isolde, and Hans' children too, so he invited them all to move in with him, even Hans. Hans did not seem to object, but Cosima did. She wanted to marry the composer since she was producing the illegitimate children of Wagner with alarming regularity. But Hans was happy to live in Munich and conduct there while visiting his wife and children at Triebschen.

In Triebschen, Wagner's son Siegfried was born on June 6, 1869, (legally a bastard). Hans seemed to raise no object to the composer's relationship with his wife. Cosima was writing letters to the king maintaining the innocence of their relationship and insisting

An 1865 photograph of Wagner (Music Division, The New York Public Library for the Performing Arts, Astor, Lenox and Tilden Foundations).

that she was still Hans' wife even though she was not living with him anymore. While he was conducting in Munich, and making more and more enemies, she was living in Triebschen, Switzerland, with the composer, and they were having more children, and Hans apparently did not object to giving them his last name. Cosima wanted to divorce Hans and marry Wagner and dedicate her life to him — which she was doing already. She also liked acting like a mother and bossing around Wagner like a naughty child, which he both yearned for and hated.

Wagner was writing his next opera, *Meistersinger*. After composing so many operatic tragedies, Wagner yearned to write a comedy. After the birth of Siegfried, Wagner composed the famous "Siegfried Idyll" for Cosima's birthday and she awoke on her birthday,

17. The Triangle in Triebschen: 1865–1870

Christmas Day 1870, to the sounds of that wonderful composition with themes from the Ring cycle interwoven into the rest of the music. An orchestra played the music on the staircase leading to their bedroom. Wagner really was living like a prince now, thanks to the generosity of the king, Ludwig II.

Wagner once said that the only time he was ever really happy in his life were his eight years at Triebschen. He and Cosima often thought of those years as the happiest time of their lives together. They both liked living in the country rather than in a large city, and they both liked playing the lord and lady of the manor. The king paid their rent and gave them a regular allowances so they could hire servants and live like wealthy aristocrats, all of which they both wanted. But during many of those years in Switzerland they were living as adulterous lovers and had produced a bastard son. This situation did not seem to bother Wagner, but Cosima was getting anxious and wanted their relationship to be legal before the law. Wagner was happy with the situation, and so was Hans; he would visit them from Munich where he was still the main pianist to the king.

Wagner and Cosima were now living in sin openly according to the Catholic church, and Cosima was a Catholic. They already had one child together, Isolde, who had been born in Munich, and Cosima had two children with Hans — Daniela and Blandine. The very next year, in 1866, their second daughter, Eva, would be born in the house at Triebschen. Three years after that, their only son Siegfried was born there.

In 1866 Minna died in Dresden; her doctor and Wagner's friend, Dr. Pusinelli, notified Wagner via telegram. Wagner sent his condolences but did not attend the funeral — he said due to an illness. Now the impediment to marriage to Cosima was Hans, who did not want to grant Cosima a divorce. She sent him many begging letters, like the following: "You will never know how I have struggled and what I have suffered, and it is impossible for me to describe the consternation I felt when it became clear that the project of a life a trois was unrealizable."

Cosima's letter to Hans indicates that he was not so naïve but knew exactly what was going on between the three of them. He knew that her last three children, the ones with the Wagnerian names of Isolde, Eva, and Siegfried, were not his children. Finally, though, he agreed to a divorce so that Cosima could legally become Wagner's wife.

Meanwhile King Ludwig was feeling desperately lonely and missing his only friend. As the king wrote to Wagner:

> I have not given up hope: better times will come, everything will calm down here, the Friend will return and inspire me with his dear proximity, we will go on with our art-plans, the School will be founded, the festival theater will rise in its undreamed-of pride and splendour ... I hope, believe, love. No, no, what began so divinely shall not end thus. I will do as you desire, will govern firmly, like a King in the fullest sense of the word. But why must we remain apart, each living on for himself? I have a presentment that you will never find peace abroad.... I implore you, let a few months go quietly by, and many things will be quite different.... Then, I hope and believe, your return will have no political significance.

The king was desperate without his beloved friend Wagner near him, but for Wagner it must have come as a relief to be away from the court politics of Munich, with Cosima and the children, and living in the high Alps. It was during the first Triebschen years that Wagner and Cosima also met the brilliant young academic Friedrich Nietzsche, a professor at nearby Basel University. Wagner and Nietzsche became the best of friends—genius and disciple. Both were born in Saxony and both were attracted to each other. Nietzsche adored Wagner (at this point), considering him the greatest artist alive. Wagner enjoyed the adulation, and the stimulating conversation with Nietzsche, who became like a member of the family. For both Wagner and Nietzsche, 1869 became a crucial year: That year when he was only 24 years old, Nietzsche got his position as a professor at the University of Basel, Wagner had finally a son (Siegfried), and Wagner invited Nietzsche to visit him at Triebschen.

King Ludwig yearned to visit his court composer in Switzerland and, despite the political damage it did him, he repeatedly visited Wagner and Cosima there. He often came disguised to avoid the press, and Wagner was undoubtedly happy to see him despite the worsening situation in Bavaria. Without the king's support, Wagner would never have been able to live in such a lavish house and have such an aristocratic lifestyle. The king dreamed of permanently leaving Munich and living with the Wagners in Triebschen, and he even thought of abdicating and living with his beloved composer. But Wagner and Cosima urged him not to do this—since they undoubtedly realized that their money from the king would be jeopardized if the king were no longer the king. But the king snuck out of Bavaria several times to visit Wagner in Switzerland—once at a time when Bavaria was at war with France.

This was the period of the building of railroads in Europe, and Germany and Switzerland were particularly quick to do this. Thanks to the new railroads in Switzerland, the king could get to Wagner within five hours and the king soon bought his own railroad car. Nietzsche was teaching at the University of Basel, fifty miles from Luzern and within two hours with the new railroad. They were all amazed at the speed of travel thanks to the new railroads. They had all been used to traveling by stagecoach, especially Wagner since he was older. The railroads were soon used for military actions since they were much faster than horses.

By 1870 Bavaria was at war with France, dragged into that war by France and Prussia. Emperor Napoleon III had declared war on Prussia on July 16, 1870, and attacked the country—the biggest mistake of his career. By late 1870 the Iron Chancellor Count Bismarck and General Molke had conquered Paris and announced a unified Germany with the Prussian king, King Wilhelm I, as emperor of all of Germany. This occurred on January 18, 1871, in the hall of mirrors in Versailles. Some people were eager to join the new kingdom, but many in Bavaria wanted to maintain Bavarian independence and not be part of the new Reich. The king was in a very delicate situation since indirectly his own throne was threatened by the new Prussian Kaiser. But King Ludwig was receiving money from a secret fund from Berlin, so many of his grandiose castle plans were possible thanks to money coming from Bismarck. If this fact had been known at the time, that would have been enough to have the Bavarian parliament push Ludwig off the throne. The king was in a position of divided loyalties since he had financially become the pawn

17. The Triangle in Triebschen: 1865–1870

of Prussia. The Bavarian parliament had refused to support any more of his artistic plans for either Wagner or the new castles.

Wagner and Cosima wrote to the king from Switzerland urging him to maintain his throne, that he was the man that Germany needed, not the Prussian king or Bismarck. They told him he world be the savior of a new spiritual, artistic Germany which only King Ludwig II could inspire and so the king did not abdicate. But given the grim realities

Wagner and his son Siegfried (1880). Siegfried would eventually be in charge of the Bayreuth festival and a composer of operas (Music Division, The New York Public Library for the Performing Arts, Astor, Lenox and Tilden Foundations).

which were to follow after Wagner's death, Ludwig II might have been better off abdicating. By the time King Ludwig was pushed off the throne in 1886, he was virtually bankrupt and the Bavarian parliament no longer wished to support a king who did not want to go to any political meetings, did not want to live in Munich, and who appeared insane to many people in court.

One of the things that developed was a secret agreement with Bismarck that the Prussian government would support the Bavarian monarch's expenses provided that Bavaria became part of the unified German Reich. Ludwig II never much liked this, but he needed the money for his grandiose artistic plans. This secret "Guelph Fund" was a bribe that Bismarck sent every year to Ludwig II in order to have him support the German Kaiser, Wilhelm I, a Prussian king. In fact, at the treaty of Versailles in 1870 which ended the Franco-Prussian war, it was Ludwig II who wrote to William I, urging him to become the Kaiser in a new, unified Germany. At the time he wrote to his brother that he did not want to do this but felt forced to because of the political situation and his finances. Wagner wanted King Ludwig to become the new Kaiser, but the idea horrified Ludwig II.

But these eight years in Switzerland were a very productive time for Wagner for it was in Triebschen that he composed more of the Ring and all of *Meistersinger*— plus the texts, of course. He was also planning for an opera after the Ring, to be called *Parsifal*, and then an opera to be called *Die Sieger,* based on the life of Buddha, but this he did not live to complete.

Cosima's own attraction to the older Wagner undoubtedly reflected her love and need for her often-distant father. Cosima rarely saw her father when she was a child since he was usually touring as a pianist. He too was a musical genius, and she wanted to devote her life to helping another musical genius. When she married Hans von Bülow, she thought she had found that genius. But the marriage, though it produced two children, soon showed many stresses. Cosima was so unhappy with Hans that several times she wanted to kill herself to get out of the marriage. She even got into a suicide pact with one of Wagner's pupils, Karl Ritter, in her desperate unhappiness with Hans. Cosima asked Karl to drown her and then himself since they were both unhappily married, but then they decided not to go ahead with their plans.

Part of the problem was undoubtedly her growing conviction that Hans was not the musical genius she was looking for. He was not in the creative category of someone like Liszt or Wagner; Cosima dismissed Hans as a good pianist and sometimes competent conductor. He tried to write music himself, but Cosima always deep in her heart felt that Hans's musical compositions were third-rate stuff. Hans himself came to agree with her. So she left Hans while she was still married to him and moved into Wagner's house on the Briennerstrasse in Munich and became his mistress — much to the horror of her parents, especially his father Liszt. Cosima, a very liberated woman of her time, refused to let society and social traditions dictate to her. But she was the child of very liberated parents, Franz Liszt and Marie D'Agout, people who committed adultery and produced illegitimate children despite the consequences.

In 1870, Hans finally agreed to a divorce, and Wagner could finally marry his mistress,

17. The Triangle in Triebschen: 1865–1870

the mother of his three children. There was always some mystery about the parenthood of those children; it annoyed Wagner that he was often thought to be the grandfather of the children instead of the father. One of the children, Isolde, would eventually sue her mother over her paternity — a case she lost and Cosima won when she asserted that Isolde was the child of Hans von Bülow and so could not inherit Bayreuth; Cosima wanted the festival to go only to Siegfried. Wagner wrote the "Siegfried Idyll" soon after his son's birth and had it performed in Triebschen as a birthday gift to Cosima in 1870.

In 1869 Cosima began her famous diaries about her existence with Wagner and this has been a very useful source on their lives together. Cosima tries to be accurate and historical but of course her own point of view inevitably gets into the way of objectivity, assuming that is possible at all. She kept that important diary from her move into Triebschen until Wagner's death in Venice in 1883. They certainly indicated a woman who had a masochistic streak in her and was willing to do anything to please her husband Wagner, whom she refers to as the master. This was also the period when the Franco-Prussia war began, and Wagner wrote "Eine Kapitulation," enjoying the defeat of France and hoping for a Germany which was finally unified. Wagner's nasty celebration of the defeat of France and the victory of a united Germany offended many, but this is understandable given his own victimization by France since his birth in Leipzig.

Cosima must have been a very busy woman since she had to raise five children in addition to all her other duties in the house in Triebschen. Now in Switzerland she became Wagner's official secretary, handling much of his correspondence and even advising him on his compositions and legal issues connected with the stagings of his operas. Now Wagner's operas were being staged frequently in Germany and some neighboring countries. During Wagner's years in Triebschen, the king also asked Wagner to write for him the story of the composer's life since he was interested in anything about Wagner. To satisfy the king, Wagner dictated his memoirs to Cosima, and this project eventually became *Mein Leben,* Wagner's autobiography from his birth until the year 1864. This book was published years after Wagner's death and remains one of the most interesting autobiographies in the history of music, and a fascinating look at how Wagner saw the development of his own life. Cosima was responsible for most of this project. Wagner's autobiography ends with the following passage describing his rescue by King Ludwig II:

> The next day I received Herr Pfeistermeister, the Cabinet Secretary of His Majesty the King of Bavaria, in my room. He began by expressing his great pleasure at having found me here thanks to some fortuitous directions, after having hunted for me in vain in Vienna and finally even in Mariafeld on Lake Zurich. He brought me a note from the young King of Bavaria, together with a portrait and a ring as a present. In words which, though few, penetrated to the core of my being, the young monarch avowed his great admiration for my art and his firm resolve to keep me at his side as a friend forever, to spare me any malignant strokes of fate. At the same time, Herr Pfeistermeister notified me that he had instructions to conduct me to the King at once, and asked for my permission to announce to his master by telegram that I would be there the following day.... On the same day I had received the most urgent warnings from Vienna not to return there. But my life was to have no more of such alarms. The dangerous path on which destiny now beckoned me to the highest goals would not be free of

worries and troubles of a kind hitherto unknown to me; but under the protection of my exalted friend the meanest cares of subsistence were never to touch me again.

But Wagner's autobiography would continue in the diaries of Cosima, and her diaries begin with her life in Triebschen and end with the death of her husband in Venice in 1883. Both Wagner's autobiography and Cosima's diaries would constitute one of the most remarkable memoirs in the history of music. Cosima was responsible for both these documents.

During his years at Triebschen, Wagner also met a young musician called Leopold Damrosch. He visited Wagner several times in Switzerland and was already a Wagner fan and a serious musician. Ultimately Damrosch did what Wagner had sometimes dreamed of doing: He emigrated to America and became a professional musician there. He conducted the premieres of most of Wagner's operas at the Metropolitan Opera in New York in the earliest years of that company, the last twenty years of the 19th century.

Another layer of Wagner's personality, and probably the most basic of those many layers, was his dedication to his art. More than anything else he wanted to create wonderful music dramas, and he did create them despite the obstacles. He agreed with Schiller that drama remained the most powerful and important of the arts, and that it could transform a society. Wagner's ten great operas—from *Dutchman* to *Parsifal*—have become part of the standard repertory of all the major opera houses in the world. All of these elements of Wagner's personality grew and changed as he was living happily in sin with Cosima and their children in lovely Switzerland. He loved his wife and children and he composed some of the happiest music ever written for his only comedy, *Meistersinger*.

When Nietzsche first started visiting Wagner and Cosima at Triebschen, he was a young professor at the University of Basel. They had wonderful discussions about Schopenhauer and other philosophers and current events. Nietzsche learned so much from Wagner: about the death of God, cynicism towards all organized religions, the theory of the superman, and differences between Dionysian and Apollonian art. Wagner's fascination with ancient Greek tragedy soon entered Nietzsche's thinking as well. Nietzsche turned many of Wagner's ideas into wonderful essays and they became his own philosophy. Nietzsche was especially interested in Wagner's most recently

A caricature of Wagner with the seeds of a linden tree (André Gill, Paris, 1869).

17. The Triangle in Triebschen: 1865–1870

staged opera, *Tristan und Isolde*, and wrote about several of Wagner's operas in his essays. Wagner and Nietzsche were becoming the two most important writers and thinkers alive during the middle and end of the 19th century, and they certainly learned from each other.

Wagner composed and wrote despite the wars and traumas going on around him — he felt very safe in Triebschen. He liked living in sin with Cosima, but when they were finally able to marry, he liked being married to her too — for a while. Meanwhile he was talking about staging his Ring cycle and finishing up *Parsifal*, plus he had a new project in mind: *The Victors*. He was a busy man.

18

Meistersinger Premiere in Munich: 1868–1871

Wagner's *Die Meistersinger von Nürnberg* became the greatest comedy in the history of German opera. Since he was known for tragic opera, trying to write a comic opera of enormous scope was a new venture for him, and he was determined to do it. His biggest fan King Ludwig was very curious to hear excerpts from it, so he visited Wagner in Triebschen despite the fact that a war throughout Europe was looming.

Once King Ludwig's engagement to his cousin Sophie was publicly announced and then rescinded, he seemed to become more unstable. He did not even want to go to the opera or the theater since people were always staring at him. House lights were kept on during performances before Wagner changed all that with the opening of his new theater at Bayreuth. That was the first theater to close the house lights so all the audience could see was the stage — something Wagner wanted the audience to do. And modern inventions like electricity were making this all possible now. But Bayreuth was lit by gas until much later in the 19th century. Ludwig was especially eager to see the whole Ring cycle staged and especially *Meistersinger* now that Wagner was steadily working on it in Switzerland. Increasingly, the king wanted Wagnerian performances just for him — with only a few friends in the audience — so he did not have to feel everyone in the audience staring at him.

Wagner interrupted the composition of the Ring yet again to compose *Meistersinger*, which had its premiere in Munich on June 21, 1868. There were many connections between Wagner's opera and Shakespeare's *A Midsummer Night's Dream*; both works were comedies involving love stories and happy endings. Despite the fact that he was persona non grata in Munich, Wagner was allowed to direct and work to stage this new opera there.

The premiere of *Meistersinger* was more successful than the premiere of *Tristan* because that opera was much more difficult and revolutionary. *Meistersinger* seemed more like a normal operatic comedy with a love story, a happy ending, and some wonderful tunes — something most opera goers want to hear. This premiere became the high point of the relationship between King Ludwig and Wagner and seemed to justify the king's patronage of the composer. Both men were at the premiere and both received standing ovations. The opera also involved the attraction of a young woman, Eva, to an older man, Hans Sachs. Wagner quotes from his own music in *Tristan* when Hans Sachs says that Eva must

18. Meistersinger *Premiere in Munich: 1870–1871*

marry a man of her own age, Walter von Stolzing. But at the time, of course, Wagner himself was living with the much younger Cosima. The historical Hans Sachs in Nuremberg himself married a much younger woman after the death of his first wife. Clearly some of the themes in this new opera reflected aspects of Wagner's own life.

Wagner may be persona non grata in Munich, but his works could still be performed at its royal opera house. The composer was allowed to visit the capital and supervise rehearsals so Wagner began to work on the premiere of *Meistersinger*. He again had insisted that Hans von Bülow conduct. Angelo Quaglio designed the sets and was given a large budget for this premiere. Wagner moved to Munich for a time to hear singers and cast the opera. The most difficult role was clearly Walter von Stolzing, the tenor, though this part was easier than Tristan. Wagner had learned from all the difficulties of casting Tristan to be less demanding of his Heldentenors.

An 1870 drawing of Wagner by Franz von Lenbach (Music Division, The New York Public Library for the Performing Arts, Astor, Lenox and Tilden Foundations).

He often thought that Ludwig Schnorr von Carolsfeld would have been perfect for the role of Walter, but he was dead and his poor wife Mathilde was slowly becoming insane. Wagner was also coaching Hans von Bülow on conducting this comic score and sleeping with Han's wife Corinna.

The Munich Royal Opera provided Wagner with a lovely production, many rehearsals, and a wonderful cast of singers. Some of the singers had performed at the Munich premiere of *Tristan*, and some members of the orchestra were Wagner fans, though some hated his music. Franz Betz became Wagner's Hans Sachs; he had been his Kurvenal in the *Tristan* premiere three years earlier. Mathilde Mallinger sang Eva with great success and Frau Sophie Dietz sang Magdalena to great acclaim. Schlosser sang David and Gustav Hoelzel became the original Beckmesser. As for the tenor role of Walter von Stolzing, Franz Nachbaur sang it well, though he was not Wagner's first choice. The Munich opera had provided Wagner with an excellent cast for this premiere and the public responded very favorably.

Wagner's opera is set in German Renaissance Nuremberg, reflecting the English Renaissance of Shakespeare. Wagner's opera remains his least mythic and most realistic work. There were multiple performances of the opera despite the summer heat, and the king's patronage seemed to be finally justified in a popular success. Most of the reviews in the Munich papers were positive, and other German cities like Vienna and Berlin wanted to stage the work after its success in Munich. Finally, Wagner was becoming a popular success all over Germany and more and more people there wanted to hear the music of the future.

One of the fascinating things about this greatest of comedies in the history of German opera is that it tries to reconcile the divisions between Christians and Jews in a very subtle way. If you look at the names in the opera, the heroine is called Eva, the primordial mother in the Old Testament, and she marries Walter von Stolzing, St. Walter being one of the saints of the new religion, Christianity. It is interesting as well that when Walter sings the Prize Song and wins the vocal contests in the final act, he is presented with the medal of King David, another one of the heroes of the Jewish Old Testament. What Wagner seems to be suggesting here is the union of Christian and Jew, though all the characters are really Christians. Wagner seems to be suggesting that intermarriage will solve the racial and religious problems in Germany, and the ending of the opera points to a glorious new future without any religion but only love among people. The opera ends with the inclusion of all religions, suggesting a united Germany. The opera, after all, premiered three years before the start of Germany's position as a unified country, thanks to the Hohenzollerns and to Count Bismarck, and the ideals of that period undoubtedly influenced Wagner during the writing of *Meistersinger*. While he would eventually become

"Wagner and Hanslick." Wagner parodied the pedantic critic Eduard Hanslick in the opera *Meistersinger* (Music Division, The New York Public Library for the Performing Arts, Astor, Lenox and Tilden Foundations).

18. Meistersinger *Premiere in Munich: 1870–1871*

disgusted with a unified and imperial Germany, the democratic ideals of Bismarck were reflected in the opera.

Modern Germany, finally a democracy, insures separation of state and religion, and religious freedom for all peoples. And Hans Sachs' final monologue in the last act of the opera is an attack on German imperialism. Hans Sachs insists that the greatness of Germany lies not in its conquests but in its art — "heilige Deutsche Kunst," as he says, holy German art. Wagner's comedy ends with a utopic vision of love and a community united through art.

Meistersinger was set in Nuremberg during the German Renaissance when the craft guilds were central to the power structure in the town; this seems like a very middle class opera, with only one aristocrat, Walter, who has a lot to learn. The opera has some similarity to *Tannhäuser* since both have singing contests, though that opera ends in tragedy while *Meistersinger* ends in comedy. During a time when Germany was being reunified by the Prussian state under Prince Bismarck and under the banner of the Hohenzollern royal family — Wilhelm I was crowned in Paris in 1871 — Wagner's new opera was glorifying German art, though not the German state. It is German art that is holy, says Hans Sachs, and not any German state. Wagner's anti-nationalistic but chauvinistic opera has Hans Sachs clarify its meaning: Sachs is a popular German-Jewish name after all, and it is the historical name of the Renaissance poet and cobbler in Nuremberg with people like Albrecht Durer and Tilman Riemanschneider all working in Germany, specifically Nuremberg, at the time. The glorification of so much significant art coming from one town certainly celebrates both the time and a unified German nation at the end of the 19th century.

Some critics have argued that Beckmesser is based on the Viennese critic Eduard Hanslick and that he is supposed to be a Jew in the opera. But he is never identified as a Jew, and Hanslick is clearly a German name, and the critic was not Jewish. No one in the opera calls this character a Jew — he is clearly a part of the Christian community in Nuremberg. Beckmesser makes a telling contrast with another great classic of the 19th century, Charles Dickens's novel *Oliver Twist*. In its original edition, the villain Fagin is called "Fagin the Jew" and Dickens describes him as a Jew who makes his living by corrupting homeless Christian boys and trains them to be pickpockets. Fagin the Jew turns poor little Oliver Twist into a pickpocket and makes a good living off him. During the English Renaissance, Shakespeare's *Merchant of Venice* presented as its villain Shylock the Jew, who demands his pound of flesh when his debt to Antonio is due. Both Fagin and Shylock are demonic but interesting uses of the Jew as villain. Wagner certainly never did anything like this, despite the fact that Wagner was anti–Semitic. Life clearly is complicated since within ten years of this premiere, Wagner became famous for developing a circle of Jewish fans and Jewish followers at his home in Bayreuth.

Wagner and Cosima lied to the king to get more and more money out of him, but they delivered the goods as well. They provided the king with a Wagnerian premiere about every five years, and they were all major works; the greatest works Wagner was to compose were under the patronage of the Bavarian monarch. King Ludwig enable Wagner to stage *Tristan*, compose and stage *Meistersinger*, finish and stage the Ring, and start the

Bayreuth Festival in 1876 for the premiere of the Ring (though the first two operas were first staged in Munich, to Wagner's fury), and compose and stage *Parsifal*, Wagner's final work for the stage. Would Wagner have created those compositions anyway? It is difficult to say because he was a driven man and he could always work with rarely a pause in his productivity, but certainly the king's patronage enabled him to be extremely productive and change the genre of opera forever. The Bayreuth Festival still stages new productions of Wagner's works over a hundred years after the death of the composer and despite all the horrendous upheavals in the history of Germany since the composer's death in 1883. Despite pauses during World War I and World War II, the festival is still going strong and tickets have become very hard to get.

These years were also years of political turmoil, especially in Germany. Just two years after the premiere of *Meistersinger,* the Franco-Prussian war of 1870 began, and it ended with the defeat of France and the unification of Germany — the reuninification, one should say, because since the fall of the Holy Roman Empire and Charlemagne, Germany had been a series of independent city states like Prussia, Bavaria, Thuringia, etc. But in 1870 France declared war on Prussia and was defeated within a year; in the next year, 1871, Bismarck made his monarch, King Wilhelm I, emperor of all of Germany. After the defeat of France in 1871, the Prussians occupied Paris and in the halls of mirrors in Versailles, the new German kingdom was declared with the Hohenzollern Wilhelm I declared the new Kaiser. It was King Ludwig II who wrote a letter asking Wilhelm to be Kaiser of the new, united Germany. Several areas of Germany were allowed to keep their own king and had special and separate powers, and Bavaria and its king were part of this arrangement. But increasingly Bismarck was subsidizing Ludwig II of Bavaria with a million marks a year, which served to force Bavaria into a unified Germany under Wilhelm I. Wagner was originally a strong supporter of German unification but soon disliked what he saw of the new unified German state. He especially got to hate Otto von Bismarck, the new prime minister. Wagner wanted a German state that would support the arts, especially his art, but that German state refused to give Wagner and his projects, like the creation of the Bayreuth festival, any money.

Originally Wagner was a big fan of the new Germany and the new Kaiser but he quickly became disaffected and realized that King Ludwig II was his only generous patron. Wagner wrote a nasty parody celebrating the defeat of the French and Emperor Napoleon III, "Eine Kapitulation," and Wagner hoped that the new German emperor would be a patron of the arts for all German artists. The German Kaiser, when they met, did not offer Wagner any money, not even a pfennig. Only Ludwig II gave him the large amounts of money he requested for both his lavish lifestyle and his artistic ambitions. Wagner certainly created a unique institution when he created his festival at Bayreuth for here he wished to stage all of his own mature works and provide a meeting place for artists from all over the world. The festival has been a Mecca for Wagner fans ever since. Wagner's revolutionary festival and revolutionary new theater there made German art an international attraction for the new Germany, but that state refused to support the Bayreuth festival.

18. Meistersinger *Premiere in Munich: 1870–1871*

But Wagner remained very interested in the movement for German unification and wrote articles on it, and he even wrote the Kaisermarsch for the new Kaiser in the hope of ingratiating himself. It did not work since the new Kaiser always remained suspicious of Wagner and was not a big fan of his operas either. But Wagner always had King Ludwig II in his corner — not the case with the new German Kaiser.

The staging of the premiere of *Meistersinger* was complicated by the fact that the opera house was in Munich but Wagner was living in Triebschen. Wagner moved to the Bavarian capital a month before the premiere of the opera to supervise the staging, and he wrote letters to the management of the theater. The scenic designers also came to Triebschen with sketches of sets and costumes so that Wagner was consulted on every aspect of the production, including the singers chosen to sing the main roles. Angelo Quaglio again designed the premiere production; it was a hit and got a standing ovation at its premiere and got many performances. Wagner could have stayed in Triebschen, where he said on many occasions how happy he was, and continued to have his operas staged in Munich. With the new railroads Wagner could be in Munich within half a day. Wagner had a wonderful situation in Triebschen with the mountains of Switzerland all around him, but something drove him to leave his latest refuge. In the meantime, he was visiting Munich and seeing the king there. While the king would have preferred that Wagner live in Munich, he lived nearby in Switzerland so the current situation was not impossible.

King Ludwig II must have known the truth about the relationship of Wagner and Cosima by now, but now that they were legally married, they could stop all the lying that they had been doing. The king must have had few illusions left about them at this point. On some level, the king came to hate Cosima since she wrote so many lying letters to the king, asserting the innocence of her relationship to Wagner and her loyalty to Hans. The king undoubtedly did not want to see her, but he remained obsessed with his favorite composer and he was eager to see the Ring cycle.

But in the meantime good things were happening in Munich as well. Certainly two high points were the premieres of two of Wagner's greatest operas in Munich, *Tristan* and *Meistersinger*. *Meistersinger* was especially a happy event because the performance was a popular success for both Wagner and the king. This opera, arguably the greatest operatic comedy in German opera, had a very successful premiere at Munich's main opera house, then called the Hoftheater but now called the Bavarian National Theater. The opera was a glorification of "heilige Deusche Kunst"— or holy German art. The opera was also a glorification of Wagner's main source for his libretto, Shakespeare's *A Midsummer Night's Dream*. There are many similarities in these two works, and Wagner was a lover of Shakespeare for his entire life. His second opera was *Das Liebesverbot*, or *The Ban on Love*, was based on Shakespeare's *Measure for Measure*, and his greatest comedy, *Meistersinger*, was based on Shakespeare. Wagner sometimes said that he was trying to combine Beethoven with Shakespeare, and this was the recurrent motif of his operatic career as a composer.

What a life Wagner had! He moved from the extremes of poverty to wealth, moved all over Europe, staying at the best hotels and eating in the best restaurants, and meeting some of the most famous people at the time, including artists and monarchs. When he met Queen Victoria and Prince Albert, they told him they liked his music despite what the music critics said in London.

With the very successful premiere of *Meistersinger* in Munich, the relationship between king and artist was at its high point. Both were in the same box at the royal opera house in Munich, now called the Bayerische Statsoper (Bavarian State Opera). They had both accomplished so much in terms of Wagner's artistic success, which cast a good light on both artist and king. But there were other premieres in the future: the Ring cycle and *Parsifal*.

Towards the end of Wagner's years in Triebschen he developed another idea — the Bayreuth Festival. He came to feel that the opera houses in Europe were totally incapable of staging his Ring cycle. He needed a new theater to stage its premiere, a new opera house that would revolutionize the opera houses in Europe. His works were unique and could not be staged in just any ordinary theater, which reflected some narcissism. Wagner had a vision of a summer opera festival in the little town of Bayreuth, in Franconia — a part of Bavaria to the north of Munich. Bayreuth was also close to Berlin, the new capital, and Dresden and Leipzig. Bayreuth was very close to Nuremberg, the site of his comedy *Meistersinger*. With Germany united in 1871, this was the time for a German festival connecting the north of Germany with its southern province, Bavaria.

Wagner's obsession with love, sexuality, and women became arguably the most recurrent theme in his operas. Redemption through woman became a dominant theme. *Meistersinger* focuses on three men (Walter, Beckmesser, and Hans Sachs) who love the primordial woman, Eva. In the Western tradition of theater, comedies end in marriage — with the belief that marriage is a happy ending and that the couple will live happily ever after as a result of this marriage. Redemption through the love of a woman was a recurrent theme in Wagner's operas, and Wagner had finally produced a comedy on this theme. Here Wagner was probably influenced by Goethe's *Faust*, whose final line is "das ewig weibliche zieht uns hinab" (the eternal feminine leads us on). Men are obsessed with the search for the female — perhaps a return to mother?

It surely seems incredible that within five years Wagner could produce the great operatic tragedy *Tristan und Isolde* and the great operatic comedy *Meistersinger von Nürnberg*. These two operas are arguably the two greatest operas in German opera, and in two separate genres, comedy and tragedy. Wagner's range impressed even the people who hated his music.

19

Hans, Cosima and King Ludwig: 1870–1874

"My honor is at stake!" — Cosima

Wagner seemed to be subconsciously attracted to triangular attachments — as in his obsession with Mathilde Wesendonck and other husband Otto. Wagner now was in love with Cosima von Bülow, born Liszt, but he was also in a way in love with her husband Hans. Hans has been Liszt's piano student and became Wagner's conducting student — and both Hans and Cosima were young enough to be his children. But Wagner also loved Hans and wanted him to be his conductor and conduct his premieres, so clearly he trusted all his scores to Hans, an ardent Wagnerian who felt that Wagner was the greatest composer in the world. Thanks to Wagner, Hans moved from being a promising piano student to a world-famous conductor. And as Cosima began to fall in love with Wagner, she also revealed the unhappiness of her marriage to Hans, despite the fact that she already had two children with him. Wagner seemed to love them both and wanted this adulterous affair to continue as it was, with both of them lying. Hans seemed to want it to continue too. Were they all in bed with each other? There were rumors to that effect in Munich, but the documents that survived seem to indicate that Cosima loved only Wagner at this point and not Hans any longer. She was so unhappy in her marriage to Hans that at one point she formed a suicide pact with Karl Ritter, who was also very unhappily married. They planned to meet on the shore of a lake and drown together. Ultimately of course, this did not happen. But one of the things that bound Wagner to Cosima is that they were both in some ways suicidal personalities. Friends of theirs commented that there was a wild streak to both of them. Both also liked triangular relationships of some kind.

Why was Cosima unfaithful to her husband Hans von Bülow within five years of their marriage? In her diaries, Cosima frequently lamented her unhappy marriage to Hans, and she frequently asked her children to forgive them. The five children she had by the two men must have been often confused by who their father was and why there were so many articles in the newspapers about the family. The family movements from Berlin to Munich to Switzerland and the sudden appearances of either Wagner or Hans von Bülow must have terribly scared the five children. Several of those children had very unhappy marriages in their adult years since they were clearly adversely affected by the marital chaos around them.

Cosima was raised in Paris and spoke better French than German for much of her life. When she married Hans, she thought she was marrying another great genius on a par with her father, and in fact a pupil of her father, but Hans turned out to be an excellent pianist and conductor but not much of a composer. There were probably other difficulties in the marriage — perhaps sexual ones. Cosima soon felt that her marriage was a mismatch and that she was doomed to be unhappy for the rest of her life with Hans. Then she met a real musical genius and great composer, Wagner. On some level she wanted to sacrifice her life to the support of a musical genius, as in her worshipful attitude to her father Franz Liszt. On another level, Hans was a musical genius too — after all, he became one of the greatest pianists and conductors of his time. Liszt was in many ways cruel to her and her brother Daniel and sister Blandine. Liszt kept her in Paris with her cruel governess, and Cosima was forbidden to see her mother Marie D'Agoult, who was also living in Paris. Liszt was not a very good father to his children, all illegitimate and all neglected. Cosima's relationship with Wagner presented her with both a lover and a father figure, something she longed for.

When Cosima met Wagner, he was unhappily married to Minna, and in fact they were no longer living together. Since Hans took Cosima to visit the Wagners in Switzerland for their honeymoon, Cosima got to see how unhappy Wagner's marriage was. She saw the horrible arguments between Wagner and Minna and must have realized that this was another classic mismatch, like her own marriage eventually became. At that point in his life, Wagner was living outside Zurich with Minna in Asyl, on the Wesendonck property near their mansion. Meanwhile, Hans and Cosima were on their honeymoon and visiting Wagner at Asyl.

Wagner became convinced that the whole Ring cycle should have its premiere in a special new opera house constructed just for this occasion. He did not want any of the four Ring operas to be staged in Munich, despite the fact that the king now owned the copyright to the whole Ring cycle. King Ludwig II had supported Wagner throughout his eight years in Switzerland, and Wagner had agreed to grant him the copyright on all his subsequent operas. When Wagner came to Munich, he repeatedly tried to visit King Ludwig, but the king was so angry that he refused to see him. The king wanted those two operas staged in Munich, and he did not want to see Wagner or hear any more demands from him. At this point, the king saw Wagner and Cosima as narcissistic "theater people" and wanted to avoid them. This reaction generated in Wagner and his new wife a fear that their money from the king would cease.

Now that Wagner was legally married to Cosima, he became tired of dealing with the neurotic Hans von Bülow and unhappy with his conducting. Wagner had heard the conducting of a new young musician, Hans Richter, and began to think of him as the man who should be conducting the premiere of his Ring cycle. Wagner certainly helped many promising young conductors, and now that he had made Hans von Bülow internationally famous, he thought that he could do the same thing for Richter. Wagner was also impressed with the young Hungarian conductor Anton Seidl and felt that he too could be trained to conduct the Ring cycle and help with the musical preparation by coaching some of the singers.

19. Hans, Cosima and King Ludwig: 1870–1874

The king insisted on Munich for the premiere and was becoming more annoyed with his favorite composer. While he continued to love Wagner's operas and also to love the man, he felt that Wagner was too demanding and often too duplicitous. Ultimately the king and Wagner "met halfway" in terms of the Ring. The first two operas, *Das Rheingold* and *Die Walküre*, were staged in Munich while the last two, *Siegfried* and *Götterdämmerung*, were first staged in Wagner's new theater in Bayreuth.

Das Rheingold premiered on September 22, 1869, in Munich under the baton of Franz Wüllmer; the *Die Walküre* premiere, also in Munich, was on June 26, 1870, with the same conductor. Richter conducted the Bayreuth premiere of the entire Ring in 1876. The king became annoyed at the first two premieres because Wagner tried to sabotage them by not assisting much in these performances and writing nasty letters to the conductor Wüllmer since he felt he was incompetent. The king felt that this conductor did a fine job with the first half of the Ring cycle. The king also wrote letters to Wagner urging him to be more supportive of these performances in Munich. During these years, the king developed a theory of "theater people" and the difficulties of dealing with these narcissists, and he began to see Wagner as part of this hostile tribe. But the king stuck to his guns and the first half of the Ring cycle first appeared in his capital, Munich, and his own opera house, the Hofoper. He had paid the composer for these operas and wanted to see them as soon as they were completed, and he wanted to see them in his own capital, Munich.

Probe in Bayreuth (Richard Wagner), a drawing of Wagner at rehearsal, by Adolph von Menzel, ca. 1875 (Music Division, The New York Public Library for the Performing Arts, Astor, Lenox and Tilden Foundations).

While Wagner raged at these premieres and urged his friends not to attend them, the king was very pleased and many in the audience enjoyed the operas as well. A few days before the premiere of *Rheingold*, Wüllmer got the following letter from Wagner:

> Hands off my score! This is my advice to you; if not, the devil with you. Confine your activities to conducting singing clubs.

But the conductor followed his orders from the king and the premiere went well, despite the generally negative reviews from the press. Some of Wagner's most ardent fans were there and were pleased with the results. The cast received a good round of applause in Munich. August Kindermann was Wotan, Sophie Strehle sang Fricka, Heinrich Vogl sang Loge, and Seehofer was Erda. The performance of *Rheingold* was repeated several times and all the performances were sold out. The king was very pleased with the results.

The 1870 premiere of *Die Walküre* was much more successful than the premiere of *Rheingold*. This second opera even got a few good reviews from the local press. Wüllmer conducted yet again and got a very loud ovation. The king promoted him to a higher position in the royal opera to reward the conductor. Vogl sang Siegmund this time and his wife sang Sieglinde; Kindermann sang Wotan again, and Sophie Stehle was the Brunnhilde. There were also several performances of first *Rheingold* and then *Walküre* so that the king and the Munich audience would hear the first half of the Ring cycle in the correct order.

Wagner had foolishly reissued his "Judaism in Music" under his own name—not under a pseudonym—even though Cosima, the king, and others had urged him not to do so. Wagner's friends had often told him he was the best opera composer in the world yet he kept getting negative, nasty reviews in the French and German press. Wagner said that these negative reviews were a result of a Jewish plot against him. But if Wagner did not write and reissue his anti-Semitic essay, he would not have such a large groups of Jewish enemies in the press. Wagner never seemed to see the connection here between his own hateful views and the enemies he had earned.

Writing about the Ring premieres in Munich, Ernest Newman wrote:

> Wagner did all he could to dissuade his personal friends from going to Munich, and in some cases succeeded. But Liszt was there, and the two Mendes and Mme. Mouchanoff. The *Valkyrie* made a great impression; even the journalists most hostile to Wagner had to admit that it was a work of "gigantic talent," as the Munich *Neueste Nachrichten* handsomely described it. Wagner was thus proved to be completely wrong in his forecast that the production would damage irreparably the prospects of the Ring as a whole: on the contrary, it whetted the public appetite for the complete work. Once more one has the feeling that there had not been very much wrong with the Rhinegold production of 1869 except with regard to some of the machinery; and, as has been pointed out ... some of the scenic problems of the work have never really been solved from that day to this.

Catholic Bavaria had a constitutional monarchy, not an absolute one, and most of the citizens would not countenance more public sexual scandal in their royal family, the Wittelsbachs. The Catholic political party in Bavaria had significant power, and they resented Bavarian money going to Protestants like the Wagners and wanted funding for the completion of more proposed churches in Munich and elsewhere in Bavaria. (Munich already had some gorgeous baroque and rococo churches like St. Michael Church, the Theatiner Church, and the Asam Brothers' Church.)

The Bavarian press pointed out that Wagner had the lifestyle of a prince and that the king and their funds paid for all this luxury. Their tax money was going to support a very extravagant man, who was not even a Bavarian. The Bavarian newspapers were

19. Hans, Cosima and King Ludwig: 1870–1874

themselves making a lot of money out of the Wagner situation. Some Bavarians defended the Saxon composer but others got to hate him.

Wagner was happy to generate all this publicity for himself and his latest opera. He realized that all this newspaper coverage was selling tickets. His performances were selling out, as he liked to point out to his friends, despite the negative newspaper reviews.

Wagner seemed to have the ability to have people fall in love with him, people of both sexes, including his king. Wagner also had the ability to develop a group of fans who would go anywhere to hear a performance, and this is still the case. There are a group of Ring-heads who will go anywhere to hear a Ring cycle, and these fans appeared as soon as the Ring was staged in Munich or Bayreuth.

But during the horrible sexual scandal and political conflicts with the king and the government in Bavaria, Wagner was able to continue to work. He wrote more of the music of the Ring and was desperately trying to complete the Ring cycle now that the first half had been staged, though not under his supervision; in fact, the success of the first half of the cycle encouraged him to finish the last two operas and stage them. Wagner was one of the most productive composers in the history of the art form, and he continued his heavy burden of work despite his domestic affairs, public scandals, and growing old age.

France declared war on Prussia on July 19, 1870, a month after the *Walküre* premiere in Munich. Soon after the declaration of war, the other German states joined with Prussia in this war, as they were forced to do because of mutual alliances among them. So a unified group of German states was being attacked by France, and under Prussian direction they counter-attacked. By January of 1871 France was defeated, Paris surrounded, and the Germans occupied the palace of Versailles. In the hall of mirrors there, a unified Germany was finally declared and established. King Ludwig II wrote a letter urging the Prussian king to become Kaiser of the unified Germany to the general enthusiasm of most of the German people. Especially in Bavaria there was a fear of Prussia, and many Bavarians wondered why their king was offering the imperial crown to Wilhelm I of Prussia.

Wagner and Cosima wanted their patron, King Ludwig II, to be the new imperial Kaiser of the new, united Germany. But King Ludwig was absolutely not interested in this. He would rather go to the theater and opera, and he tired of being king of Bavaria. If ever there was a monarch who should not have been a king, it was Ludwig. But Wagner did approve of the movement toward a unified Germany, now finally achieved.

During his final years at Triebschen in Luzerne, Wagner received a very weird letter one day from a Jew named Josef Rubinstein. Ernest Newman tells the story very well:

[Rubinstein] had introduced himself to Wagner in February 1872 in a letter from Kharkov in which he lamented the disabilities and dangers to which his race was subject in the Germany of that epoch. He had not only contemplated suicide but attempted it, he said. So he had decided to write to Wagner, who perhaps could help him, though not, he hoped, out of simple pity, not out of the mere desire to save him from suicide.

"Could I not be useful to you in connection with the production of your *Nibelungen*? I think I comprehend the work, even if not entirely. So I hope for help from you, help I urgently need. My parents are rich and would supply me with means to go to you."

Richard Wagner

>Whereupon Wagner had invited him to Triebschen, treated him kindly, and afterwards taken him with him to Bayreuth, which he made his home, off and on, until Wagner's death.

Wagner was so moved by the letter and its statement of personal suffering that he wrote back and invited Rubinstein for a meeting. Wagner was even more moved by a man who was Jewish, homosexual, and suffering. You would think this would be the kind of person Wagner would avoid and ask to leave, but instead Wagner offered his a job and a home — in his own house, Triebschen. Rubinstein was Wagner's personal employee and friend for the rest of Wagner's life. Even when Wagner moved to Bayreuth, Rubinstein was invited to continue living with the Wagners in their home and continue his employment. When Wagner went to Italy in the winter, Rubinstein was considered part of the family and invited to join them. Wagner became a kind of loving father-figure. When Wagner died, Rubinstein was so distraught he returned to Triebschen, where he first met Wagner, and there committed suicide. He is now buried in the Jewish cemetery in Bayreuth, in the town where Wagner was buried. Rubinstein repeatedly wrote to his parents about Wagner's kindness and generosity to him and his lack of feelings of racism of any sort.

While Cosima sometimes got annoyed with Rubinstein's sometimes difficult personality, she followed Wagner's orders and treated him with kindness as a member of the family. This indicates that Wagner was capable of great acts of kindness. As one of his biographers said, Wagner was anti–Semitic in theory but never in practice. He furthered the careers of many Jewish friends and musicians whenever he could — people like Joseph Rubinstein and Hermann Levi. Wagner was a loving friend to many gay men from his days in Paris during his La Boheme existence with a group of starving German artists. He liked gay men at a time when they were being jailed in London and Berlin.

Wagner was a mixture of the good and the bad, the desirable and the undesirable — like the rest of us only more so since he was also a musical genius of the first order. His operas had a revolutionary effect on the theater and opera of his times and well beyond that. His influence on opera and the other arts was immense and would continue well into the new century and even into our own time. Now in the 21st century, we are living in a Wagner Renaissance when his operas are being more performed than ever before. Wagner was demanding and sometimes sadistic but he was also a loving friend to many people, often Jewish people who defended him throughout their lives.

Now Josef Rubinstein was part of a group of young men that Wagner called the "Nibelungen Chancellery." They were helping him complete his masterpiece, the Ring cycle. After the successes in the Munich premieres of his first two Ring operas, Wagner became more determined to finish the Ring and stage it before he died. He was in his late fifties now, and he was wondering if he had enough time left.

20

The Idea of Bayreuth — The Premiere of the Ring: 1873–1876

"I have finally seen Walhalla completed!"— Wotan

As Wagner approached his sixtieth year, he dreamed of owning his own theater and staging his own works in ideal circumstances with ideal singers, conductors, sets, and costumes. His dream was an opera house in a small town in Germany where he could stage model performances of his old operas and model premieres of his new operas.

He also knew that fulfilling that dream demanded a lot of money. For most of its history, opera had to be subsidized by a king or a duke or by the state (in ancient Greece). From what we know of Greek tragedy, it was much closer to our opera since it included music and singing and an orchestra plus a chorus.

Wagner also developed revolutionary theories of theater and opera house design. He wanted a new kind of opera house with perfect acoustics, one which reflected the world of a modern democracy — with comfortable seats for all and without a royal box and rows of ascending boxes to reflect the power and wealth of the royal and aristocratic families in Europe. Wagner's grandson, Wolfgang Wagner, has stated on several occasions that if Wagner had been alive in the 20th century he would be directing films since that art form could create what theater could not create onstage.

Wagner also used a symphonic approach to opera, his overtures suggesting not the beginning of a typical opera, but the beginning of a symphony. This demanded a large symphony orchestra, which also costs much money. This of course delighted some people and annoyed others — after all, they were in an opera house, not a concert hall.

In Zurich, Wagner told friends about his dream of building a revolutionary theater, staging his Ring cycle in a model performance, and then burning the theater after one performance. That in a nutshell was his dream: create the perfect theater world and then destroy it. But after building such a revolutionary new theater for a revolutionary new opera, why burn down the theater? This image reflected the suicidal part of his personality — a desire to destroy both himself and his world.

Wagner generated a new project, bigger than any of his earlier ones, for establishing a Wagner festival in Bayreuth, a small town in Franconia, for the ideal performance of his own operas and for the premieres of his mighty Ring cycle and his planned *Parsifal*, and any future operas he was planning like the Buddhist opera *Die Sieger*. And with his proposed new opera festival in Bayreuth, Wagner also established a Wagnerian industry with societies and critics around the world working on his life and operas.

He often wrote about the ideals of Greek tragedy, which many argue is where opera began since those performances had a musical component which ultimately was lost. The chorus in Greek tragedy and comedy was often sung, and the acoustics in those ancient, gigantic Greek amphitheaters would have favored music rather than spoken drama. Wagner's essays repeatedly glorified the ideals of ancient Greek tragedy and the plays of Aeschylus, Sophocles, and Euripides. This was the kind of drama he wanted to create in his Ring cycle, modeled in many ways on the *Oresteia* of Aeschylus. A cycle of four plays with an interconnected plot is what he produced when he wrote his Ring cycle — rather like the cycles of plays which the Greek tragic writers produced.

His revolutionary theater concept included a theater that was not about status and power and golden horseshoes and royal boxes to reflect the power of the king and the aristocracy. He wanted a democratic theater where the focus was on the stage, not the royal box, not on chatting with one's neighbors in the audience and noticing who was sitting with whom and what people were wearing and the valve of the costumes and jewels in the audience. He wanted a people's theater in which there would be no distractions from the stage, not even distractions coming from the conductor and the orchestra pit. He wanted a dark auditorium so that the audience would not focus on each other but only on the stage. This new theater would have good sight lines and good acoustics for all, like a Greek amphitheater And such a revolutionary theater he wanted to build in Bayreuth, a pretty little town in Germany halfway between Berlin and Munich, the two largest cities in Germany.

He wanted only his own operas performed there. He dreamed of a summer festival in a small town away from the capitals, so that the audience's focus would be on the works themselves. This, Wagner considered a theatrical Valhalla, and for millions of Wagner fans today, that is what it has become, though alas without air conditioning.

The stage and auditorium Wagner designed for Bayreuth do look like an indoor version

A caricature, "Wagner Versus the Critics" (ca. 1875).

20. The Idea of Bayreuth—The Premiere of the Ring: 1873–1876

of a Greek amphitheater with the orchestra pit under the stage. The acoustics are wonderful with a warm intimate sound and real resonance throughout the theater.

Another aspect of Wagner was a showman, a man who could put on great shows and attract thousands of people to see them. He was a man of the theater, an actor, a director, a theater designer. Friends often commented on his ability to act and to read his librettos to large audiences and mesmerize them. He was a showman who could put on the best shows imaginable and create new kinds of intriguing shows and entrance audiences. Though some people hated his revolutionary new operas, others loved them. He and his operas immediately attracted both fans and detractors — people were not neutral about Wagner and his works. Wagner was what the Germans call a Macher — a mover and shaker who was capable of creating and staging new works of art which mostly succeeded with the public.

Wagner and Cosima were now legally man and wife. To celebrate this, at Cosima's next birthday, on Christmas Day 1870, Wagner arranged to have his "Siegfried Idyll" played to her as she awoke. He rehearsed the musicians secretly and in advance of the surprise performance. The musicians performed the piece by the door of the couple's bedroom in Triebschen and the whole house got to hear this sublime music. This moving musical tribute to Cosima, based on the music of Wagner's next opera *Siegfried*, was also a musical tribute to their son Siegfried — and this performance became one of their happiest memories of their time in Triebschen. They would both later describe this period as the happiest time in their lives together. This house near Luzern is now a Wagner museum with interesting memorabilia of Wagner's time there. This Swiss paradise, however, would not last since the very next year the family started packing and in 1872 moved to a hotel in Bayreuth. Wagner and Cosima were determined to establish the Bayreuth Festival for the premiere of the complete Ring in Wagner's new festival theater.

After this came the campaign to build the new theater and establish the festival at Bayreuth, something that would make them both happy and bitter given the cost — it undoubtedly shortened Wagner's life as he was approaching the biblical end of the human life span, 70 years. Their dream was to stage the complete Ring in a new festival theater in 1875, and the foundation stone for the new theater was laid in 1872.

Wagner had visions of his Ring cycle premiere in Bayreuth and getting money from all over Germany so that his new opera festival at Bayreuth might become a symbol for German unification and German nationalism. However, all Wagner's planning and development of the Wagner societies through 1871 and 1872 finally produced very little money. Wagner's organizational skills were immense, but the rumors about his princely lifestyle had spread throughout Germany thanks to the newspapers, and not many Germans wanted to contribute. Many felt that the Bayreuth Festival effort was a result of the composer's egomania, and they were right. King Ludwig II himself felt that Munich had one of the most beautiful opera houses in all of Germany and the complete Ring cycle should have its premiere there, where the first two Ring operas had already had debuted. But the stubborn Wagner disagreed and was determined to establish a new summer opera festival for his works in Bayreuth.

Richard Wagner

By the time Wagner and his wife and children moved to Bayreuth in 1872, his life (and theirs) would change forever as they became international celebrities. Wagner wanted to found the first summer opera festival in Europe in a specially constructed revolutionary new opera theater. He hoped that his new theories of the Gesamtkunstwerk — or combination artwork — would be staged there and would change the history of opera forever.

Bayreuth had the largest theater stage in all of Germany, in the Margrave's Opera House. It could be used for concerts as part of the Wagner festival. Perhaps Bayreuth could be the place for his new opera festival, where his Ring would have its premiere. Also, when he looked at a map, Bayreuth had several advantages. It was a small city so there would be no competing events and people who came there could study his works. Also, the town was in Franconia, a northern part of Bavaria, under the rule of his patron, King Ludwig II.

Wagner contacted Friedrich Feustel, a prominent banker in Bayreuth, who set up a meeting between the composer and Bayreuth's mayor and other dignitaries. As Wagner presented his ideas, the men were very receptive since they envisioned thousands of tourists coming to Bayreuth for the festival and pumping millions of marks into the local economy. They already had the house where the writer Jean-Paul Richter had lived many years ago, but it did not attract many tourists. A whole Wagner festival could do wonderful thing for the local economy.

Also at this time Wagner wrote his "Kaisermarsch" to celebrate the newly unified nation. So on his 59th birthday, on May 22, 1872, the foundation stone was laid for the new festival theater and construction began — despite a pouring rain. Wagner had about ten years of life left, but those ten years were his most productive.

He immediately approached his patron, King Ludwig II, who was dubious about the idea; the king had hired an architect, Wagner's friend Gottfried Semper, to design a new opera house for Munich dedicated to the world of Richard Wagner. That opera house would not be built in Munich but it might be built in Bayreuth. But ultimately King Ludwig himself could not get the money necessary to build such a new opera house since he was still constructing his new castles.

So Wagner decided that he would raise the money, build the new theater in Bayreuth, and show the world what opera should really look like. He developed the idea of starting a society of patrons, all of who would contribute to the Bayreuth festival and in exchange get a ticket to the premiere of the Ring. He first planned this for the summer of 1875, but he was forced to delay this for one year so that the Ring had its premiere in the summer of 1876.

By 1872 Wagner had designed and started construction on Wahnfried, his opulent home in Bayreuth. Some of the money contributed to the Bayreuth festival was being channeled into Wagner's lavish new home, and by 1874 the family was able to move in. Wahnfried is now a Wagner museum and a very interesting place to visit. It had been bombed during World War II but was restored in 1976.

Ultimately, Wagner had to appeal to his patron, King Ludwig II, for funds for the new opera house, and the king agreed to a loan, which saved the project. The Wagner

20. The Idea of Bayreuth—The Premiere of the Ring: 1873–1876

house became the center of operations for the new festival and Wagner used it to entertain visitors and donors. Right behind the house, one can now see the graves of Wagner and Cosima—and this grave has no religious symbols of any kind on it, not even a simple cross.

So Wagner had to start a marketing campaign, and that is precisely what he did. He would go from city to city all over Germany, Austria, and the rest of Europe to conduct his works, especially excerpts from his new Ring cycle to try to get support for his proposed Bayreuth festival, where he wanted the complete Ring cycle to be staged under his management and perfect conditions. He knew he could always make money conducting so he would conduct performances and include excerpts of his own works, especially the new Ring cycle. That would interest audiences in his new work and perhaps get them to give money to the cause and come to Bayreuth to hear the music of the future. One had to admire his determination and his efforts to build this revolutionary new theater for his own works. He was not only conducting but also listening to singers around Germany and trying to cast his Ring cycle—which by the way he had still not finished composing. Toward the end of his life, Wagner told his wife that their blood was in that new theater, and indeed it was.

They kept moving from city to city in Germany and around Europe, and Wagner's conducting whetted people's appetite for his new music as they tried to raise funds for the proposed new festival at Bayreuth. Part of the problem with this traveling and raising funds is that Wagner insisted on staying at the best suite at the best of hotels and going to the best restaurants in town. He entertained hundreds of people on a princely level,

A caricature, "Wagner with Plato and Shakespeare" (1876).

and he got a lot of people curious about his music and about the new festival. But he did not raise much money.

Bayreuth was not a particularly old town by German standards, especially when compared to nearby Nuremberg and Bamberg, towns from the 14th century with lots of lovely architecture to prove it. Bayreuth was a very young town that had the Margrave's opera house, the Fantasie palace nearby, and not much else. Wagner had a plan for bringing potentially millions of people to the town with a new summer festival around just one composer in a specially built new theater for the performances.

Meanwhile Wagner had to finish composing the last two operas of the Ring cycle. He needed the help of the Nibelungen Chancellery, young men who were also musicians. As he composed, he turned over his manuscripts to Josef Rubinstein to turn into printed score. Hans Richter he now wanted to listen to singers and lead rehearsals and conduct the premiere. He wanted his friend Friedrich Nietzsche to write about the Bayreuth enterprise, and he wanted Heinrich Porges to write on the rehearsals for the Ring. As Rubinstein corrected the proofs for the printed scores, the singers were given these to rehearse their roles. Meanwhile, Wagner had made final discussions on cast and helping with the rehearsals of the orchestra, the singers, and the chorus.

Wagner, now in his sixties, was also developing heart palpitations and angina attacks. The effort took its toll on him and Cosima. Wagner was in his sixties when he started the Bayreuth Festival in 1876 and he only lived seven years longer. The effort undoubtedly shortened his life.

What was his marriage to Cosima like? The best source on his marriage was his wife's diary. The picture of Wagner that emerges from Cosima's diary is that of a very insecure and demanding man who was easily angered. He wanted to be treated with the greatest of care and was in many ways like a demanding child. There must have been a masochistic streak in Cosima, though the 19th century especially expected wives to dedicate themselves to their husbands.

From what Cosima reports in her diary, if she showed too much affection to her children or especially her father Franz Liszt, this would generate a jealous rage in Richard. Why was Wagner so jealous? If her diaries show anything, they show that hers was a slave-like devotion to her husband, and she would blame herself if Wagner found fault with her. But he was so demanding of her and so jealous and insecure in her love.

Life at Bayreuth must have been very difficult for Cosima since Richard could be so demanding, and he was so often angry with her for her alleged neglect of him. But Cosima was also convinced that he was the greatest composer alive, and she had been raised to worship her father, Liszt, also a distant and demanding man who kept her away from her own mother, Countess Marie D'Agout. Liszt and Wagner had much in common in terms of needing mother figures in the women they fell in love with.

Despite these personal and financial problems, the Ring cycle—which Wagner had begun twenty-five years ago while he was living in Dresden—finally had its premiere in Bayreuth during the summer of 1876. Thanks to the monumental efforts of Wagner, Cosima, and the young men of the Nibelungen Chancellery, the Ring in its entirety was

20. The Idea of Bayreuth—The Premiere of the Ring: 1873–1876

finally on stage, with Hans Richter conducting the premiere and most of the subsequent performances in Bayreuth.

On August 13, 1876, *Das Rheingold* had its premiere in the Fespielhaus, *Die Walküre* had its Bayreuth premiere on August 14, *Siegfried* on August 16, and *Götterdämmerung* on August 17—all four operas within a week, as Wagner wanted. Richter conducted all four performances with Franz Betz singing the Wotan, Georg Unger the Siegfried, Amalie Materna the Brünnhilde, Karl Hill the Alberich, and Albert Niemann as Siegmund. The miracle had been achieved and the whole Ring had finally been staged in Bayreuth—three cycles were given that summer in Bayreuth. This cycle has been called the greatest, longest, and most profound work in the history of musical theater. The twenty-five-year project begun in Dresden had finally been achieved in Bayreuth in 1876 and several complete cycles were given there. King Ludwig II attended the dress rehearsal, really a private performance just from him, hugged Wagner, and left immediately. Their project had been finished and staged at last.

One of the aspects of Wagner's personality was his desire to revolutionize opera through giving jobs to his friends. His revolutionary new theater at Bayreuth would give status and employment to many of his friends, often Jews, who would owe their whole careers to his encouragement. There were of course many layers to Wagner's personality, but some of those layers were kindly and generous, especially to Jews. Josef Rubinstein, Hermann Levi, Angelo Neumann, Hans von Bülow, and Hans Richter owed much of their careers to Wagner. Wagner helped many people to develop their talents and their careers in the arts; Wagner's anti–Semitism was clearly about stupid theories and not about people.

Many of his friends came to these Ring cycles—people like Otto and Mathilde Wesendonck, Malvida von Meysenbug, and Camille Saint-Saëns. Most of his friends loved the results, though the performances gave Friedrich Nietzsche migraine headaches. The Russian composer Tchaikovsky came but was not so impressed. The press remained by and large hostile to the Bayreuth performances, but others enjoyed them. The Kaiser came, congratulated Wagner, but left before the end of the cycle. King Ludwig enjoyed the dress rehearsal very much and dreaded meeting anyone there and left immediately. He was by now becoming more and more of a recluse and avoiding his official duties as monarch. King Ludwig considered the festival a great success, and Wagner promised to repeat the cycles the following year. Wagner congratulated the cast and orchestra players and backstage crew but said, "Next time we will do it all differently." Wagner had seen tremendous upheavals in Germany during his lifetime, but now Germany was a unified country and his Bayreuth festival, he felt, was a celebration of that and German musical and theatrical culture in general.

After the festival, when he was alone with his family in Wahnfried, he fell into a deep depression. This often happened after one of his premieres, and he felt that everything in the Bayreuth Ring was terrible and all was a failure. But Cosima and the children reminded him how happy most of the audience members and cast were. Wagner had created a revolutionary concept at Bayreuth.

21

Wagner and Nietzsche: 1876–1880

"May blood-brotherhood spring from our bond today!"—Gunther

The relationship between Wagner and Friedrich Nietzsche remained very complicated and changeable. This relationship was a major one in both their lives. Arguably, Wagner was the century's greatest opera composer and Nietzsche its greatest philosopher. It developed into love very quickly and ended in mutual hatred toward the end. Both men's needs in friendship were inevitably going to be changing as they aged. By the end Nietzsche seemed to hate Wagner but not Cosima, whom he continued to write to, but Wagner and Cosima never seemed to voice any hatred of Nietzsche—more disappointment. They felt they had been betrayed by their foster-son. This relationship began as a very close and loving one and ended in Nietzsche's severing the friendship, much to Wagner's annoyance.

Both men were betrayed by women in their own families—and the Nazis. Nietzsche's sister Elisabeth had become a Nazi, as did Wagner's daughter-in-law Winifred, the wife of his son Siegfried, and so turned the geniuses' work into racism and propaganda for the Nazis. Both men would have been appalled but could not defend themselves since these horrible events occurred after they were dead. Betrayals within a family are at the core of most of the Greek tragedies. Wagner's wife Cosima and his daughter-in-law Winifred (both women not born in Germany) emphasized his anti–Semitism after his death, while his noble, democratic side was ignored by these women.

Wagner died in 1883 and Nietzsche died in 1901, and by the time the Nazis took power in 1933, both geniuses became propaganda for the Third Reich. The Nazis were a group of racists and thugs who wanted to surround their criminal, apartheid regime with intellectual grandeur so they appropriated both Wagner and Nietzsche, helped by family members of those great geniuses, especially Winifred Wagner and Elisabeth Nietzsche.

Nietzsche wrote to a friend about when he first met the composer:

I was presented to Richard and say a few reverential words. He wants to know exactly how I came to be so well up in his music, abuses horribly all performances of his operas with the exception of the famous Munich ones, and makes fun to the Kapellmeisters who call out amiably to their orchestras, "Gentlemen, now some passion! My dear fellows, now a bit more passion!" Wagner imitates the Leipzig dialect very well. Before and after dinner he played all the most important parts of the Meistersinger, taking the various voices; he was very exuberant. He is indeed extraordinarily lively and fervid: he speaks very rapidly, is very facetious, and makes a company of this entirely private kind very gay.

21. Wagner and Nietzsche: 1876–1880

The philosopher found Wagner great fun; Nietzsche wrote to Wagner while he was living in Switzerland and Wagner very quickly responded to him with an invitation to visit him in Triebschen. Wagner himself had never gotten a degree and was undoubtedly flattered that a professor at the University of Basel was writing a fan letter to him. At this point Nietzsche was considered a Wunderkind since he had gotten a professorship at age 25 due to his published essays. When they met, they immediately liked each other since Nietzsche was a young, highly educated fan there to flatter Wagner, who certainly enjoyed such flattery. Both men were from Saxony and both really liked Greek tragedy and Shakespeare — high points in the history of drama for both the composer and the philosopher. Both men also adored the philosopher Schopenhauer, another bond between them.

When they met, Nietzsche was a man of 25 who had had a very difficult relationship with his father, a Lutheran minister; Nietzsche was undoubtedly attracted to father-figures. Wagner yearned for a son and Nietzsche seemed to be the son he was looking for — bright, highly educated, and loving all of his compositions. In June of 1869, Wagner's own son Siegfried was born, and Nietzsche was there to celebrate the new arrival. When Wagner composed the "Siegfried Idyll" as a birthday present for Cosima in 1870, Nietzsche was there to prepare the surprise gift for Cosima. He helped Wagner gather the musicians to rehearse the music and then perform it on the staircase outside Cosima and Wagner's bedroom on Christmas morning.

Nietzsche visited the family at least twenty-five times in five years, often staying for the weekends. Why did the relationship get so ugly within ten years after the height of its happiness? Both Wagner and Cosima wrote to Nietzsche, especially Wagner, and these letters record a complex but often loving relationship. Part of the attraction was undoubtedly intellectual, and they certainly had some exciting intellectual discussions, Wagner often voicing his admiration for the philosopher Arthur Schopenhauer, whose book *The World as World and Representation* he much admired. Nietzsche was fond of this philosopher as well, and was mentioning him in his classes. All of Nietzsche's aesthetics can be traced to the ideas of Richard Wagner.

And Nietzsche learned so much from Wagner. As long as he was a young man, he would very willing to learn from the great man, whom he considered the greatest composer alive. Much of Nietzsche's early thinking, and early writing, came from Wagner's ideas and their discussions together. Nietzsche's obsession with ancient Greek art and Greek tragedy, came from Wagner. Also, his theories of the differences between Dionysian art and Apollonian art came from Wagner's own thoughts on the matter. Nietzsche's early theories of aesthetics, and his essays on this topic, like "The Birth of Tragedy from the Spirit of Music," came from Wagner and his theories about the nature of art. Nietzsche's own atheism came from Wagner as well, and Wagner's discussions about the downfall of the gods in his *Götterdämmerung*. Wagner's theories of atheism came to be accepted by Nietzsche, as well as Wagner's theories of ordinary people and exceptional people who were able to create art and philosophy, which Nietzsche turned into *Mensch und Ubermensch*, or man and superman. As long as Nietzsche was willing to be a disciple, the relationship was very happy since Wagner loved to have disciples around him, and he was personally very fond of the young Nietzsche. The rejection of religion became one of their favorite topics and the necessity of looking to humanity rather than to the supposedly sympathetic gods recurred in their discussions, as it would in their essays. Both men also saw art as the modern substitute for religion. Wagner's great sense of entitlement because he was a great composer, these ideas became the model for Nietzschean man and superman — as they appear in his philosophical novel *Also Sprach Zarathustra*. Narcissism became an aspect of both their personalities — neither one was a particularly humble man. They thought of themselves as uniquely gifted individuals above most people and entitled to certain exceptions from common rules of behavior.

Nietzsche himself had a very strained relationship with his own father, who had rather rigid Lutheran beliefs and wanted his son to enter the ministry and become a clergyman, something which Nietzsche early rejected. He became famous quite early for this atheism and his stricture "Gott ist tot," "God is dead," a statement from his philosophical novel *Also Sprach Zarathustra,* which soon became one of his own famous quotes and which would have horrified his father. He got this from Wagner because Wagner too was an atheist who sometimes used religious themes, but ultimately to attack religion. Wagner himself was not a churchgoer and had deep suspicions about people who did attend church. While some Jews have felt his operas were anti–Semitic, some people, especially the tenor Jon Vickers, have argued Wagner's operas are really anti–Christian, parodies of Christian rites. Nietzsche also tended toward extreme positions — rather like a borderline personality type — so in the beginning Wagner was the most wonderful person alive and the greatest genius of music and theater in the entire 19th century. When the relationship soured, Wagner was demonized by Nietzsche: Wagner became the most awful opera composer alive, a Jew, and a French decadent. Nietzsche never sought the middle ground in people or ideas. This approach made his writing more interesting and engaging, but it narrowed his view of humanity and tended to simplify his ideas. It was impossible for Nietzsche to see the pros and cons in any person or intellectual position.

The reasons why the relationship soured were complicated. Wagner liked having young disciples around to agree with him and thought him the greatest composer around. There were people like Joseph Rubinstein around and others to do this. But Nietzsche himself was interested all his life in extreme rather than moderate positions. In the beginning, Nietzsche viewed Wagner as the greatest artist alive, his example of the Dionysian artist, but by the end of his life he viewed Wagner as an evil man and a fake.

Wagner liked gay men. Many of the friends Wagner had in Paris were gay men — people like Kaitz, Anders, and Lehrs. Toward the end of his life, Wagner became attached to the Russian Paul Joukovsky, who was an openly gay man, something very rare in the 19th century. He talked frankly with Wagner about his homosexuality and the rights homosexuals should have. Wagner became one of the first people to defend gay liberation — the idea that homosexuality is not a disease and that gay people should have all the rights of other people. Since Wagner was a man of the theater, he was used to working with gay people and this was never a problem for him.

While Nietzsche was not gay, Wagner clearly loved him as a friend of the family. He asked him to do favors for him and for Cosima, and Nietzsche was very happy to oblige. He bought special gifts for Wagner — gifts for Cosima and the children — and helped him in many ways. Cosima would ask Nietzsche to do some shopping for her. He was really a member of the family and always stayed in their house when he visited Luzern.

I think there were several reasons for the end of the Wagner-Nietzsche friendship. First, Nietzsche got older and less and less comfortable in the role of young disciple. He himself was getting to be a middle-aged man, not a youth any more. And he must have gotten tired of doing Wagner and Cosima's little errands and gift-buying. When he was middle-aged, he probably wanted disciples himself and was no longer comfortable in the role of Wagner's disciple. Also, Nietzsche, as an important philosopher of the 19th century, probably got less comfortable agreeing with Wagner, who did not like to be disagreed with. Wagner's narcissism was legendary so he was not comfortable with disagreements and Nietzsche must have gotten tired of curbing his desire to argue with Wagner and present his own point of view. Especially as Wagner got older, he seemed less able to tolerate disagreement and liked to run things in his household at Triebschen and then at Bayreuth. It is not uncommon for older people to become inflexible, and that certainly happened to Wagner in his final ten years.

Another major reason was undoubtedly Bayreuth. As long as Wagner was in Triebschen in Switzerland, there was a family house and Nietzsche was the happy guest, in fact the chosen foster-son. Nietzsche was in many ways the first son of the Wagner household, and Wagner and Cosima liked treating him that way, and the philosopher liked *being* treated that way. But when Wagner moved to Bayreuth, all of a sudden he was in charge of a cause and an institution, the Bayreuth Festival, and an enterprise that had to be funded. Wagner's house, Wahnfried, became the center of the cause to get people to donate to the new Wagner festival and the building of the new festival theater in Bayreuth. Wagner's main source of money was King Ludwig II, but the king had said he did not want to support Bayreuth. Nietzsche probably did not want to be used for this cause, though Wagner wanted him to write on behalf of the new Bayreuth enterprise. His earlier works, like "The Birth of Tragedy Out of the Spirit of Music," reflected Wagner's theories. There Nietzsche presented Wagner's *Tristan und Isolde* as the perfect example of Dionysian art, something Wagner would have found flattering and helpful to the cause. Wagner wanted Nietzsche to use his genius and his considerable writing ability to further the Wagnerian cause of Bayreuth and the Bayreuth festival theater. Wagner began suggesting Wagnerian topics for future books by Nietzsche, books which would help the Bayreuth cause, which of course was really the cause of Richard Wagner. Certainly Nietzsche began to feel that he was being used by the Wagners — which was true — and he began to resent it. He did not want to dedicate his life and his genius to the cause of Bayreuth, especially since he became suspicious of Bayreuth and of Wagner's last opera, *Parsifal*.

Nietzsche wanted to become a Wagner himself, a Wagner for a new philosophy just as Wagner was writing a new kind of music, "the music of the future" as Wagner liked to call it. For a while Nietzsche actually believed he was as good a composer as Wagner, though when he sent some of his compositions to Hans von Bülow, he swiftly and tactlessly told Nietzsche how little he thought of those compositions. Nietzsche began to show signs of the insanity which would ultimately overtake him. He died insane, due to syphilis, in a sanitarium in Switzerland in 1901 after a series of horrible medical problems — attended by his sister Elisabeth.

Nietzsche was at the premiere of *Parsifal* in 1882 and it nauseated him. He saw the opera as a defense of Christianity, though it certainly was not. Nietzsche saw *Parsifal* as an example of Wagner returning to the cross, despite the fact that the composer had consistently been anti–Christian, especially anti–Catholic, in his discussions with Nietzsche. Since the philosopher was also very anti–Christian — probably because his father was a Lutheran — he saw *Parsifal* as a rejection of all that Wagner had previously stated about his religious beliefs. But was *Parsifal* really a Christian opera? Most devout Catholics and Protestants do not think so, but the opera does have a Christian element. Some have argued that it is actually a parody of the Mass and an attack on Christianity, but it does use the old Christian legend of the Grail and the search for the Grail — and that was enough for Nietzsche, who saw the opera as Christian, or an old man's return to his Christian roots after he was too old to pursue the Roman goddess Venus. The Grail legend was one of the most important myths to come from medieval Europe and naturally Wagner was attracted to it — but not to encourage Christianity. Some people thought so at the time, but we now see the Buddhist and anti–Christian elements in the opera. But Nietzsche refused to see this and insisted that *Parsifal* was Wagner's final acceptance of Christianity — a deathbed conversion, he called it to his friends. This was not all that unusual, but this was not what the opera was really about, though some pious Christians thought that the opera really was a defense of Christianity. The Good Friday music in particular seemed to reflect the Easter season in *Parsifal*. Wagner saw that some people perceived this opera as a reflection of Christian belief, and he did not disagree with them since this helped ticket sales. Wagner saw *Parsifal* (in part) as his way of supporting his family after his death since he wanted the opera performed only at Bayreuth. Copyright laws would protect *Parsifal*— but only until 1903, when the copyright ran out in America and the Metropolitan Opera immediately staged its version of the opera and had a hit on its hands.

Another thing which made Nietzsche quite angry was a letter Wagner wrote to Nietzsche's doctor when he was first hospitalized with mental instability and eye problems. Wagner wrote to the doctor that these conditions might have been caused by excessive masturbation on Nietzsche's part, which of course made the philosopher quite angry. Philosophers are not supposed to be wanking, as the English say. Of course, Wagner was following medical practice at the time — that excessive masturbation lead to mental illness and blindness. These problems added to the complexity of this relationship and Nietzsche's increasing resentment of Wagner and the Bayreuth enterprise.

So the philosopher got to hate Wagner and even his operas — though not always. Nietzsche's last two works, "Contra Wagner" and "Human, All Too Human," attack Wagner personally, attack Wagnerian opera, and even attack Bayreuth. He attended the first festival in 1876 and his memories of that first festival are generally very negative. He wrote

21. Wagner and Nietzsche: 1876–1880

that his favorite new opera was Bizet's *Carmen* and not any of the Wagnerian operas. He announced that only operas from Mediterranean countries were worth hearing. He visited Wagner at Bayreuth once with a copy of one of the Brahms scores (Brahms was part of the anti–Wagner movement in Vienna headed by Eduard Hanslick). Clearly at this point Nietzsche was provoking Wagner rather than complimenting him—as the philosopher had done earlier. This was not helping his friendship with Wagner but it became a declaration of independence on Nietzsche's part.

For the rest of his sane life, Nietzsche's reactions to Wagnerian operas remained strangely mixed since he both hated them and loved them. He once wrote to a friend after hearing the overture to Wagner's *Parsifal* that this was the most sublime music he had ever heard.

The story is told that when Nietzsche was sent to an insane asylum toward the end of his life, he said that Cosima Wagner had sent him there. Even after Wagner had died in 1883, Cosima continued to receive love letters from Nietzsche, some of them pathetically insane. Even though Cosima did not answer those letters, she kept them since they reveal that Nietzsche's bond with Wagner remained and indicated that he may have loved Cosima more than Richard. He had probably loved them both and had helped them raise their children in Switzerland, but how many friendships really last in life? As people and their needs change, friends usually are lost in the process. Where are the snows of yesteryear, as the poet said?

Perhaps Gabriel Monod, a Frenchman who had attended the first Bayreuth Festival in 1876, summarized Wagner best:

> On everyone who comes near him he exercises an irresistible fascination, not only by reason of his musical genius,

"The Music of the future," a caricature of Wagner by Vincent Brooks, Day & Son published in the May 19, 1877, edition of *Vanity Fair* (Music Division, The New York Public Library for the Performing Arts, Astor, Lenox and Tilden Foundations).

187

or the originality of his intellect, or the variety of his learning, but above all by the energy of temperament and will that emanates from every fiber of him. You feel that you are in the presence of a force of nature, unleashing itself with almost reckless violence. After seeing him at close quarters, at one moment irresponsibly gay, pouring forth a torrent of jokes and laughter, at another vehement, respecting neither titles nor powers nor friendships, always letting himself be carried away by the first thing that comes into his head, you find yourself unable to be too hard upon him for his lapses of taste, of tact, of delicacy; if you are a Jew, you are inclined to forgive him his pamphlet on "Judaism in Music," if a Frenchman, his farce on the capitulation of Paris, if you are a German, all the insults he has heaped on Germany.... You take him as he is, full of faults — no doubt because he is full of genius — but incontestably a superior being, one of the greatest and most extraordinary men our century has produced.

Surely Gabriel Monod accurately describes Wagner's intensity and his lack of tact, but also his genius. Both Wagner and Nietzsche were geniuses and had their own work to do; in the case of Wagner, he had to get *Parsifal* written and staged at Bayreuth, and there was not a moment to lose since Wagner undoubtedly knew that he was a sick man whose heart was not working well. By the last three years of his life, Wagner was having angina pectoris attacks often, so he must have known that his remaining time was short. Wagner was in pain much of the time he was composing and trying to stage what would become his final opera, *Parsifal*, though he was also working on *Die Sieger*, which would have been his next opera, not to mention the thousands of letters he wrote during this period to get *Parsifal* staged at Bayreuth and continue the operation there. Wagner also had five children to worry about and try to support. After the Ring cycles were over at Bayreuth, Wagner was inundated with bills and debts.

By now Wagner was an old man and he needed a lot of praise and a lot of help to get through his difficult and painful days. He was hardly the first artist who needed incessant praise, especially from women. Wagner's insecurities about himself and his talents must have been monumental or he would not have needed so much praise or been so quick to attack highly successful people like Meyerbeer or Mendelssohn or Verdi who had become great successes right before or during his own career. One wishes that Wagner were more generous to other composers, but he was too insecure and envious.

One of the most liberated of women, Malwida von Meysenbug, became Wagner's close friend. She visited him at Bayreuth, and he visited her while she was living in Italy. Wagner was not a male chauvinist, though he did make enormous demands on his wives, especially Cosima. Malwida was a feminist in the 19th century, a liberated woman who was also a Wagner fan; they corresponded from when they first met until Wagner's death, and she attended the Bayreuth premieres of the Ring and *Parsifal*.

Cosima was also liberated in many ways, but she was a woman who wanted to serve a great musical genius. Cosima had to worship her father Franz Liszt from afar since he rarely saw her in her childhood; he was always touring and playing the piano. But as a child, Cosima loved her famous father and worshipped him. When she met her father's greatest friend, Wagner, she was prepared to worship and work for another musical genius, Richard Wagner. Cosima must have realized early in her marriage that Hans von Bülow would never become a creative genius like her father, though Hans was a great pianist

21. Wagner and Nietzsche: 1876–1880

and would eventually become a great conductor. But Cosima wanted an artist like her father, both to help and to worship. Nietzsche would become a great philosopher, so naturally both Richard and Cosima found him interesting and encouraged him. Many of Nietzche's early ideas came straight from Wagner and his theories, but Nietzsche would have wanted to develop along his own lines and so had to break the tie with Wagner.

To the end of his life, Nietzsche, mute and living in a mental asylum, wrote pathetic letters to the one he called his true love, Cosima Wagner. Wagner's sudden death at the age of 69 was much quicker and kinder and involved less anguish than what Nietzsche was forced to endure in his final ten years.

By the time Nietzsche died in 1901, he had been in a series of mental hospitals and by the end was unable to talk due to a series of strokes. At the time, he was diagnosed with the final, tertiary stage of syphilis. His friend Lou Andreas Salome was one of the first to write a book about Nietzsche, and after World War I his reputation grew, to be destroyed by Nazi propaganda. Since World War II his reputation has been restored and a clearer understanding of his life and his relationship with Wagner has emerged. Nietzsche started the rumor that Wagner was Jewish as an explanation of his notorious anti–Semitism. This rumor had been circulating in Europe throughout Wagner's career, due the terrible racism of the 19th century.

A photograph of Richard Wagner, circa 1877, taken at Elliott & Fry, a Victorian photography studio in London (Music Division, The New York Public Library for the Performing Arts, Astor, Lenox and Tilden Foundations).

As Wagner grew older, he learned to love more and more people of all types and regretted his former prejudice. He did not support a movement to deny Jews the right to vote in the new united Germany. He did not sign any anti–Jewish petitions to the new Kaiser, William I. He hired Jews to perform at Bayreuth and remained true to his Jewish friends, especially Josef Rubinstein and Herman Levi, who wrote lovingly of Wagner and denied that he was anti–Semitic.

A year after the Ring premiere, Wagner got a lucrative offer to conduct a series of concerts at London's Royal Festival Hall during the summer of 1877. London was a city he disliked, primarily because of all the fogs and all the poverty he saw there. On his latest visit, the critics were ready for him; most of them were Mendelssohn fans and were determined to pan all the concerts Wagner conducted. The critics even made up malicious lies about him, to make him appear awful to the British public. Nevertheless, a small group of artists, intellectuals, and musicians came to his concerts and were amazed at his new approach to conducting, and the new sounds he was getting from the orchestra. They were also impressed with the excerpts of his own music he added to the programs — once again, Wagner's marketing. Despite the critics, the concerts were well received by the public. Queen Victoria and Prince Albert once again invited him to visit them at Buckingham Palace. The writer George Eliot (Marian Evans legally) and George Henry Lewes visited Wagner, as did many other writers, painters, and intellectuals. Wagner's 1877 visit to London and his conducting became a major artistic success, though not a financial success.

During these concerts Wagner was writing desperate letters to his king and his banker, Friedrich Feustel in Bayreuth, threatening to sell Wahnfried, his house in Bayreuth, and the Festspielhaus, and move with his entire family to America. The king was horrified, but then Wagner, once back in Germany, was approached by his friend Angelo Neumann with an offer to tour European capitals, including London, with the Ring cycle and most of the original cast. Such a tour could pay off the Bayreuth debts and support another festival there. Wagner happily signed a contract with Neumann.

22

Parsifal: 1881–1882

"I don't know my name!"— Parsifal

Almost immediately after the Ring had its premiere in Bayreuth at the Festival theater in 1876, Wagner began work on *Parsifal*, which would be his final work. He was dissatisfied with the Ring production and depressed about the results, but at least the Ring had had its premiere. As he told the cast afterwards, "Next time we will do it all differently," which suggests the multiple approaches possible with the Ring and his own dissatisfaction with what he and his production team had come up with. Often after a premiere of one of his works, Wagner felt depressed about the results, even after his most revolutionary premiere, the Ring.

With *Parsifal* Wagner yet again created a new kind of mystical, profound opera with a shimmering orchestration. He once said that the art of composition was actually the art of transition, and *Parsifal* especially displayed Wagner's genius and subtlety when moving from one motif to another in both the orchestra and in the singing voices of his characters onstage. Wagner now was using the legend of the Grail, though in a Wagnerian rather than Christian way. Wagner's image of Amfortas' wound that will not heal was a wonderful symbol because everybody has one — a psychic wound which does not seem able to heal and which is still painful.

In many ways, Wagner had planned out his entire artistic life as a composer as a young man. Even while he was a Kappelmeister in Dresden he had planned a *Parsifal* opera. His early cantata, "Liebesmahl der Apostel," sounds like a first draft for *Parsifal*. Wagner also borrowed from Liszt's *Christus* for his *Parsifal*, and he cheerfully admitted this to Liszt. Even the Ring cycle was planned by Wagner back then, so clearly Wagner had planned much of his artistic life early, and he even suggested that *Parsifal* would be his final work. In many ways he seemed to be moving from Christianity to his theory of art as the new religion after the death of the gods. Like Freud and Marx, Wagner increasingly thought that humanity would be happier without God and without religion of any kind.

But with *Parsifal*, Wagner finally had his own theater at Bayreuth with exactly the festival establishment he wanted, though he did not have the money to run it. He had given up on most opera audiences and said that most operas during his life were written for tired businessmen; he wanted to write operas for real Wagner enthusiasts who were willing to make the hadj to his new Mecca, Bayreuth. He knew that his patron, King Ludwig II, was eager to hear anything he composed, he knew he had a lot of fans, and he knew that if he worked hard he could raise the money to stage *Parsifal* in model circumstances and he would not have to start begging other opera houses in Germany to stage the work, as he had had to do so often before. He probably would have to beg the king and other wealthy patrons for money, but he was now used to that. He must have dreamed about the festival being self-sufficient financially and maybe even turning a profit every year, and in his manic moments he probably thought this would be possible, though it never was.

Parsifal was the only opera Wagner composed for the theater at Bayreuth, and the acoustics there remain perfect for this opera. Hearing *Parsifal* at Bayreuth is a little like dying and going to heaven for Wagner fans since the opera sounds so wonderful in the theater where it had its premiere. Wagner knew the acoustics of the Bayreuth house and had them in mind when he wrote his final opera — and the wonderful combination of the orchestra and chorus sounds especially shimmering in that opera house. Wagner became more reasonable in his demands on his tenor so that the role of Parsifal is not as difficult as Tristan and Siegfried. Wagner realized that casting the role of Siegfried had been so difficult for him in 1876 so he made less vocal demands for the tenor role of Parsifal — and thus it was easier to cast.

Current productions of Wagner's operas at Bayreuth generally begin with the director's concept rather than Wagner's stage directions, and these days one approaches Bayreuth productions with a certain skepticism, but the acoustics there remain as wonderful as ever. Hearing *Parsifal* at Bayreuth becomes a unique listening experience; the productions themselves have become increasing weird in the 21st century, though weird can sometimes be wonderful too. But the sound in that opera house at Bayreuth remains particularly suited to *Parsifal*, and Wagner wanted the opera only performed at Bayreuth. He called his final opera a "stage dedication festival play." Wagner hoped that *Parsifal* being staged only at Bayreuth, his express wish, would insure that his family would have an inheritance to live on.

He had three children with Cosima, and two from her marriage with Hans von Bülow, and he undoubtedly wanted to protect them from poverty. But why didn't he write a will to clarify his thought on this topic? Partially this may have been a denial of his own likely death from a heart attack and his plans for the future, including his newest opera project, *Die Sieger*, and partially it was anger at Cosima and his family. His subconscious anger at the people who loved him most was yet another product of his stressful childhood and his subconscious and conscious resentments. As Wagner indicated in the first act of *Tristan und Isolde*, love always comes mixed with hate, and that was certainly true of his own strong emotions.

But it was very frustrating for Wagner that the king did not want to come to Bayreuth for the premiere of *Parsifal* but instead wanted the opera staged for him in Munich, something which Wagner did not want to allow. Wagner's stream of love letters to the king included his frustration at not having the king at Bayreuth for the premiere of *Parsifal*. As Wagner wrote to the king while he was working on *Parsifal*, "You are right, my dear, heaven-sent Lord, to remind me so often, with pride, of the finest virtue you are conscious

22. Parsifal: 1881–1882

of possessing—fidelity. To each of my poetic conceptions you have brought your own seed of life."

Wagner's sexual metaphor must have enchanted the king. He did come to many of Wagner's dress rehearsals, which were in effect performances just for the king. The king loved private opera performances, especially since before Bayreuth the house lights were kept on during performances and many eyes were often on him in the royal box. The king liked that at Bayreuth no one could see him because there was no royal box and the theater was completely darkened during performances so there were no distractions from what was going on onstage. That meant the king could enter the Bayreuth auditorium after the house lights were dimmed. The king was becoming more of a recluse and did not want to be seen in public, not even for Wagner his favorite composer. But Wagner of course wanted his king and patron at the premiere of what he must have suspected would be his final opera.

Amalie Materna, his Brunnhilde in 1876, became his Kundry in this opera's premiere on July 26, 1882. Hermann Winkelmann sang Parsifal to the composer's satisfaction. The Amfortas was Theodor Reichmann, and Gurnemanz was sung by Emil Scaria. His conductor for the premiere was Hermann Levi, despite his being Jewish. Wagner made the career of several Jewish musicians despite his stupid racism. King Ludwig II was a big fan of Levi, and Wagner had to admit that his conducting of *Parsifal* was the best. Wagner could not resist torturing Levi a bit, and made a joke of trying to get him to convert, but he wanted Levi to conduct the premiere of *Parsifal*, which he did.

Parsifal became an international sensation and made news in both Europe and the Americas. The press was becoming a bit less hostile to Wagner as he approached his seventieth year. During the last performance, Wagner secretly entered the orchestra pit and took over the conducting from Levi for the last scene, and this would be the last time the composer ever conducted. Wagner's staging of the opera remained for about 50 years at Bayreuth, until Winifred Wagner replaced it with one by Heinz Tietjen. Whenever *Parsifal* was staged at Bayreuth, Cosima wanted only Levi to conduct, and he had become a friend of the family. Until his death in 1900, only Levi conducted *Parsifal* in Bayreuth. But the original sets must have been rags after 50 years. Younger people felt that even though Wagner and Paul von Joukowsky had designed the original production of *Parsifal*, it was time for a new production and a new look for that opera, and Tietjen designed a new production in the '30s despite the scandal to the old aunties of Bayreuth, Siegfried Wagner's old lady sisters who still wanted to influence artistic decisions there.

The text and the music for *Parsifal* seemed to come very easily to the composer; he set the opera in Monsalvat, Spain, one of the few European countries he had not visited before but still wanted to see. He wanted the Hall of the Grail to look like Sienna's magnificent cathedral, which it did thanks to von Joukowsky's set designs for the original production. The ideas and the music in the opera repeated some of his earlier obsession but also tried to say new things and explore new territory. He had ideas for other operas, but his correspondence to the king suggests that he knew this would be his final opera and the final product of his artistic legacy.

Richard Wagner

Wagner started his Wagner associations to provide support for Bayreuth, but ultimately it was the generosity of King Ludwig II and other wealthy patrons that kept the enterprise afloat. Now Bayreuth is supported primarily by the Bavarian government. Wagner had wanted to stage the Ring cycle there every summer, but he did not have the capital so the next Bayreuth festival would be for the premiere of *Parsifal* and he was hoping more money would appear to finance that. It was gradually dawning on Wagner that his festival would never be profit-making and would instead have to be supported by the king or some foundation.

Wagner also always felt that he wanted common ordinary people to attend his festival at Bayreuth. He thought that his operas should attract an audience of everyone, but he gradually learned that most common, uneducated people much preferred the music of the Viennese Strausses — and that they considered Wagner's operas too long and complicated. Most Germans wanted dance music, not music drama; they wanted operetta and not grand opera. These facts profoundly disappointed Wagner, who wanted to write music for the common, everyday person and not for an upper-class, educated elite. But these are the realities of Wagnerian opera.

In the meantime, Wagner and his family really enjoyed living at Wahnfried, his home, which he had designed, within walking distance of the festival theater and bordering on the king's park in Bayreuth. Wagner spent a fortune on creating this palatial house — the best and largest house in the city — and decorating it in busy Victorian style, typical of his period. He had created a real establishment for himself and his family with servants and governesses for the children. Wagner really was living like a prince now, thanks to the charity of his patron King Ludwig II, who rarely wanted to visit him there. Wagner himself often wanted to avoid Bayreuth's cold winters by going to Italy for a few months — once again traveling like a prince, staying at the best hotels, going to the best restaurants, and traveling with his wife, his family, his servants, his personal valet, plus his group of gay friends like Josef Rubinstein and Paul Joukowsky. This princely lifestyle was underwritten by the generosity of the king, who was developing his own financial problems due to his elaborate plans to keep building new castles in Bavaria. But the king still had the secret stipendium, the Guelph fund, from Bismarck.

Rather than the theme of salvation through a woman, here Wagner would explore the theme of the femme fatale, though of course he had also done that with his Isolde — the woman who was dangerous and attempting to kill the hero. But the orchestral color of *Parsifal* would be different, most subtle in terms of orchestration and more transparent and ethereal. There is an undulating, watery sound to *Parsifal*, rather like the watery sound in *Tristan und Isolde*. Wagner was always a master orchestrator, and he is at his most subtle in *Parsifal* and captures the spiritual, metaphysical world of this opera. He continues to use his famous methods of leitmotifs and moving from one to another of those leitmotifs. Wagner's interest in Buddhism and its spirituality clearly influenced his thinking on *Parsifal*— the search for the Grail becomes the search for spiritual wholeness and enlightenment, which is not exactly a Christian theme.

Nietzsche felt that Wagner was reverting to Christianity in this opera, and he was,

22. Parsifal: 1881–1882

but the Christianity is Wagnerian rather than orthodox and has much more to do with Buddhist enlightenment. While the Ring was of this world, *Parsifal* would be more from the search for another world, at least in terms of tonal color. The music shimmers and moves effortlessly from one key to another and from one theme to another in a quiet, undulating, magical way. *Parsifal* can be fascinating just in terms of musical transitions, and Wagner himself said that composition is the art of transition. The music has an ethereal quality which prefigured the impressionist sounds of Debussy. Wagner would also use the chorus in a new way to give tonal variety and ethereal sounds in this his final opera. The Grail music, the Good Friday music, and the final scene remain haunting. The Flowers Maidens and Kundry become captivating in the second act. It is also interesting that even in *Lohengrin* Wagner mentions Parsifal, the father of Lohengrin, so these two operas can be compared and contrasted very easily.

In *Parsifal* Wagner also presents the theme of the death-wish, suicidal characters like Amfortas and Kundry — reflecting the suicidal lovers Tristan und Isolde. But the atmosphere of the Grail brotherhood surrounds *Parsifal*. What is Wagner presenting here? Is this his defense of Christianity, as Nietzsche asserted, or a new form of Christianity connecting it with Buddhism? Wagner certainly knew how to be both suggestive and mysterious in his operas. He must have intended a conscious ambiguity here, which adds to his opera's fascination.

But most of the settings for *Parsifal* were the result of his frequent trips to Italy, where he went every winter for his last three years to avoid the Bayreuth winters. More and more he was sick of Germany, sick of Franconia, and sick of Bayreuth, and yearning for the land where the oranges and lemons bloom, as Goethe said, Italy.

In Italy he especially liked traveling with the young Russian von Joukowsky, who drew and painted wonderfully and was the kind of fan which Wagner liked to have around him. Joukowsky traveled with his gay lover Peppino, an Italian musician who had to be supported financially. Peppino sang Neapolitan songs to the Wagner family, all of whom enjoyed them.

The gardens of Rapallo, near Naples and on the Amalfi coast, particularly impressed the composer, and he and Paul decided that they had found Klingsor's Magic Garden for the second act of *Parsifal*. Wagner had von Joukowsky draw some sketches of the garden to act as the stage setting for the second scene of the second act of *Parsifal*. Wagner also loved the main cathedral in Sienna, which he thought would be the perfect setting for the temple of the Grail — used in the final scenes of both Acts 1 and 3 of *Parsifal*, and von Joukowsky's drawings of the interior of the cathedral in Sienna did form the basis for the sets of *Parsifal* at Bayreuth. The cathedral at Sienna, arguably one of the most gorgeous examples of Italian Gothic architecture, was the model for the temple of the Grail for the first production of *Parsifal* in Bayreuth, and Joukowsky designed these sets to Wagner's specifications.

Wagner tried to connect *Parsifal* with Christianity, but this was marketing once again, since the opera's Christianity was denounced by clergymen at the time of the premiere. But Wagner's marketing helped to sell tickets; he wanted to connect the opera with the spring Easter season since that would attract press and produce publicity for Bayreuth.

Wagner wanted his final opera performed only at Bayreuth, but once the copyright ran out in Germany in 1913 the work could be staged anywhere and was. Ten years earlier, on December 2, 1903, the Metropolitan Opera staged the work to great acclaim; the production toured other American cities, much to Cosima's displeasure. Once beyond copyright, even the opera houses in Germany were staging the work on their own stages. *Parsifal* became a major success even in Paris, ironically enough since Wagner never had any success there. Cosima was furious at this development and wanted Bayreuth to keep its monopoly on performances at Bayreuth. She wrote to German legislators to pass a law to keep this monopoly for the Bayreuth Festival and the Wagner family, but the Berlin legislators did not pass such a law and *Parsifal* fell into the public domain all over Europe, even earlier in America because of its own copyright laws.

During the rehearsals for the premiere of *Parsifal*, Wagner had a mild flirtation with Carrie Pringle, one of the English flower maidens, and this added some pleasure to the rehearsal period for him. He developed this relationship and started a correspondence with Pringle partially to annoy Cosima; this sadism was part of his personality. People who are treated sadistically as children, as he was, can become sadistic in their relationships with others.

Many of Wagner's friends came, including Malwida von Meysenbug, Hans von Bülow, and Judith Gautier. There was a special performance for people who contributed a substantial sum to support Bayreuth, and Wagner was there and spoke personally to this audience. Elisabeth Nietzsche came to these performances with a group of Nietzsche's friends, but he did not come. As he wrote to his sister: "I am very glad you are going. You will find all my friends there. But you must excuse me: I assuredly will not go unless Wagner invites me personally and treats me as the most honored of his festival guests."

Nietzsche was still angry at Wagner and becoming increasingly arrogant in his views. Several months later, Nietzsche wrote to his sister Elisabeth:

> Certainly the days I spent with him in Triebschen, and through him in Bayreuth (1872, not 1876) were the most beautiful of my life. But the all-compelling power of our tasks drove us asunder, and now we cannot draw together again; we have become too alien to each other. When I found Wagner I was indescribably happy. I had searched so long for a man higher than and superior to myself. In Wagner I thought I had found him. I was wrong. Now I can no longer compare myself with him: I belong to another order. For the rest, I have had to pay dearly for my Wagner-enthusiasm. Has not this nerve-shattering music ruined my health? And the disillusion and the parting from Wagner, did not this endanger my life? Has it not taken nearly six years to recover from this grief? No, Bayreuth is impossible for me! What I wrote you the other day was only in jest. But you at any rate must go to Bayreuth. It means a good deal to me.

Right before the 1882 festival, Wagner was very pleased that his stepdaughter Blandine married a Sicilian nobleman, Count Biagio Gravina. Wagner had already visited Sicily, where the couple met, and remained very fond of his new son-in-law.

22. Parsifal: 1881–1882

Wagner called *Parsifal* a stage dedication festival play, and that very peculiar title has religious overtones. What Wagner was suggesting was that this work was religious, but religious in a new sense: Now people will worship art, and art will become the new religion. By implication Wagner was rejecting traditional religions and presenting the work of art as the new religion. With the final opera of the Ring, *The Twilight of the Gods*, and *Parsifal*, he was suggesting the new religion would be the religion of art, and by implication Wagner was rejecting all organized religions. *The Twilight of the Gods* suggests the death of God and religion, and by the end humanity is on its own and better off without the gods. The new kind of opera Wagner was writing with *Parsifal* would be dedicated to the stage, suggesting the stage itself and what is presented on it as the new religion of the future. Art and the stage would become the new art form Wagner implied, and he wanted Bayreuth to be one of those stages. And he wanted the search for enlightenment despite the temptations of the world, to be found in art — the grail brotherhood being a symbol of artists and thinkers search for enlightenment. This clearly reflects Buddhist teaching rather than orthodox Christian thought. Wagner here also reflects the ideas of Schiller, who wanted to connect theater with its origins in ancient Greek drama, where the altar of Dionysos was placed on the stage.

Wagner's very tomb suggests his skepticism about all religions and the existence of any God: He did not want any religious symbols placed on his tomb, and there are none. Instead, Wagner suggests that art has become a new religion, providing the only enlightenment and fulfillment we can ever get. Wagner's suspicion of all religions prevented him from becoming a church-goer, though he did go to churches, especially when he was in Italy, to see the art. After all, Titian's *Assumption of the Virgin* was in Venice's Church of the Frari. Wagner visited that painting whenever he was in Venice. He did not attend religious services when he was there — or anywhere, for that matter.

What did the original audience make of the opera and what was the critical reaction? The reviews were mixed with some critics being overwhelmed by the new opera and its unique sound and other critics being bored and annoyed by what they saw and heard. This should hardly be surprising given the revolutionary opera *Parsifal* was. Wagner uses some aspects of Christian mythology, like the search for the Grail, and connects it with mythologies from other religions, like Buddhism, but in a uniquely Wagnerian combination. The undulating sounds from the orchestra generate a unified vision and a search for a life without polarities, a life as a unified whole. If anything, the opera presents a form of Manichaeism — the medieval heresy that neither God nor the devil are omnipotent but are in constant conflict and God wins some battles and Satan others. Instead, both halves here are parts of a view of life as constant struggle, which also appears in the philosophy of Schopenhauer.

Parsifal seems to be about the search for some sort of brotherhood and some sort of enlightenment and spiritual life, but Wagner left everything very vague since he wanted as many people as possible to be fascinated by the opera. Was the brotherhood a symbol of celibacy? Well, we know that Parsifal would father a son called Lohengrin so that does not seem possible. Is it male-only — that kind of brotherhood? Kundry is invited into the temple of the Grail at the end, but she dies there soon afterwards. But poor Kundry has been seeking death for the entire opera so it would be kind to give her her most ardent wish at this point at the end of the opera. Wagner was always fascinated with the suicidal personality since he himself was suicidal for much of his life.

The Grail brotherhood in *Parsifal* seems to offer the audience some sort of communal friendship and some sort of profound enlightenment and to solve their most secret yearnings, to heal the audience in some way. What exactly is the Grail offering us? Wagner was shrewd enough to realize that to be ambiguous is best so that most of the audience would be fascinated, and also because Wagner himself was not sure what the Grail promised. Perhaps Wagner shared Henry James' theory of conscious ambiguity — a secret that most artists undoubtedly knew. Henry James was a friend of Paul von Joukowsky, who offered to introduce James to Wagner, though James declined because he said he did not know enough German. If an audience member could understand everything about a work of art, that audience member would then become bored with it. But if the work of art was consciously ambiguous, if the audience member or reader could never quite understand exactly what was being suggested, such a work of art would remain eternally fascinating. Wagner had much earlier, from his first work, realized that to give out mixed messages in a work of art is a way of making many different types of people respond to it since people will read into a work of art what obsesses them. Wagner was at his most consciously ambiguous in *Parsifal* and that has made it fascinating. Wagner was a genius at giving out mixed messages in his operas. Just when we think we understand them, contrary evidence appears to make us doubt our theories about the work. And so we continue to wonder about them. This quality is especially apparent in *Parsifal*, with its recurrent symbols of the Grail cup and the spear — phallic and yonic symbols which reappear in this opera. Is this the search for a balance of the male and female within ourselves? Is this the search for a redemption which will unify all the conflicting parts of our complex personalities? Is this a search for a redemption through self-awareness and self-integration? These were the questions being asked after the premiere of *Parsifal* in 1882 in Bayreuth, and continue to be asked.

The Metropolitan Opera in New York was the first company to break Bayreuth's monopoly on *Parsifal* when they staged it in 1903, when it was no longer under copyright protection in the United States, and the production became the hit of the Met season that year. The production was so successful that the Met even toured with its *Parsifal* so that many Americans got to hear the opera and became fans. One no longer had to go to Bayreuth to hear Wagner's final opera. In 1913, when the opera went into the public domain in Europe, other opera companies there and around the world staged *Parsifal*.

Wagner was now a sick man, having a series of heart incidents which must have worried Cosima very much. He could not conduct the whole score of *Parsifal*, even though he undoubtedly wanted to, because of his worsening health. He had several heart attacks during the rehearsals for his final opera. He must have known that he was in fact dying and that this would be his final opera, despite the happy face he put on for Cosima and

22. Parsifal: 1881–1882

his friends at Bayreuth. Other people commented at how exhausted Wagner seemed during the summer of 1882. But he had plans for another opera, *Die Sieger, the Victors*, based on his new fascination with Buddhism, once again turning religion into art rather than becoming a member of any religion.

Wagner's friend Angelo Neumann wanted to tour Europe with *Parsifal*. Neumann had had great success touring Wagner's Ring production and had introduced many cities, including London, to the Ring. Neumann wanted to do the same for *Parsifal,* and Wagner hesitated for a while and then said that he wanted to keep this opera for Bayreuth. Neumann said he understood. According to Ernest Newman:

> His prevailing mood was of profound depression. He had had more than one severe attack of asthma and cramp during the festival. In one of the early August days Scaria [the singer] had been the witness of a terrifying scene. He was alone with Wagner in one of the rooms at Wahnfried. Suddenly the Meister was seized by one of his worst heart spasms; purple in the face, he sank on to the sofa and made convulsive movements with his hands as if he were fighting off an invisible enemy. The crisis passed: "I have escaped death," he said in a faint voice. It was only his courage and his desire not to dishearten his artists that kept him going in the latter stages of the festival. "He told me he longed for death," Cosima recorded in her diary.

After sixteen performances of *Parsifal,* the second Bayreuth festival ended. After the final performance, as Wagner and Cosima were returning to their home, Wahnfried, Cosima recorded in her diary:

> Our return home was silent and solemn. I think we can give thanks, though assuredly what we have achieved has been at a heavy cost, and we have sacrificed to it almost all our lives' comfort. To be sure, this activity is a necessity to Richard, and notwithstanding all the griefs it brings with it, the only one suited to him.

By the fall of 1882 Wagner was exhausted since he had staged and directed the premiere of *Parsifal* despite his worsening health. He was approaching his seventieth year and that must have been a sobering experience for him. He dreaded another winter in Bayreuth, so he decided to take his entourage with him and go to his beloved Venice, where he had written most of *Tristan und Isolde*. Perhaps he thought that if there was any place on earth where he would like to die, it would be in the watery city of Venice. Water imagery had figured so often and so prominently in his operas — especially *The Flying Dutchman, Tristan,* and the Ring — so what better place to die than in the lagoons of beautiful Venice? He could return to see one of his favorite paintings, "The Assumption of the Virgin" by Titian in the Church of the Frari. That painting had given him the idea for both the Liebestod at the end of *Tristan* and the Immolation Scene at the end of the Ring. Maybe he could repair his health in the warm climate of Italy since he feared another German winter would kill him. Buddhism's promise of some sort of personal afterlife connected with water and rebirth seemed promising at this point in his life.

Wagner's yearning for something other than the world was a basic and recurrent concern in his life. His operas became attempts to create a fantasy world which embodied his own concerns, which were general enough to embody the concerns of most other people. The yearning—whether it was the knights of the Grail or the flying Dutchman—was always yearning for something which was ultimately impossible.

Wagner founded a journal called the *Bayreuther Blatter*, or *Bayreuth Journal*, and wrote articles for it. He made his young friend Hans von Wolzogen its editor, and the journal, which began in 1878, published essays on Wagnerian topics by many authors. He also developed a friendship with Count De Gobineau, a French racist who wrote a very famous book at the time, *On the Inequality of the Human Races*. Wagner enjoyed talking with him though they usually disagreed since when De Gobineau kept repeating the importance of race, Wagner would usually answer by emphasizing the importance of money, class, and property; these, he felt, were the things that had to be eliminated in a just society.

To yearn to be something we are not, to yearn for someone we cannot obtain, to desire what we can never have, these are all part of Wagner's personality and are themes in his operas. Wagner wanted to create a new kind of integrated art which combined all the other arts. Wagner had often commented that most art in the 19th century, especially opera, was written for bored businessmen. Wagner wanted to create a new kind of symphonic music drama which would contain compelling characters and compelling ideas and real drama. Wagner wanted to create the kind of great art which the Greek dramatists and Shakespeare had created, not a series of catchy tunes connected by a ridiculous plot.

23

Death in Venice: 1883

"What a beautiful, watery city!" — Richard Wagner

When Richard Wagner died in Venice in 1883, it was headline news throughout Europe and America. He had become a world figure in terms of international musical culture as it existed in the 19th century. In many ways, Wagner staged his own death and it was a suicide. He was used to staging his own musical dramas in Bayreuth so why not stage his own death? As he approached his seventieth year, he seemed old and exhausted and he was constantly in pain — and he particularly dreaded the winters in Bayreuth. It was time for his final Italianiesche Reise, or Journey to Italy, to quote Goethe. What better placed than Venice to stage his own death and funeral — he was a naturally born actor and stage director, something he had done his entire life.

In Venice, Wagner was particularly fond of going to Florian, the great restaurant and café on the Piazza San Marco which is still in business. Many artists and writers used to gather there for their morning cappuccino and cakes. Wagner also liked visiting one of his favorite paintings, Titian's "The Assumption of the Virgin," in the church of the Frari in Venice. Bellini's gorgeous "Madonna and Child" was in that same church.

Wagner died at the Palazzo Vendramin-Calegeri, which still exists on the Grand Canal in Venice and which is now the casino of the city. The palazzo now contains a small museum, housed in the rooms where Wagner actually died and includes some furniture and objects when the Wagner family was living in that part of the house. Wagner would rent one of the most beautiful palazzi in one of the most beautiful spots on Venice. He had received a special grant from his great patron Ludwig II for this, and Wagner was not one to squirrel away money for a rainy day. At the time he was surrounded by his wife Cosima and his and Hans van Bülow's children, plus some Italian servants. Liszt was in Budapest when Wagner died; he came soon afterwards to comfort his daughter Cosima. Liszt died in Bayreuth in 1886, the same year that King Ludwig died. Liszt is buried in the Bayreuth cemetery, in a tomb designed by his grandson Siegfried Wagner years after Liszt's death when Siegfried wanted to become an architect and before he took over the running of the Wagner festival from his mother, who lived on into her 90s. Cosima and Siegfried Wagner died in the same year, 1930. He survived his mother by about six months. Some in Bayreuth had always considered Siegfried Wagner a momma's boy and gay, which he was; though he did marry Winifred Williams, an Englishwoman, and produce five children with her. But all this occurred years after Wagner's death: Fidi (the family nickname for Siegfried) was five years old when his father died.

As he aged, Wagner's politics more and more reflected his left-looking politics during the Dresden revolution of 1849. There he was at the barricades with Michael Bakunin and the other revolutionaries fighting for equal rights for everyone, not just the aristocrats and the royal family. He wanted to keep the Saxon monarch, but with guaranteed rights for all people of every race and religion, including Jews. Though that earlier, revolutionary Wagner got ignored by Cosima and the Bayreuth circle after Wagner's death, he himself retained that stance to the end of his life. His political and social ideals were self-contradictory, like so much of his personality in general. He was both a democratic idealist and a racist — he had his good angels and his bad angels. Both his leftist and rightist ideas lived together simultaneously, but his articles in the *Bayreuther Blatter* leaned more and more to the right. Partially this was encouraged by Cosima who was herself very conservative. Racism was unfortunately an ugly part of European intellectual history, particularly in the 19th century when Europeans needed an excuse for their imperialism and colonialism. The 19th century found Britain and France grabbing land all around the globe, and Germany wanted an empire too — something Wagner always found repugnant in the Prussian Kaiser. Wagner had no sympathy for imperialism and colonialism. In Hans Sachs' final monologue in *Die Meistersinger*, Wagner made clear his disgust with the German empire and German imperialism thanks to the new Kaiser. What Wagner believed in was "holy German art" and nothing else.

Wagner sabotaged efforts to deal with his heart condition, according to his doctor, Friedrich Keppler:

> He suffered from advanced hypertrophy of the heart, especially in the right ventricle, with consequent degeneration of the cardiac tissues. There was also a fairly extensive dilation of the stomach and an inguinal hernia on the right side; this had been greatly aggravated for a long time by an unsuitable truss, so that the first thing I did was to order him a better one.
> The pains from which he suffered in the last months of his life came principally from disorders of the stomach and bowels, and particularly from advanced matorism: these occasioned — though secondarily, by direct mechanical constriction of the chest as a result of much gas in the stomach and intestines and by reflex action of the nerves of the stomach and heart — painful derangements of the heart's action, leading eventually to a rupture of the right ventricle. It is self-evident that the innumerable psychical agitation to which Wagner was daily disposed by his peculiar mental constitution and disposition, his sharply defined attitude towards a number of burning questions of art, science and politics, and his remarkable social position did much to hasten his unfortunate end.

There was a rumor in Venice that Wagner was having an affair with a flower maiden, Carrie Pringle. She did write to him and he did meet her in Venice, but he was probably too sick for sex at this point in his life, though he certainly enjoyed the adulation of a fan who was also a lovely young woman. There was also Judith Gauthier, an old fan and girlfriend who lived in Paris and who had visited him in Bayreuth and Venice.

Wagner was working on an essay, "On the Feminine in Humanity," when he collapsed. A servant ran to Cosima, who immediately sent for the doctor. By the time he

23. Death in Venice: 1883

arrived, Wagner was dead in Cosima's arms. She clung to his body for several days, yearning to die with him. Finally, her family was able to pry her off Wagner's corpse so that she could be fed and he could be prepared for burial. Hans von Bülow immediately sent her a telegram which said, "Seour, Il faut vivre"—"Sister, you must live!" He undoubtedly knew her well enough to know what she would have wanted to do.

The attending physican wrote in his report about Wagner's condition in his final days:

> The medical treatment I gave him consisted of massage of the abdomen and the fitting of a proper truss; I avoided medicinal treatment as much as possible, since Wagner had a bad habit of taking promiscuously, and in considerable quantities, many strong medicines that had been prescribed for him by physicians whom he had previously consulted [Newman, IV, 705–06].

Was this Wagner's attempt to kill himself? We have already seen that suicide was such a major theme in his

An 1883 portrait of Richard Wagner, inscribed below left as "Letzte Aufnahme nach dem Leben" (the last picture taken from life). A.V. Gross, Bayreuth, Photographer (Music Division, The New York Public Library for the Performing Arts, Astor, Lenox and Tilden Foundations).

operas and that Wagner himself was often suicidal in his own life. His taking his medicines promiscuously may have been a way of ending quickly a life which was coming to an end anyway. The genius which had pushed him to produce so much work during his lifetime was now wearing him out and making him wish for the end. As Wotan says in the second act of *Die Walküre*, all he wished for now was the end.

The complexity of characterization in Wagner's operas remains one of his great contributions to the history of opera. Before Freud, Wagner realized the complexity of humanity, how love and hate go together, and how we both desire and dread getting what we want. Wagner's villains are never simple-minded forces of evil but complex human beings who are often the most sympathetic of beings. Wagner's operas indicate his understanding of human complexity and human suffering. He also knew about the power of our childhoods and how they influence our entire lives. Wagner also instinctively knew about how our subconscious minds can control and contradict what we are consciously aware of doing and wanting. It is a shame that Freud was so unmusical and had no interest in either music or opera because he would have found that many of his theories were being portrayed in Wagner's operas, which were being performed in Vienna and London when Freud was living in these cities years after Wagner was dead.

Wagner did not leave a will, which would have left Cosima and his children in a very difficult situation, to say the least. Why did he want them to suffer? Was he angry particularly at his wife and if so, why? It is significant as well that he was working on an essay on the nature of women when he had his final heart attack. That essay was centrally concerned with the nature of women, and especially the maternal in women. As he was dying, he had been once again writing about women and motherhood. He seems to have spent his entire life looking for a mother-figure since his relationship with his own mother was so problematical. How ironic that he got to hate the very woman who was most nurturing to him, his wife Cosima; he tortured her with his needs and got to hate himself for not being able to control his own self-contradictory and overly demanding needs for a woman. He must have also felt guilty for this very behavior, which he could not control. The power of the subconscious mind, so apparent in his operas, continued to sabotage his desire to be a good husband and father. His subconscious needs continued to drive him to test Cosima's love for him, and he hated himself for this.

Wagner certainly wrote some of the best roles in opera for women. He often presented liberated women like Isolde and Brunnhilde. He was a great friend of Malwida von Meysenbug, a very liberated woman who was also a fan and corresponded with Wagner for years and was at Bayreuth to attend performances. Wagner in both his operas and in his life supported women's freedom and liberation, though he was not always kind to the women he loved, especially Minna, Mathilde Wesendonck, and Cosima.

Wagner's death was reported in all the major European and American newspapers and was followed by a Venetian gondola funeral. Gabriele D'Annunzio claimed to be one of Wagner's pallbearers in Venice, and that may have actually happened since he was in Venice at that time—the winter of 1883. Wagner's body floated down the Grand Canal in a funereal gondola, with his wife and his son Siegfried on it, going to Venice's train station. Franz Liszt, though not there, did write two piano compositions describing the funereal gondola. The body was then transported by train through Italy, over the Alps, and to Munich, where there was a funeral service. King Ludwig said, "This artist whom the whole world now mourns, it was I who was the first to understand him; it was I who rescued him for the world." The body was then transported by train to Bayreuth for another funeral service and burial behind Wagner's house at Wahnfried. His pallbearers in Bayreuth were primarily, but not exclusively, his gay male friends: "Snow was falling as the cortege made its way to the place in the garden where Wagner had prepared his own tomb years before. Twelve men bore the coffin there—Muncker, Feustel, Gross, Wolzogen, Seidl, Joukowsky, Wilhelm, Porges, Levi, Richter, Standhartner and Niemann, while the four children grasped the corners of the pall" (Newman 716). There are no religious symbols of any kind on the grave, not even a cross, in keeping with Wagner's rejection of all organized religions. That grave contains the bodies of both Wagner and

23. Death in Venice: 1883

Cosima and is a silent testament to Wagner's ultimate rejection of all religions and his belief that art was the only real religion for all modern people.

Many people thought that with Wagner's death, the Bayreuth Festival would come to an end, that this was the composer's intention. But those people failed to reckon with the planning skills of his widow, who became determined that the festival should continue after the composer's death. That the Bayreuth festival survived all the horrors of German history and is still in operation now is a testament to Cosima. She was left with five children and with not much money and with debts, but she sought to raise the funds to continue the festival and maintain it for her son Siegfried. She got the festival on a sound financial footing, got funding from various state and private sources, and kept the festival going for many years after Wagner's death.

Cosima lived long enough to see the Bayreuth Festival established as an annual summer event, and to see all of her children married, even her son Siegfried, whom she must have come to realize was homosexual. She wanted Siegfried to marry and produce children to continue the Wagner legacy and establish a Wagner dynasty, and Siegfried did this. He married the Englishwoman Winifrid Klindsworth, and they had five children in quick succession. Once she was in control, after Siegfried died a few months after his mother in 1930, Winifred Wagner helped support her friend Adolf Hitler and the Nazi party, which resulted in a disaster for both Germany and the world, and for Bayreuth. She herself became a member of the Nazi party. But the Bayreuth Festival survived even this, and started again in the summer of 1951 under the leadership of Wieland and Wolfgang Wagner, grandsons of the composer. So Cosima's desire for a Wagner dynasty was established and fulfilled despite Winifred.

Richard Wagner was arguably the greatest and most influential composer in the 19th century, and while the 20th century was unkind to him, the 21st century has so far been kinder to him. He was a very complicated man, probably a manic depressive, and certainly he could be cruel to people. But he could also be funny, generous, and even kind. As some of his friends argued, he was both a creative genius and a natural born clown who liked climbing up gutters in his home in Bayreuth to prove that he still had some youthful energy.

It is interesting that Cosima reports that Wagner was revising his first opera, *Die Feen*, in his last year while they were in Italy. His publisher Schott wanted to publish *Die Feen*, which had never been staged; Wagner revised the overture and various aspects of the score, but ultimately he decided not to give his publisher permission to publish it, even with his revisions. It is also interesting that Wagner was dying in Carlo Gozzi's city, Venice. And many of the themes in Gozzi's *La Donna Serpente*, the source for Wagner's *Die Feen*, would reappear over and over again in Wagner's subsequent operas, themes like the gods versus ordinary people, the woman as both source of redemption and source of all suffering, etc.

But Wagner the man, despite his great successes on the world's stages and opera houses, remained the unhappy, obsessed genius trapped in a world of extreme highs and lows. As John Stuart Mill wisely pointed out in his essay "On Human Happiness," when we ask ourselves if we are really happy, that very question will destroy any happiness we might have. One must just keep working, argued Mill, and not ask such a question, and maybe we will find some happiness. Wagner rarely did find much happiness but he created one of the greatest bodies of operas which the world has ever seen and given the world's opera companies works to destroy their budgets trying to stage.

Wagner took much from the world, but he gave the world even more. His mature operas are now in the standard repertory of all of the major opera houses of the world. His Ring cycle has become a world-wide phenomenon. All the opera companies in the world now want to stage it, and there are thousands of Ring-heads who will go anywhere in the world for a performance of the cycle. The Ring cycle remains Wagner's masterpiece, though his other six mature operas continue to hold our attention as well.

Wagner's influence on music and the other arts made Wagnerism a dominant artistic movement for fifty years after his death. His influence on the other arts, not just music, has been the subject of many books. There are Wagner societies in every major city around the world. The entire world wants to see a Ring cycle these days; it is much in the news since there are so many production of this tetralogy being staged around the world. One can spend an entire year or two going around the world to see Ring cycles in America, the U.K., Germany, Switzerland, Italy, Australia and even China and Japan.

The continuing legacy of the Bayreuth Festival and the continuing interest in Wagner and his operas has had worldwide consequences. By the bicentennial of his birth, 2013, the world was experiencing a Wagner Renaissance with many Ring cycles being staged as audiences grow for Wagnerian opera and demand more and more Wagnerian performances, especially of his Ring cycle. His whole Ring cycle has also been viewed by millions on television.

Wagner's very self-contradictory complexities add to his humanity and add to his fascination for us. Thomas Mann, Wagner's greatest literary discipline, wrote the essay "The Sufferings and Greatness of Richard Wagner." That suffering indicates the quality of much of his life and his fascination for many of us living in the 21st century. Wagner's life was complex and fascinating and conflict-ridden, his death was self-willed, and his reputation has survived the Nazi abuse of his works. By his two hundredth birthday, the world was finally able to see both the greatness and the kindness of this great musical and dramatic genius — perhaps the greatest genius in the history of art, whose masterpiece, the Ring cycle, would fascinate audiences and generate more and more productions of this and his other major works. His operas are still filling the great opera houses, and his audiences and admirers have become immense.

Conclusion: A Life of Extremes

What a dramatic life Richard Wagner endured! He wandered all over Europe, staying, at first, in the cheapest hotels and by the end at the most luxurious and gorgeous hotels and palaces in one cosmopolitan center after another: in Venice, Palermo, Berlin, Dresden, Bayreuth, Leipzig, Munich, Naples, London, and Paris. His was a life of extremes — from poverty, starvation, and even debtor's prison to aristocratic and palatial grandeur as the favorite musician and court composer of King Ludwig II of Bavaria. By the end of his life, moreover, he was considered the greatest composer in the world, though also considered by others as the worst. Simply, Wagner induced wildly extreme reactions from his audiences — who responded with love or hate for his music. From his music, listeners sensed the composer's demands on them, always to understand more of themselves — and some people found that off-putting and even intrusive. As a man, Wagner explored the same depths and heights. He went from the extreme of wishing he were dead and even of planning his own suicide to creating the glories of a novel art movement and a revolutionary new theater in Bayreuth — with performances of only Wagnerian works, produced under ideal circumstances and for an ideal audience of only Wagner's fans.

In his ten seminal operas (all products of his artistic maturity) Wagner reached a pinnacle of greatness. Today, moreover, these ten operas remain in the standard repertory of most of the main opera houses of the world. He accomplished what no other artist had, and he learned much from Franz Liszt, a friend and father-in-law yet Liszt was only three years older. Liszt indeed died three years after Wagner in 1886 in Bayreuth; He is buried in a tomb designed by his grandson Siegfried. Liszt's dying word, accord to eyewitnesses, was simply "Tristan."

At present, we are seeing around us a massive renaissance affecting both Wagner's music and his reputation. Today, in fact, no company can be considered major until it has staged a complete Ring cycle.

As a musical persuasion, Wagnerism became a most important artistic movement at the end of the 19th century and continuing into the 20th century. No other operatic composer can claim such a world-wide following of potential audiences who desire to experience his art. Wagner's concept of "mitleid" (or sympathy, in *Parsifal*) remains in all of Wagner's thought. This sympathetic philosophy is at the heart of Wagner's operas and at the center of his philosophy. Now the popular demonization of Wagner is long over and the truth of his special message must be acknowledged: Artistic freedom and secular democracy are goals we all should be striving to achieve, even those people who have been historical victims. The modern world has no place for discrimination. When will nations become truly democratic, with equal rights for all people regardless of race or religion?

Today Wagner stands foremost among opera composers; he had proved influential in every one of the arts, including film, an art that did not exist in Wagner's day. His grandson, Wolfgang, has declared that if his grandfather were alive now, Richard would be occupied in making films since only that medium could offer the means to do everything Wagner dreamed of. Modern productions of Wagner's operas often use films, and his operas have been filmed on HD film for broadcast in movie theaters and on television screens.

In Wagner's creative shadow may be identified composers like Strauss; symphonic composers like Mahler, Bruchner, and Schoenberg, painters like Renoir, and many writers such as Proust, James Joyce, E. M. Forster, Joseph Conrad, Virginia Woolf, D. H. Lawrence, and Thomas Mann. Wagner's theories of theater and opera, such as the Gesamptkunstwerk, have moreover influenced many of the theater designers and film makers who have followed him, especially in Germany, Russia, and America.

This astonishing breath of Wagner's accomplishments in music, librettos, essays, and theater design distinguish him as one of history's great geniuses. In 2013, the bicentenary of his birth, Wagner can be fully appreciated as the complex but influential figure that he was. From his rare genius, our inheritance is richer and more various.

Wagner tried to revolutionize not only opera but all the arts, calling for the Gesamptkunstwerk, or combination art work which would connect all the arts into one greater art. He tried to create in his own operas, especially his monumental Ring cycle, a work of art which included all the others — literature, music, theater, painting, and sculpture with sets and costumes all integrated into one perfect art form. His theories had implications for all the other arts, and by the end of the 19th century his theories influenced the novel, theater, poetry, painting — in fact all the other arts. While some artists were influenced by these theories, other artists rejected them and pursued other paths to creativity.

But we are now living in a Wagner renaissance. During the celebrations of the bicentennial of Wagner birth in 1813, Wagner's operas are being staged more frequently than ever before and around the world. There was a time when very few opera companies ever did a Ring cycle, but now every major opera company in the world wants to do a Ring cycle — and many have. This masterpiece has also become the ultimate test of any opera company, which can not be considered in the major league until it has staged a complete Ring cycle.

In the 21st century, there are now Wagner societies in every major city in the world — including New York, London, Buenos Aires, Berlin, Los Angeles, Milan, Rome, Chicago, Toronto, Buenos Aires, Tokyo, Hong Kong, and Shanghai. To indicate his world-wide popularity, London's Royal Opera staged four complete Ring cycles as part of the Olympic Games in the summer and fall of 2012.

What I have tried to do is use a different approach to Wagner's personality in different chapters. Each chapter in this book has presented a different layer of Wagner's complex personality; he was as complex as we all are, with the added complexity of being a genius. Freud said that psychoanalysis was like peeling an onion, layer by layer. And when one peels an onion, one weeps — and there was much to weep about in Wagner's long life. We are all so complex, Freud felt, that no one theory could explain the complexity of any individual. So each chapter has presented a different problem and a different aspect of Wagner.

Wagner's life began with warfare, the death of a parent, and repeated neglect and abandonment. But out of that suffering Wagner was able to create uniquely wonderful works of art which bring joy and understanding to us all.

Bibliography

Abbate, Carolyn. *Unsung Voices: Opera and Musical Narrative in the Nineteenth Century.* Princeton: Princeton University Press, 1991.

_____, and Roger Parker, eds. *Analyzing Opera: Verdi and Wagner.* Berkeley: University of California Press, 1989.

Barker, John W. *Wagner and Venice.* Rochester: University of Rochester Press, 2008.

Barondes, Samuel H. *Mood Genes: Hunting for Origins of Mania and Depression.* New York: W. H. Freeman, 1998.

Barth, H. D. Mack, and E. Voss, eds. *Wagner: A Documentary Study.* London: Thames & Hudson, 1975.

Bassett, Peter. *Wagner's Parsifal: The Journey of a Soul.* Adelaide, Australia: Wakefield Press, 2000.

Blunt, Wilfrid. *The Dream King: Ludwig II of Bavaria.* New York: Penguin, 1970.

Boyle, Nicholas. *Goethe: The Poet and the Age.* Vol. 1. *The Poetry of Desire (1749–1790).* Oxford: Oxford University Press, 1991.

Breton, André. *Manifestoes of Surrealism.* Richard Seaver and Helen R. Lane, trans. Ann Arbor: University of Michigan Press, 1969.

Brockett, Oscar G. *History of the Theatre.* Boston: Allyn and Bacon, 1982.

Buller, Jeffrey L. "Spectacle in the Ring." *The Opera Quarterly* 14, no. 4 (Summer 1998): 41–58.

Burbridge, Peter, and Richard Sutton, eds. *The Wagner Companion.* London: Faber, 1979.

Burian, Jarka. *Svoboda: Wagner.* Middletown, CT: Wesleyan University Press, 1983.

Burrell, Mary. *Richard Wagner, His Life and Works, 1813–1834.* London: Allan Wyon, 1898.

Chancellor, John. *Wagner.* New York: Granada, 1978.

Chapman-Huston, Desmond. *Ludwig II: The Mad King of Bavaria.* New York: Dorset Press, 1990.

Cicora, Mary A. *Parsifal-Reception in the Bayreuther Blätter.* New York: Peter Lang, 1987.

_____. *Wagner's Ring and German Drama.* Westport, CT: Greenwood Press, 1999.

Conrad, Peter. *Romantic Opera and Literary Form.* Berkeley: University of California Press, 1977.

_____. *A Song of Love and Death: The Meaning of Opera.* St. Paul: Graywolf Press, 1996.

Cooke, Deryck. *I Saw the World End: A Study of Wagner's Ring.* New York: Oxford University Press, 1979.

Corazzol, Adriana Guarnieri. *Tristano, mio Tristano: Gli Scrittori Italiani e il Caso Wagner.* Bologna: Il Mulino, 1988.

Corse, Sandra. *Wagner and the New Consciousness: Language and Love in the Ring.* Cranbury, NJ: Associated University Presses, 1990.

Cowley, Malcolm, ed. *Writers at Work: The Paris Review Interviews.* New York: Viking, 1957.

Culshaw, John. *Reflections on Wagner's Ring.* New York: Viking, 1976.

_____. *Ring Resounding.* New York: Viking, 1967.

Deathridge, John, and Carl Dahlhaus. *The New Grove Wagner* in *The New Grove Dictionary of Music and Musicians.* Stanley Sadie, ed. New York: Norton, 1984.

DiGaetani, John Louis, ed. *Inside the Ring: Essays on Wagner's Opera Cycle.* Jefferson, NC: McFarland, 2006.

_____. *Richard Wagner and the Modern British Novel.* Cranbury, NJ: Fairleigh Dickinson University Press, 1978.

_____. *Wagner and Suicide.* Jefferson, NC: McFarland, 2003.

_____, ed. *Penetrating Wagner's Ring: An Anthology.* New York: Da Capo Press, 1991.

_____, ed. *Wagner Outside the Ring: Essays on the Operas, Their Performance, and Their Connections with the Other Arts.* Jefferson, NC: McFarland, 2009.

Eger, Manfred. *Wagner und die Juden: Fakten und Hintergrunde: Eine Dokumentation zur Ausstel-

Bibliography

lung im Richard Wagner Museum Bayreuth. Bayreuth, Germany: Druckhaus, 1985.

Fischer-Dieskau, Dietrich. *Wagner and Nietzsche.* Joachim Neugroschel, trans. London: Sidgwick and Jackson, 1976.

Forster, E. M. *Howards End.* New York: Vintage, 1921.

———. *Two Cheers for Democracy.* New York: Harvest Books, 1951.

Freud, Sigmund. *Beyond the Pleasure Principle.* James Strachey, trans. New York: Norton, 1961.

Frye, Northrop. *Anatomy of Criticism.* New York: Atheneum, 1957.

Furness, Raymond. *Wagner and Literature.* New York: St. Martin's Press, 1982.

Gay, Peter. *Freud: A Life for Our Time.* New York: Norton, 1988.

Glasenapp, Carl Friedrich. *The Life of Richard Wagner.* Ashton Ellis, trans. New York: Da Capo, 1977.

Glass, Frank W. *The Fertilizing Seed: Wagner's Concept of Poetic Intent.* Ann Arbor: UMI Research Press, 1983.

Goethe, Johann Wolfgang von. *Goethe's Faust.* Translation and introduction by Walter Kaufmann. New York: Doubleday, 1963.

Goodwin, Donald W., and Samuel B. Guze. *Psychiatric Diagnosis.* New York: Oxford University Press, 1989.

Graham, Ilse. *Goethe: Portrait of an Artist.* New York: Walter de Gruyter, 1977.

Gregor-Dellin, Martin, and Michael von Soden. *Richard Wagner: Leben, Werk, Wirkung.* Dusseldorf: Econ, 1983.

Gutheil, Emil A. *Music and Your Emotions.* New York: Liveright, 1952.

Gutman, Robert W. *Richard Wagner: The Man, His Mind, and His Music.* New York: Harcourt Brace Jovanovich, 1968.

Herzeld, Friedrich. *Das Neue Bayreuth.* Berlin: Rembrandt, 1965.

Hilmes, Oleana. *Cosima Wagner: The Lady of Bayreuth.* Stewart Spencer, trans. New Haven: Yale University Press, 2010.

Holman, J. K. *Wagner's Ring: A Listener's Companion and Concordance.* Portland, OR: Amadeus Press, 1996.

Huebner, Steven. *French Opera at the Fin de Siecle: Wagnerism, Nationalism, and Style.* New York: Oxford University Press, 1999.

Inwood, Margaret. *The Influence of Shakespeare on Richard Wagner.* Lewiston, NY: Edwin Mellen, 1999.

Jamison, Kay Redfield. *Night Falls Fast: Understanding Suicide.* New York: Knopf, 1999.

———. *Touched with Fire: Manic-Depressive Illness and The Artistic Temperament.* New York: The Free Press, 1994.

———. *An Unquiet Mind: A Memoir of Moods and Madness.* New York: Vintage, 1996.

Katz, Jacob. *The Darker Side of Genius: Richard Wagner's Anti-Semitism.* Hanover, NH: Brandeis University Press, 1986.

———. *Richard Wagner: Hebrew.* Jerusalem: Markaz Zalman Shazar, 1986.

———. *Richard Wagner: Vorbote des Antisemitismus.* Konigstein: Judischer Verlag, 1983.

Kesting, Hanjo. *Das Pump-Genie: Richard Wagner und das Geld: Nach Gedruckten und Ungedruckten Quellen.* Frankfurt Am Main: Eichborn, 1993.

Köhler, Joachim. *Wagner's Hitler: The Prophet and his Disciple.* Ronald Taylor, trans. and introd. Malden, MA: Polity Press, 2000.

Kreis, Rudolf. *Nietzsche, Wagner und die Juden.* Wurzburg: Konigshausen & Neumann, 1995.

Large, David C., and William Weber. *Wagnerism in European Culture and Politics.* Ithaca: Cornell University Press, 1984.

Lawrence, D. H. *The Collected Letters of D. H. Lawrence.* Harry T. Moore, ed. 2 vols. London: Heinemann, 1962.

Lee, M. Owen. *Wagner: The Terrible Man and His Truthful Art.* Toronto: University of Toronto Press, 1999.

———. *Wagner's Ring: Turning the Sky Around.* New York: Limelight Editions, 1998.

Levin, David J. *Richard Wagner, Fritz Lang, and the Nibelungen: The Dramaturgy of Disavowal.* Princeton: Princeton University Press, 1998.

Lilla, Mark. *G. B. Vico: The Making of an anti-Modern.* Cambridge: Harvard University Press, 1993.

Magee, Bryan. *Aspects of Wagner.* New York: Stein and Day, 1969.

———. *The Philosophy of Schopenhauer.* New York: Oxford University Press, 1983.

———. *Wagner and Philosophy.* New York: Allen Lane/Penguin, 2000.

Mander, Raymond, and Joe Mitchenson. *The Wagner Companion.* New York: Hawthorn Books, 1977.

Manera, Giorgio, and Giuseppe Pugliese. *Wagner in Italia.* Venice: Marsilio, 1982.

Mann, Thomas. "The Suffering and Greatness of Richard Wagner" in *Essays,* H. T. Lowe-Porter, trans. New York: Vintage, 1957.

Marek, George R. *Cosima Wagner*. New York: Harper & Row, 1981.
Martin, Stoddard. *Wagner to The Wasteland: A Study of the Relationship of Wagner to English Literature*. Totowa, NJ: Barnes & Noble, 1982.
Mayer, Hans. *Wagner*. Ramburg: Rowohlt Taschenbuch, 1959.
Millington, Barry. "Nuremberg Trial: Is There Anti-Semitism in *Die Meistersinger*?" *Cambridge Opera Journal* 3, no. 3 (1991): 247–260.
_____. *Wagner*. New York: Vintage, 1987.
_____, ed. *The Wagner Compendium: A Guide to Wagner's Life and Music*. New York: Schirmer Books, 1992.
_____, and Stewart Spencer, eds. *Wagner in Performance*. New Haven: Yale University Press, 1992.
Minois, Georges. *History of Suicide: Voluntary Death in Western Culture*. Lydia G. Cochrane, trans. Baltimore: Johns Hopkins University Press, 1999.
Müller, Ulrich, and Peter Wapnewski, eds. *Wagner Handbook*. Cambridge: Harvard University Press, 1992.
Nattiez, Jean-Jacques. *Wagner Androgyne: A Study in Interpretation*. Stewart Spencer, trans. Princeton: Princeton University Press, 1993.
Newman, Ernest. *The Life of Richard Wagner*. 4 vols. New York: Cambridge University Press, 1976.
Nietzsche, Friedrich, and Richard Wagner. *The Nietzsche-Wagner Correspondence*. Caroline V. Kerr, trans. New York: Liveright, 1949.
Nilges, Yvonne. *Richard Wagners Shakespeare*. Wurzburg: Königshausen and Neumann, 2007.
Osborne, Charles. *Wagner and his World*. New York: Scribner's, 1977.
_____. *The World Theatre of Wagner*. New York: Macmillan, 1982.
Porges, Heinrich. *Wagner Rehearsing the "Ring," An Eyewitness Account of the Stage Rehearsals of the First Bayreuth Festival*. Robert L. Jacobs, trans. Cambridge: Cambridge University Press, 1983.
Rather, L. J. *The Dream of Self-Destruction: Wagner's Ring and the Modern World*. Baton Rouge: Louisiana State University Press, 1979.
Reinhardt, Hartmut, "Wagner and Schopenhauer" in Ulrich Muller and Peter Wapnewski, eds. *Wagner Handbook*. John Deathridge, trans. Cambridge: Harvard University Press, 1992.
Robertson, J. G. *A History of German Literature*. Revised by Edna Purdue. New York: British Book Centre, 1962.
Rose, Paul Lawrence. *Wagner: Race and Revolution*. New Haven: Yale University Press, 1992.
Ross, Alex. *The Rest Is Noise: Listening to the Twentieth Century*. New York: Farrar, Strauss & Giroux, 2007.
Scholtz, Dieter David. *Richard Wagners Antisemitismus*. Wurzburg: Königshausen and Neumann, 1993.
Schopenhauer, Arthur. *Essays and Aphorisms*. R. J. Hollingdale, trans. New York: Penguin, 1981.
_____. *Philosophical Writings*. Wolfgang Schirmacher, ed. New York: Continuum, 1996.
Shaw, George Bernard. *The Perfect Wagnerite: A Commentary on the Nibelung's Ring*. New York: Dover, 1967.
Skelton, Geoffrey. *Richard and Cosima Wagner: Biography of a Marriage*. Boston: Houghton Mifflin, 1982.
Spencer, Stewart. *Wagner Remembered*. London: Faber & Faber, 2000.
Spotts, Frederic. *Bayreuth: A History of the Wagner Festival*. New Haven: Yale University Press, 1994.
Tanner, Michael. *Wagner*. Princeton: Princeton University Press, 1996.
Vico, Giambattista. *The Autobiography of Giambattista Vico*. Max Fixch and Thomas Bergin, trans. Ithaca: Cornell University Press, 1975.
Wagner, Cosima. *Cosima Wagner's Diaries*. Geoffrey Skelton, trans. New York: Harcourt Brace Jovanovich, 1980.
_____. *Cosima Wagner's Diaries: An Abridgment*. Geoffrey Skelton, ed. New Haven: Yale University Press, 1997.
Wagner, Gottfried. *Twilight of the Wagners: The Unveiling of a Family's Legacy*. Della Couling, trans. New York: Picador, 1999.
Wagner, Nike. *The Wagners: The Dramas of a Musical Dynasty*. Ewald Osers and Michael Downes, trans. Princeton: Princeton University Press, 1998.
Wagner, Richard. *Der Fliegende Holländer: Romantic Opera in Three Acts*. Susan Webb, trans. New York: Metropolitan Opera Guild, 1993.
_____. *Die Meistersinger von Nürnberg*. Susan Webb, notes and trans. New York: Metropolitan Opera Guild, 1992.
_____. *The Family Letters of Richard Wagner*. William Ashton Ellis, trans. Ann Arbor: University of Michigan Press, 1991.
_____. *The Letters of Richard Wagner to Anton Pusinelli*. Elbert Lenrow, trans. New York: Vienna House, 1972.

Bibliography

———. *Lohengrin: Opera in Three Acts.* Stewart Robb, trans. New York: G. Schirmer, 1963.

———. *My Life.* Andrew Gray, trans. New York: Da Capo, 1992.

———. *Opera and Drama.* William Ashton Ellis, trans. Lincoln: University of Nebraska Press, 1995.

———. *Parsifal: Music Drama in Three Acts.* Stewart Robb, trans. New York: G. Schirmer, 1962.

———. *Religion and Art.* William Ashton Ellis, trans. Lincoln: University of Nebraska Press, 1994.

———. *Selected Letters of Richard Wagner.* Stewart Spencer and Barry Millington, trans. New York: Norton, 1987.

———. *Tannhäuser: Opera in Three Acts.* Susan Webb, notes and trans. New York: Metropolitan Opera Guild, 1998.

———. *Three Wagner Essays.* Robert L. Jacobs, trans. London: Eulenburg Books, 1978.

———. *Tristan und Isolde.* Stewart Robb, trans. New York: G. Schirmer, 1965.

———. *Wagner on Music and Drama.* Albert Goldman and Evert Springchorn, eds. New York: Dutton, 1964.

———. *Wagner's Ring of the Nibelung.* Stewart Spencer, trans. New York: Thames and Hudson, 1993.

———, and Franz Liszt. *Correspondence of Wagner and Liszt.* 2 vols. Francis Hueffer, trans. New York: Greenwood Press, 1969.

Walton, Chris. *Richard Wagner's Zurich: The Muse of Place.* Rochester, NY: Camden House, 2007.

Warrack, John, and Ewan West, eds. *The Oxford Dictionary of Opera.* New York: Oxford University Press, 1994.

Watson, Derek. *Richard Wagner: A Biography.* London: Dent, 1979.

Weber, Eugen. *France Fin de Siecle.* Cambridge: Harvard University Press, 1986.

Westernhagen, Curt von. *Wagner: A Biography.* Mary Whittall, trans. Cambridge: Cambridge University Press, 1978.

White, Chappell. *An Introduction to the Life and Works of Richard Wagner.* Englewood Cliffs, NJ: Prentice Hall, 1967.

Williams, Alastair. "Technology of the Archaid: Wish Images and Phantasmagoria in Wagner." *Cambridge Opera Journal* 9 no. 1 (1998): 73–87.

Williams, John. *The Life of Goethe: A Critical Biography.* Oxford: Blackwell, 1998.

Windell, George G. "Hitler, National Socialism, and Richard Wagner," in John L .DiGaetani, ed., *Penetrating Wagner's Ring: An Anthology.* New York: Da Capo, 1991.

Woolf, Virginia. "Impressions at Bayreuth." John L. DiGaetani, ed. *Opera News* 41 (August 1976): 22–23.

Wright, William. *Born That Way: Genes, Behavior, Personality.* New York: Alfred A. Knopf, 1998.

Wylie, Sypher. *Comedy.* New York: Doubleday, 1956.

Index

Aeschylus 47, 176
Albert of Britain (Prince) 168
Also Sprach Zarathustra (Nietzsche) 184
Anti-Semitism 3–4, 7, 16, 22, 25, 31, 60, 92, 98, 119, 124, 127, 165, 174, 181–182, 184, 189
Art Deco 137
Der Asyl 108
Auber, Daniel 48
Avenarius, Eduard 58, 61

Bach, J.S. 25, 27, 106
Baden-Baden, Germany 66
Bakunin, Mikhail (Michael) 73–74, 78–79, 202
Barbarosa, Frederick 76
Bath, England 66
Battle of Borodino 9
Battle of Leipzig 9–12
Baudelaire, Charles 126
Bavaria 26, 139–141, 173
Bavarian State Opera 141, 168
Bayreuth, Germany 4, 19, 37, 69
Bayreuth Festival 21, 37, 120, 157, 162–167, 171–181, 185, 187, 194, 196, 199, 205–206
Bayreuther Blatter 200, 202
Beethoven, Ludwig van 26, 29, 38, 42, 46–47, 55–57, 62–67, 70, 96, 103, 107, 120, 132, 133, 136, 137, 149, 167
Bellini, Vincenzo 29–30, 38, 45, 57, 59, 70–71, 99, 149, 201
Belloni, Gaetano 83, 121
Berg, Alban 43
Berlin, Germany 92, 129, 147
Berlioz, Hector 30, 38, 59–60, 100, 111–112, 120, 127
Bethmann, Heinrich 48
Bismarck, Otto von 77, 119, 129, 145, 157–164

Bizet, Georges 124
La Bohème 58
Brahms, Johannes 40, 135
Brazil 118
Brockhaus, Friedrich 60
Browning, Elizabeth 100, 106
Browning, Robert 100, 106
Büchner, Georg 43
Buddhism 194
Burton, Richard 3
Byron, George Gordon 74, 99

Café Florian, Venice 100, 115
Chamberlain, H.S. 6
Chancellor, John 6
Chaucer, Geoffrey 6, 31
The Claque 123
Code Napoléon 59
Congress of Vienna 25
Conrad, Joseph 120, 134
Cornelius, Peter 136
Cromwell, Oliver 75

D'Agoult, Marie 83
Damrosch, Leopold 160
D'Annunzio, Gabriele 204
Dante Alighieri 30
Da Ponte, Lorenzo 47
Death in Venice (T. Mann) 115
De Gobineau, Count 200
Desplechin, Eduard 125
Dickens, Charles 6, 7, 13, 31
Dietsch, Louis Philippe 125
Disney, Walt 65
Donizetti, Gaetano 29
Dresden, Germany 17, 25–26, 34, 49, 64–66, 75–79, 90
Dresden Court Opera 61–64

Eliot, George 6, 190
Ellis, William Ashton 135
Esser, Heinrich 135
Euripides 47
Evans, Tamara 104–105

Die Feen 37, 44, 50
Feuerbach, Ludwig 76–78
Feustel, Friedrich 178, 190
Fitzgerald, F. Scott 6, 36
Flaubert, Gustave 134
Flying Dutchman 2, 37, 44, 54–64, 114
Forster, E.M. 120, 134
France 75, 119–129
Franconia, Germany 175
Frankfurt, Germany 111
Freud, Sigmund 7, 27, 82–94, 203, 209
Friedrich August II of Saxony (King) 68–77
Die Frieschütz (Weber) 25

Gauthier, Judith 196
Gay, John 122
German Emigration 65–70
German Kaiser 166
Gewandhaus Orchestra (Leipzig) 132
Geyer, Ludwig 4, 13–19, 20–28
Glasenapp, Carl Friedrich 6
Gluck, Christoph Willibald 70, 101
Goethe, Johann Wolfgang von 22–29, 34, 82, 98, 201
Goldoni, Carlo 28, 37
Götterdämmerung 197
Gozzi, Carlo 10, 28–39, 47
Gravina, Count Biagio 196
Greek Drama 28–29, 148, 176
Grimm Brothers 65
Guadaloupe Concerts 117
Guelph Fund 145
Gutman, Robert 3

Halévy, Fromental 59
Handel, George Frideric 122
Hanslick, Eduard 136, 164
Hardy, Thomas 49
Haussmann, Baron Georges-Eugène 118

Index

Henze, Hans Werner 38
Herzl, Theodore 1
Herzog, Werner 118
Hitler, Adolf 1, 3, 10
Hoffmann, E.T.A. 22
Holocaust 31

Israel 4, 27, 31, 77
Italy 75, 98–113, 195–196, 200

Jesuits 52, 151–152
Jesus Christ 76
Jews in Music 88, 172
Jockey Club 123
Joukovsky, Paul 184, 193–195
Joyce, James 105

Kaiser William I 92
"Kaisermarsch" 167
"Eine Kapitulation" 159
Karlsruhe, Germany 132
Keats, John 99
Keller, Gottfried 102
Keppler, Friedrich 202
Kietz, Ernest 58–59, 61
Kindermann, August 172
Koehler, Joachim 3
Königsberg, Germany 49

Lablache, Luigi 56
Lachner, Franz 98
Laussot, Eugene 89–91
Laussot, Jessie 89–91
Lawrence, D.H. 120
Lehrs, Samuel 58–61
Leipzig 9, 17, 22, 25–26, 33
Leipzig University 35–43
Levi, Herman 4, 189
"Das Liebesmahl der Apostel" 67, 191
Das Liebesverbot 38, 40, 50, 167
Liszt, Franz 4, 21, 40, 79–87, 102, 137, 169, 191, 200
Lohengrin 3, 82–84, 92
London, U.K. 27, 49, 54, 75
Louis XIV (King) 148
Ludwig I (King) 140
Ludwig II (King) 39–40, 77, 80, 102, 139–143, 152, 191
Lüttichau, Baron von 65

Magdeburg, Germany 44–45, 53
Maier, Mathilde 142–143
Mainz, Germany 131
Malibran, Maria 56
Manichean Heresy 85
Mann, Thomas 7, 52, 206
Margrave's Opera House (Bayreuth) 178

Marie of Bavaria (Queen) 143–144
Marx, Karl 73–76
Materna, Amalie 193
Maximilian II (of Bavaria) (King) 142
Meeting Venus 124
Mein Leben 12, 36, 86, 100–108, 131, 147, 159–160
Die Meistersinger von Nürnberg 2, 29, 132, 152–168
Mendelssohn, Felix 93, 118, 190
Mendès, Cattule 126
Metropolitan Opera 7, 196–198
Meyer, Frederika 132
Meyerbeer, Giacomo 56, 118, 124
Meysenbug, Malvida von 88, 126, 188
Mill, John Stuart 205
Millington, Barry 1
Mitleid (Sympathy) 207
Monod, Gabriel 187–188
Monteverdi, Claudio 101
Montez, Lola 140
Mozart, Wolfgang Amadeus 35–37, 42, 47, 51, 65, 91
Mueller, Alexander 88
Mueller, Christian 26, 35
Munich, Germany 4, 98, 140

Naples, Italy 100
Napoleon 9–18
Napoleon III 75, 118, 128, 140, 156
Nazis 1, 182
Neumann, Angelo 190
Neuschwanstein Castle 148
Newman, Ernest 1, 6, 19, 54, 86, 115–116, 172–73, 199, 203
Nibelungen Chancellery 180
Nicholaischule 35
Nieman, Albert 125
Nietzsche, Elisabeth 182, 187
Nietzsche, Friedrich 14, 25, 111, 136, 156, 160, 182–189
Norma (Bellini) 71

Opera as Drama 91–95
Opera di Paris 56, 121

Palazzo Vendramin-Calergi, Venice 201
Palestinians 4, 94
Palmer, Tony 3, 17
Paris, France 11, 49, 54–57, 113–121
Parsifal 3, 31, 41, 67, 76, 86–188, 191–199
Pecht, Friedrich 58

Pfeistermeister, Count 139
Planer, Nathalie 49, 138
Plato 179
Poland 84
Porges, Heinrich 180, 193
Prague 34, 40
Pringle, Carrie 202
Proudhon, Pierre 73–76
Prussia 26, 90, 118
Puccini, Giacomo 116
Pusinelli, Anton 72, 80–88
Putzmacherin (Mrs. Maretschek) 136–137

Quaglio, Angelo 150, 163

Rapallo, Italy 105, 195
Räuber 56
Reichman, Theodor 193
Reisinger, Karl Gottlieb 65
La Revue Wagnerienne 120
Das Rheingold 171–172
Richter, Hans 170
Rienzi 38, 51, 58, 64–67
Riga, Latvia 51–55
Ring Cycle 3, 22, 78–81, 95–100, 103, 109–114, 137–141, 144–145, 173–181, 206
Ritter, Julie 94
Ritter, Karl 89–94, 115
Röckel, August 72–76, 80–88
Rome, Italy 99
Rosa, Salvatore 105
Rossini, Gioacchino 29, 38, 47, 57–60
Royal Opera, Covent Garden 1
Rubinstein, Josef 4, 173–184
Russia 49, 54, 84, 133–136

Sachs, Hans 163
Saint-Saëns, Camille 120
San Francisco Opera 7
Sandwike, Norway 54
Saxe, Marie 126
Saxony 19, 26, 63, 76, 129
Sayne-Wittgenstein, Princess Carolyne 131, 137
Scaria, Emil 193
Schiller, Friedrich von 29, 40–41, 46
Schlessinger, Maurice 57–59
Schnorr von Carolsfeld, Ludwig 132, 150
Schnorr von Carolsfeld, Malvina 132, 150
Schopenhauer, Arthur 41, 104–111, 138, 155
Schott, Bernard 131
Schröder-Devrient, Wilhelmine 41, 67–72

Index

Schubert, Franz 40
Seattle Opera 7
Seidl, Anton 170
Semper, Gottfried 152, 178
Shakespeare, William 6, 22, 28–29, 41–50, 100–115, 165
Shaw, George Bernard 6, 74, 130
Shelley, Percy Bysshe 99
Sicily 100–105, 196
Die Sieger 188
Siegfried 11
"Siegfried Idyll" 154–159
Sienna Cathedral 193
Sophocles 47
Spencer, Stewart 1
Stoppard, Tom 90
Strauss, David 41, 76
Strauss, Richard 47, 150
Stromkerl 126
suicide 22, 55, 201
Sulzer, Jacob 87
Switzerland 84–94, 102, 113–116

Tannhäuser 3, 52, 56–72, 82, 117–126, 165
Taylor, Mrs. 89–90
Tchaikovsky, Peter 100
Tedesco, Fortunata 124
Théâtre du la Renaisance 61
Thetis 54
Tichatscek, Joseph 72
Tietjen, Heinz 193
Titian/Tiziano 100, 115

Triebschen, Switzerland 19, 116, 153–155, 185
Tristan und Isolde 2, 11, 22, 31–33, 56, 78, 100–106, 116, 135–141, 147–153, 161, 168
Twain, Mark 151

United Nations 4, 27
United States 130

Venice 10, 37, 110–113, 201
Verdi, Giuseppe 7, 25, 38, 51–62, 126–133
Viardot, Pauline 61
Vico, Giambattista 106
Victoria (Queen) 168
Vienna, Austria 27, 132
Villa Pellet 144
Voltaire, François 123
Von Bülow, Hans 39, 89, 104, 136–144, 158–159, 169, 203
Von Pfordten, Ludwig 149, 152
Von Wolzogen, Hans 200

Wagner, Adolf 12, 30, 39–45
Wagner, Albert 86
Wagner, Carl Friedrich 16, 23
Wagner, Cosima Liszt 27, 40, 49, 85–89, 102–109, 144–153, 169, 180–186, 194, 201–205
Wagner, Johanna 30, 72–86
Wagner, Johanna Rosine 4, 12–33, 73

Wagner, Minna 46–55, 107–109, 124–130
Wagner, Siegfried 153, 157
Wagner, Winifred 182
Wahnfried 178–194
Die Walküre 31, 99, 103, 173
Wartburg Castle 61
water (as symbol) 65, 106
Weber, Carl Maria von 25, 42, 47, 67–71
Weimar, Germany 79–92
Weinlig, Theodor 35
Weizmann, Chaim 4
Wellington, Duke Arthur 10
Wesendonck, Mathilde 80, 102–115
Wesendonck, Otto 21, 94, 96–107
Wettin family 76
Wetzel, Christian 34
Wiesbaden, Germany 98
Wilde, Oscar 58, 130, 134
Winkelmann, Hermann 193
Wittelsbach, Otto 140, 143
Wittelsbach family 142, 172
Woolf, Virginia 120
Wüllmer, Franz 171
Wurzburg, Germany 44–48

Zionism 1, 4, 94
Zurich, Switzerland 79–85, 95–107

www.ingramcontent.com/pod-product-compliance
Lightning Source LLC
Chambersburg PA
CBHW081554300426
44116CB00015B/2882